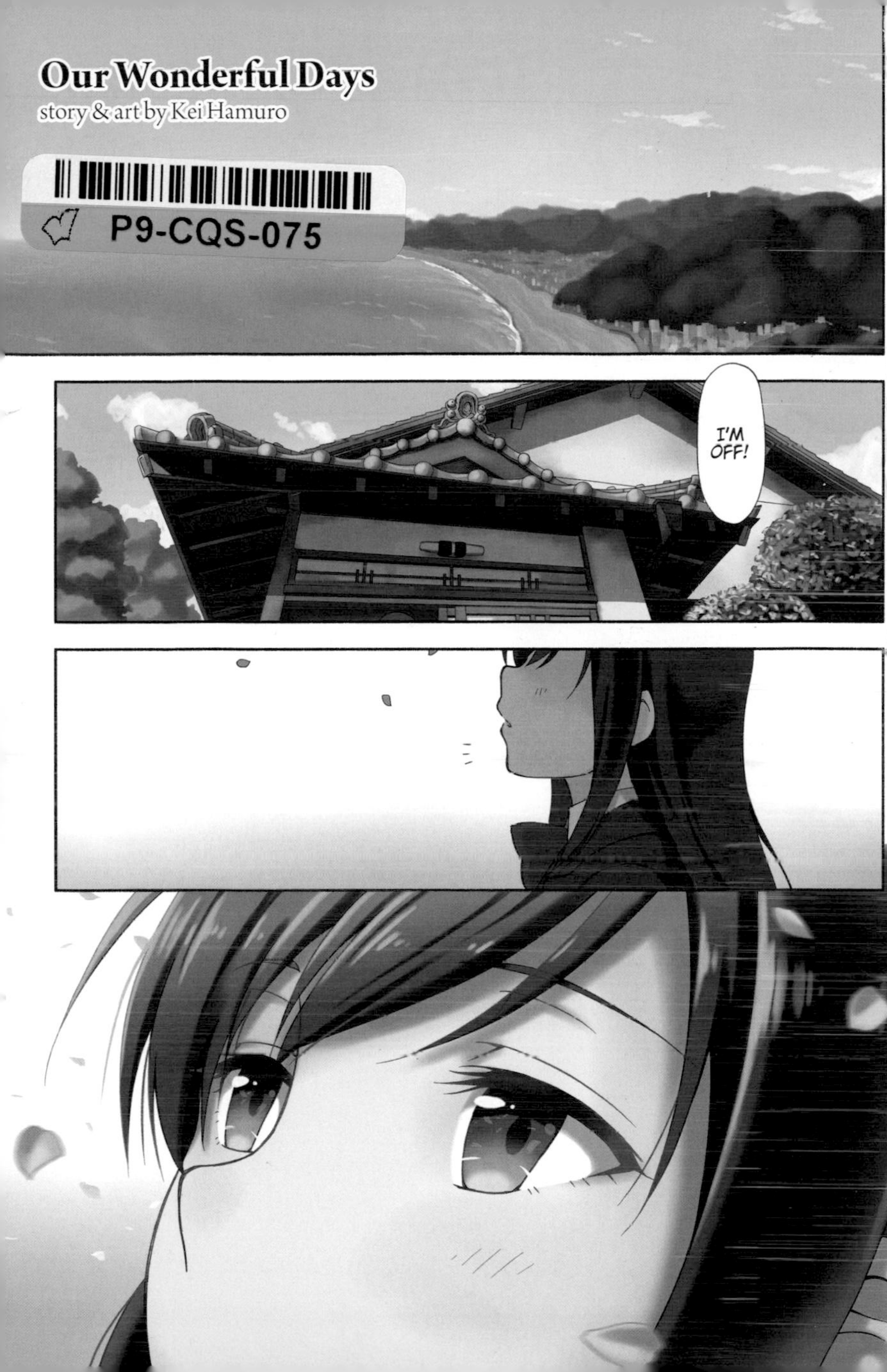
Our Wonderful Days
story & art by Kei Hamuro
I'M OFF!

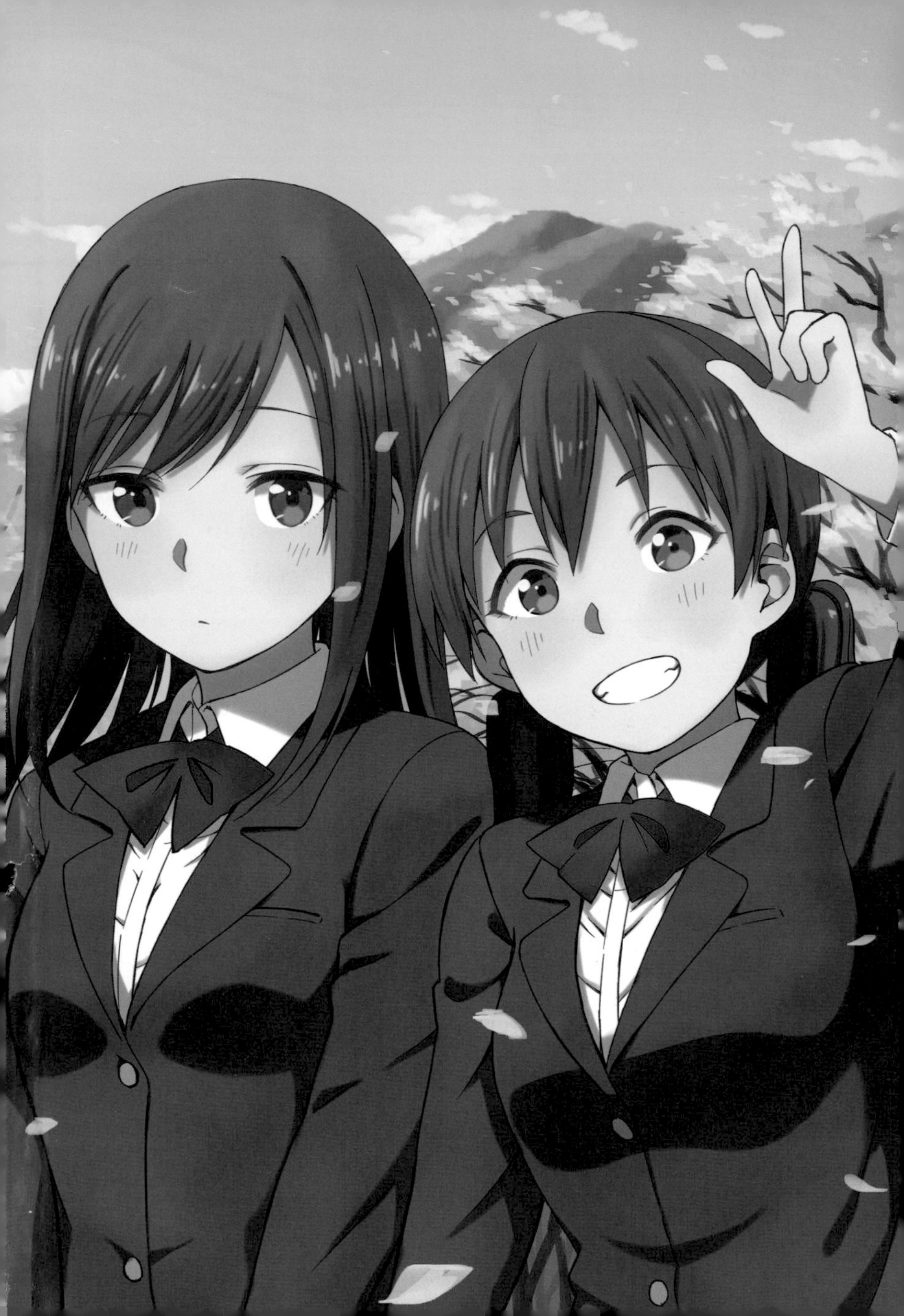

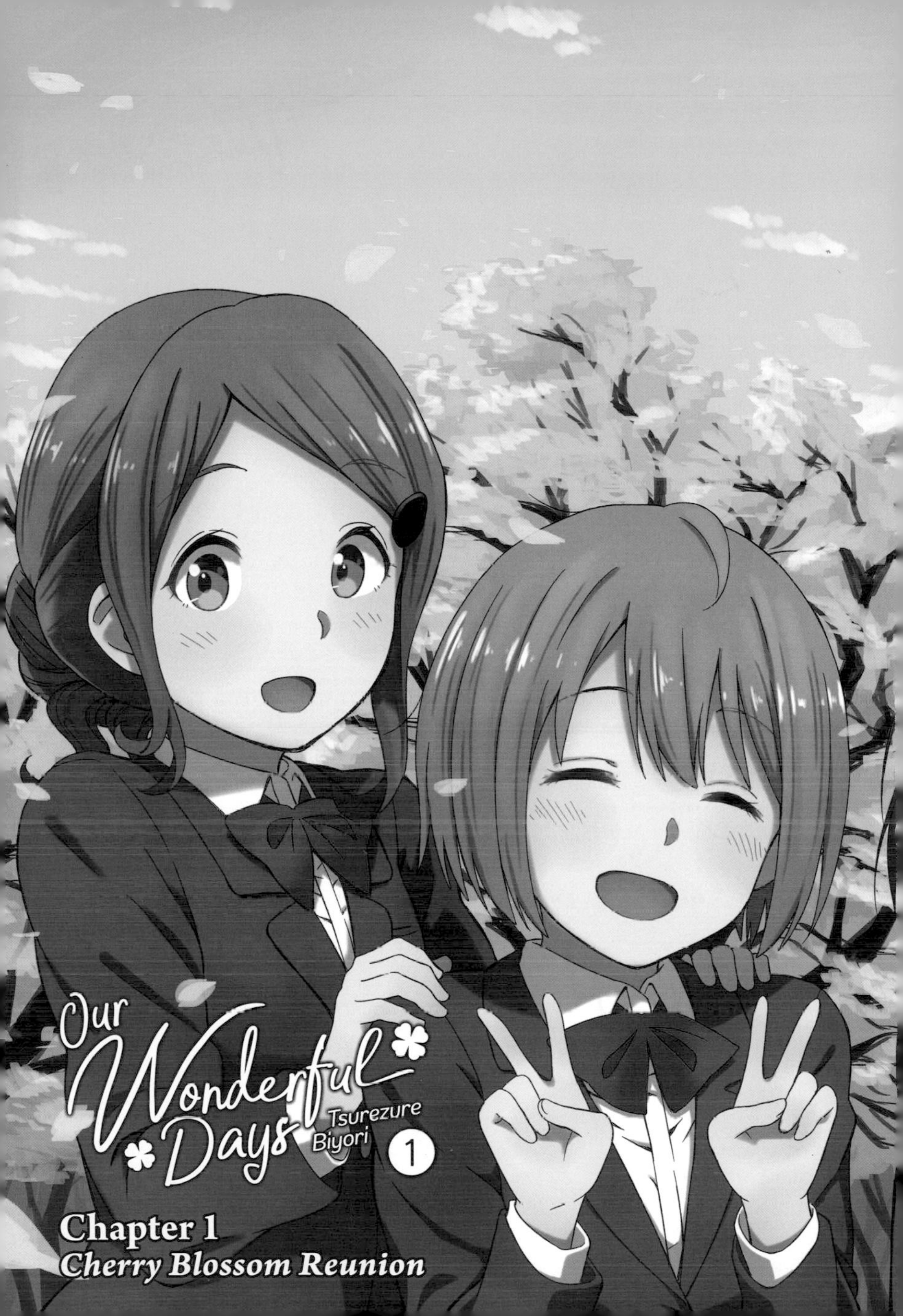
Our Wonderful Days
Tsurezure Biyori
1
Chapter 1
Cherry Blossom Reunion

Our Wonderful Days
Tsurezure Biyori 1

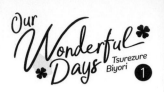

story & art by Kei Hamuro

CONTENTS

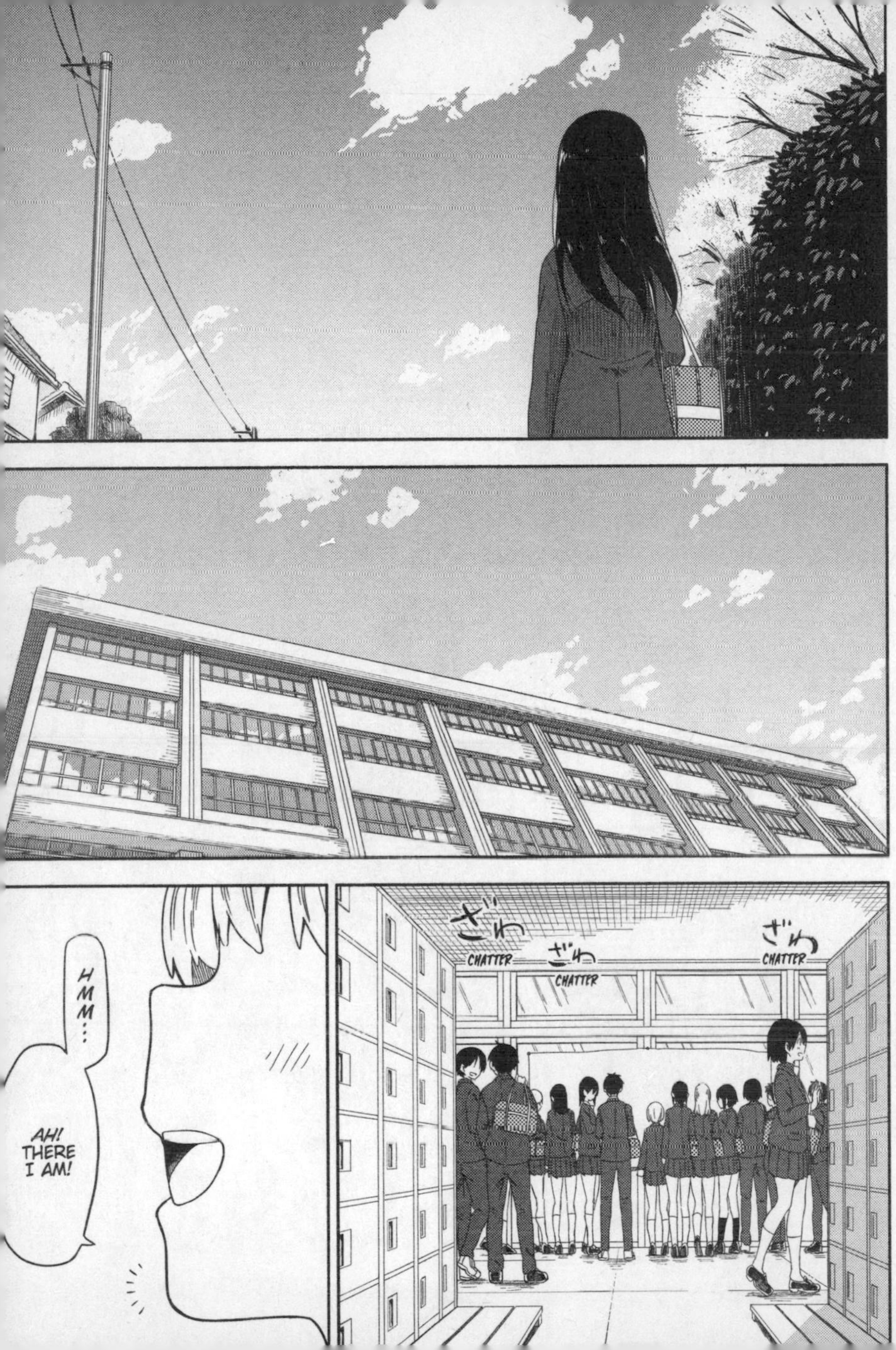
ざわ
CHATTER
ざわ
CHATTER
ざわ
CHATTER
HMM...
AH! THERE I AM!

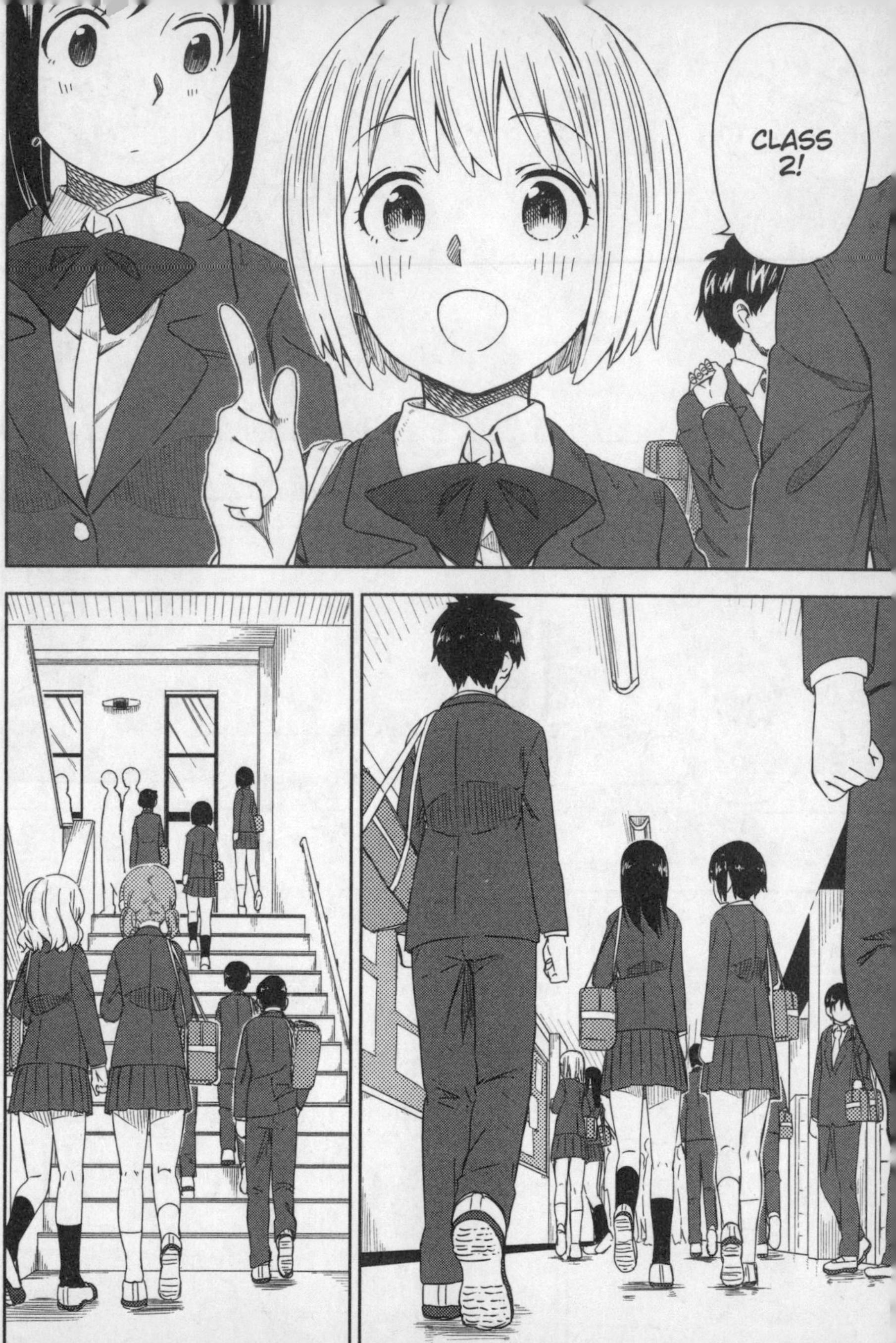
CLASS 2!

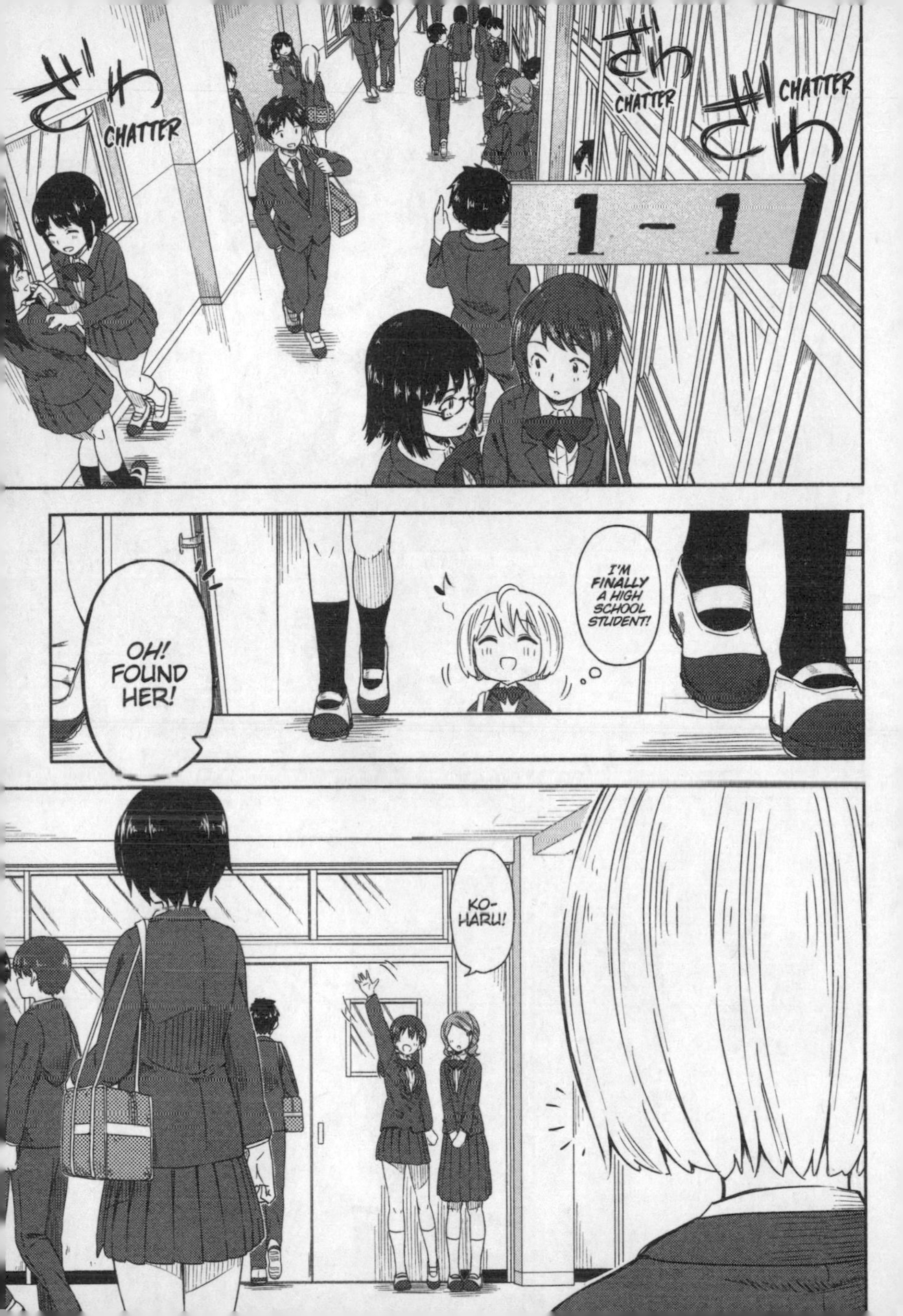
ざわ
CHATTER
ざわ
CHATTER
ざわ
CHATTER
1 — 1
I'M FINALLY A HIGH SCHOOL STUDENT!
OH! FOUND HER!
KO-HARU!

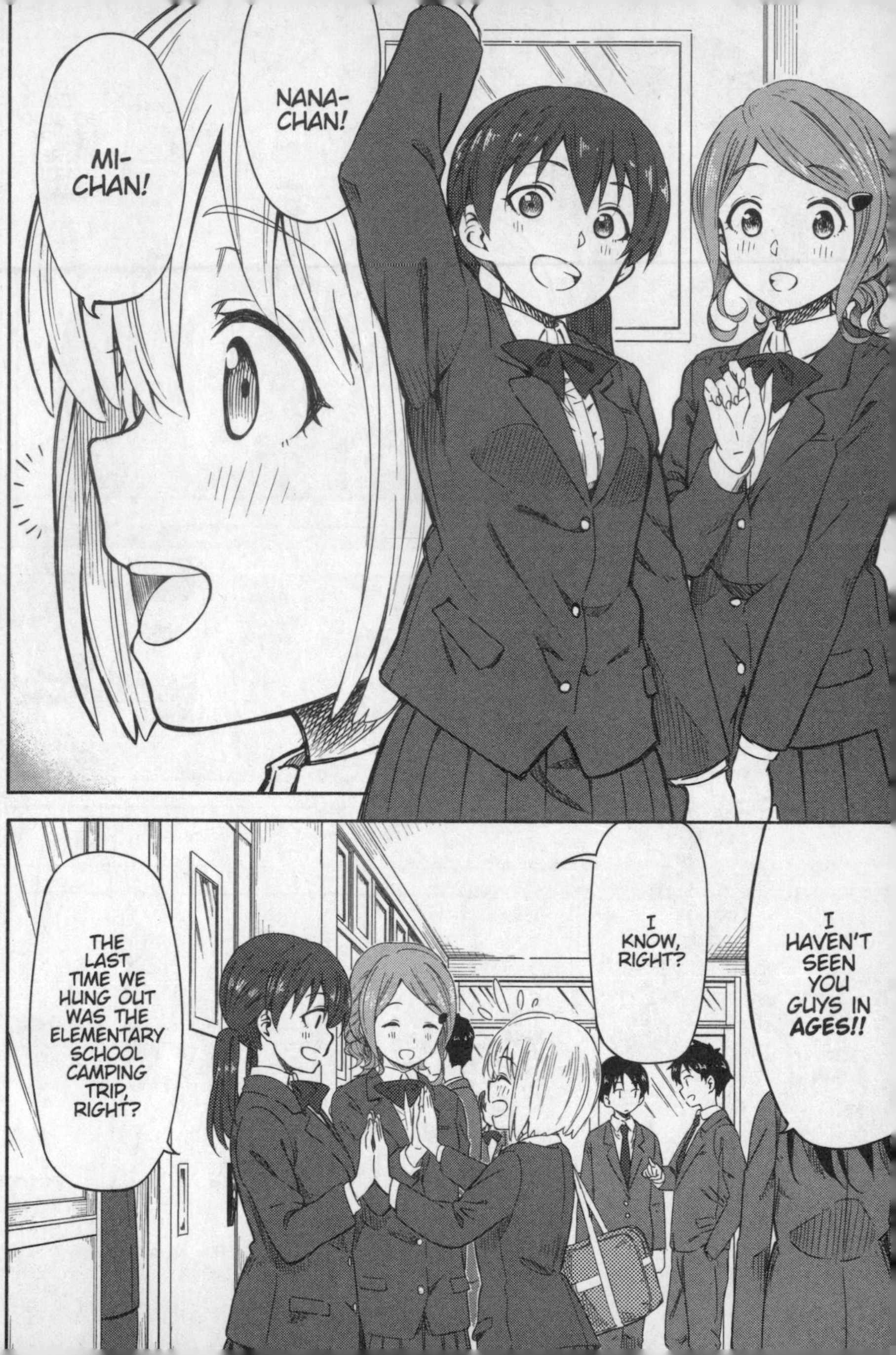
NANA-CHAN!
MI-CHAN!
I HAVEN'T SEEN YOU GUYS IN AGES!!
I KNOW, RIGHT?
THE LAST TIME WE HUNG OUT WAS THE ELEMENTARY SCHOOL CAMPING TRIP, RIGHT?

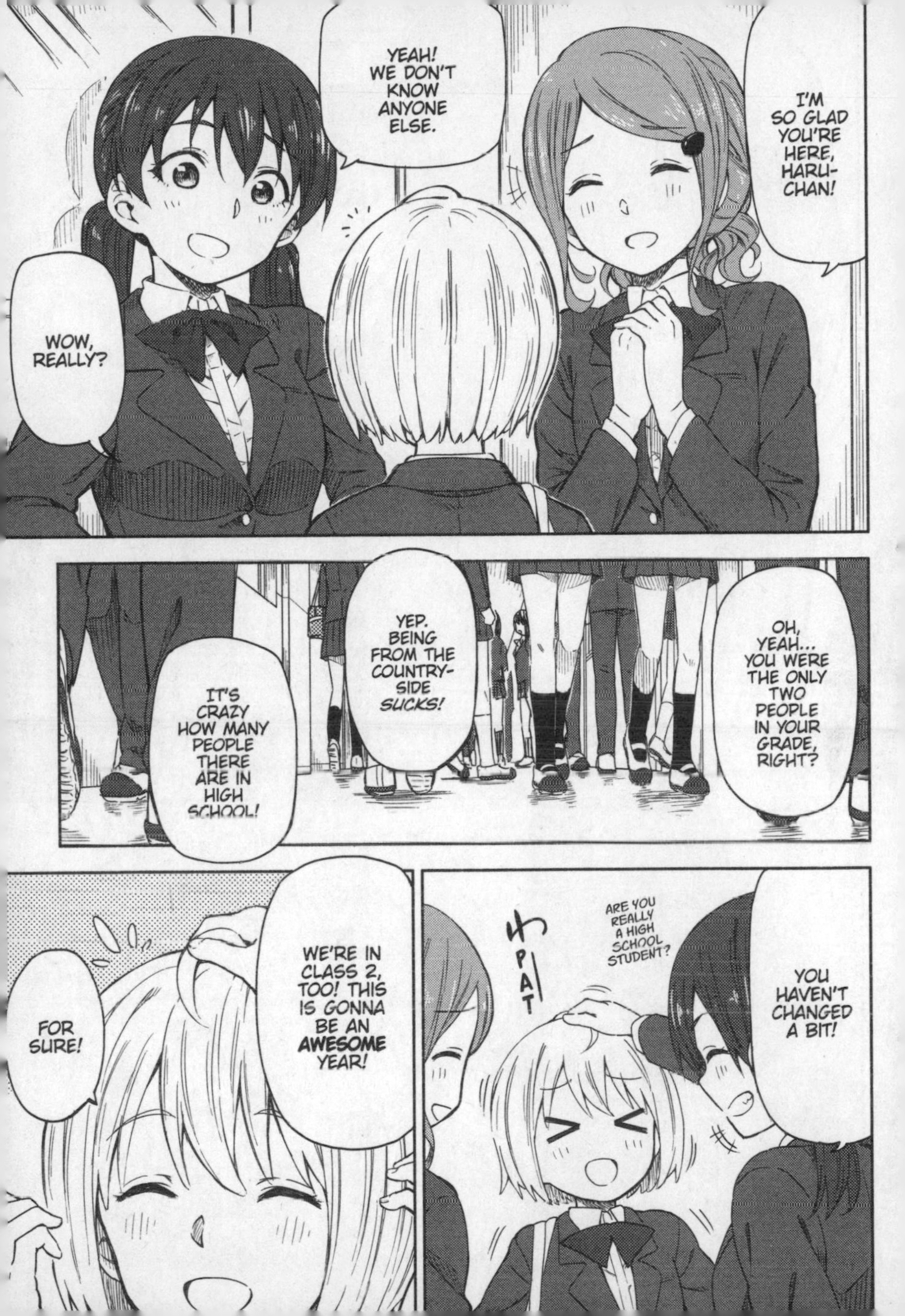
I'M SO GLAD YOU'RE HERE, HARU-CHAN!
YEAH! WE DON'T KNOW ANYONE ELSE.
WOW, REALLY?
OH, YEAH... YOU WERE THE ONLY TWO PEOPLE IN YOUR GRADE, RIGHT?
YEP. BEING FROM THE COUNTRY-SIDE *SUCKS!*
IT'S CRAZY HOW MANY PEOPLE THERE ARE IN HIGH SCHOOL!
YOU HAVEN'T CHANGED A BIT!
ARE YOU REALLY A HIGH SCHOOL STUDENT?
PAT
WE'RE IN CLASS 2, TOO! THIS IS GONNA BE AN **AWESOME** YEAR!
FOR SURE!

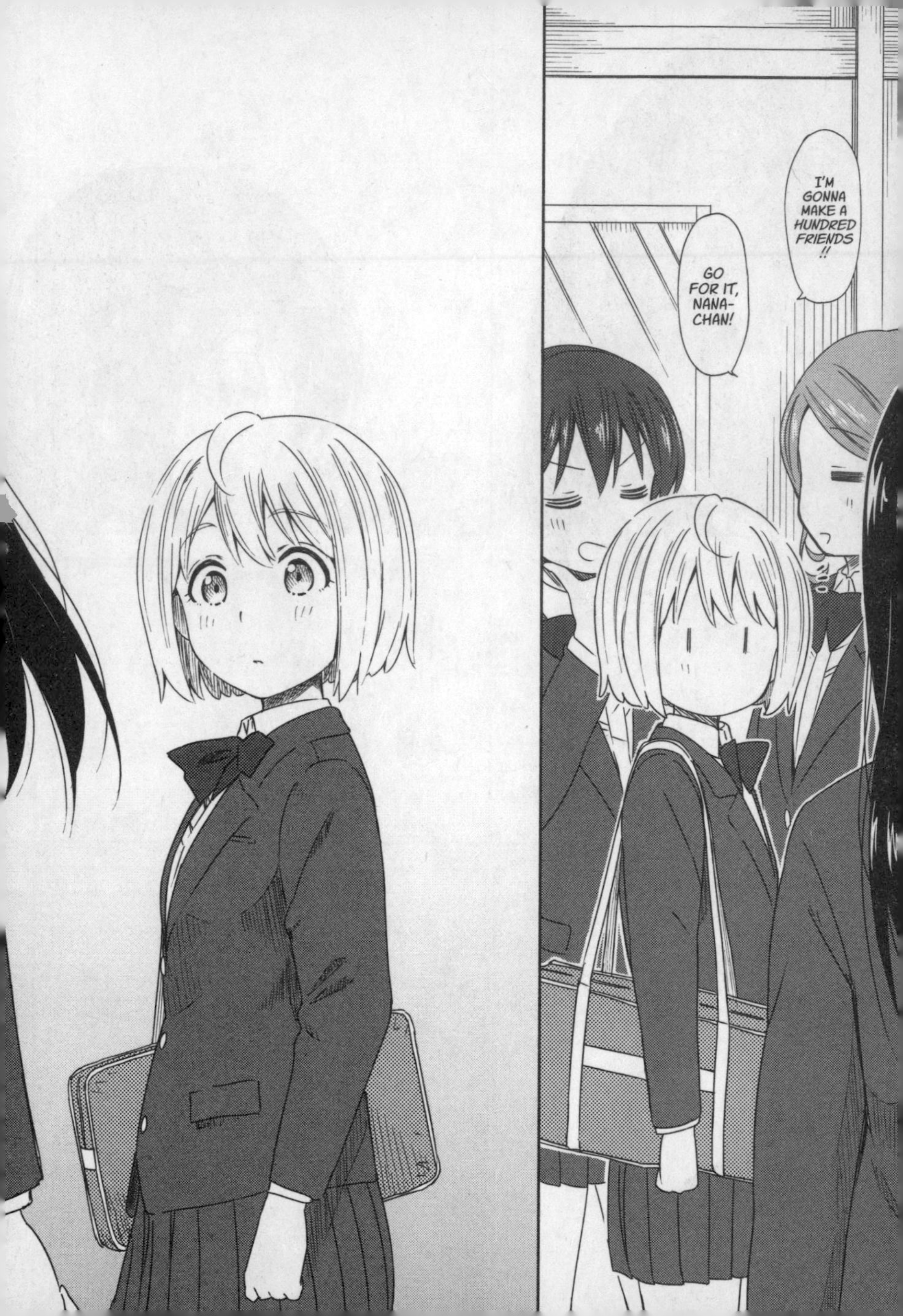
I'M GONNA MAKE A HUNDRED FRIENDS!!
GO FOR IT, NANA-CHAN!

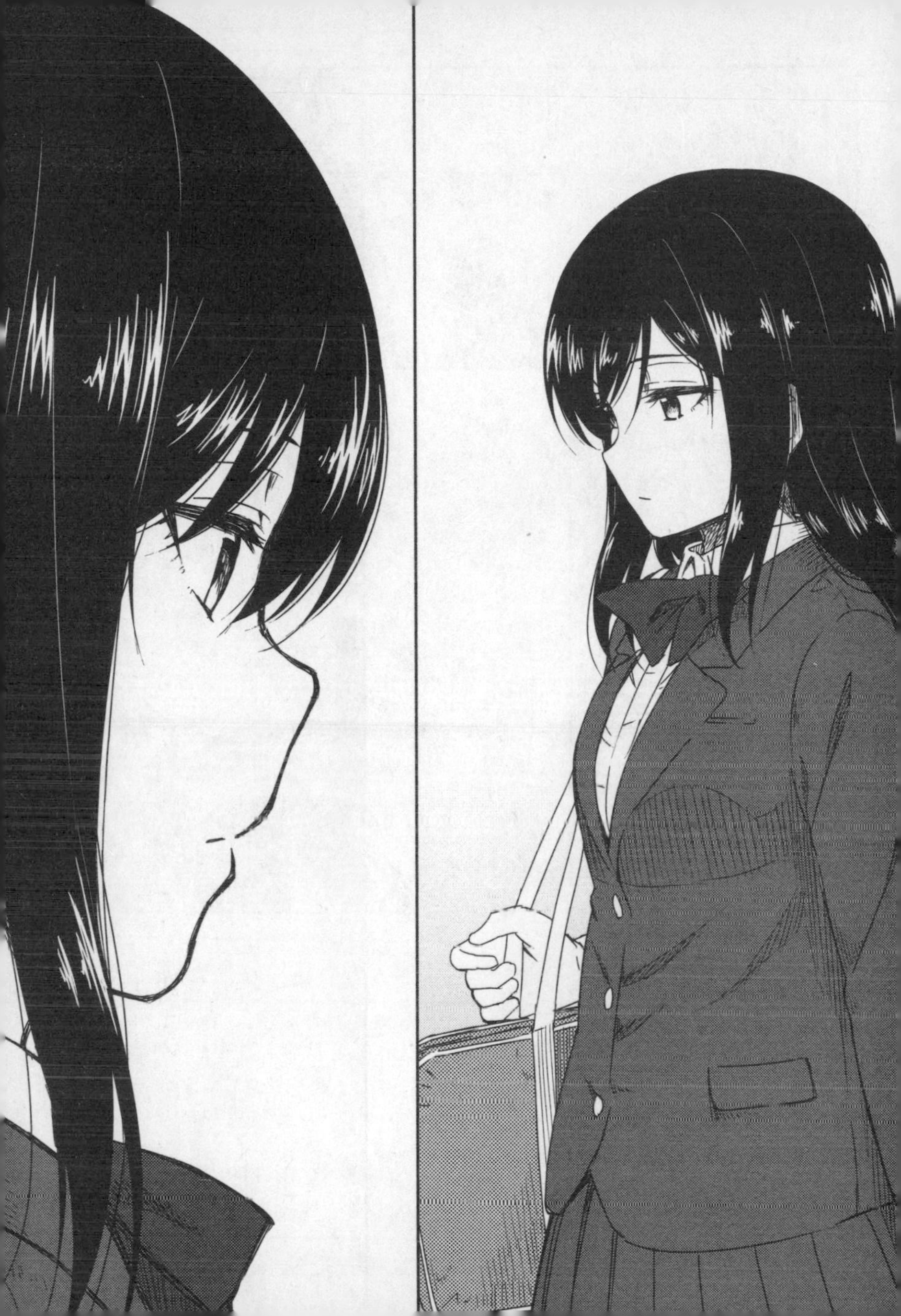

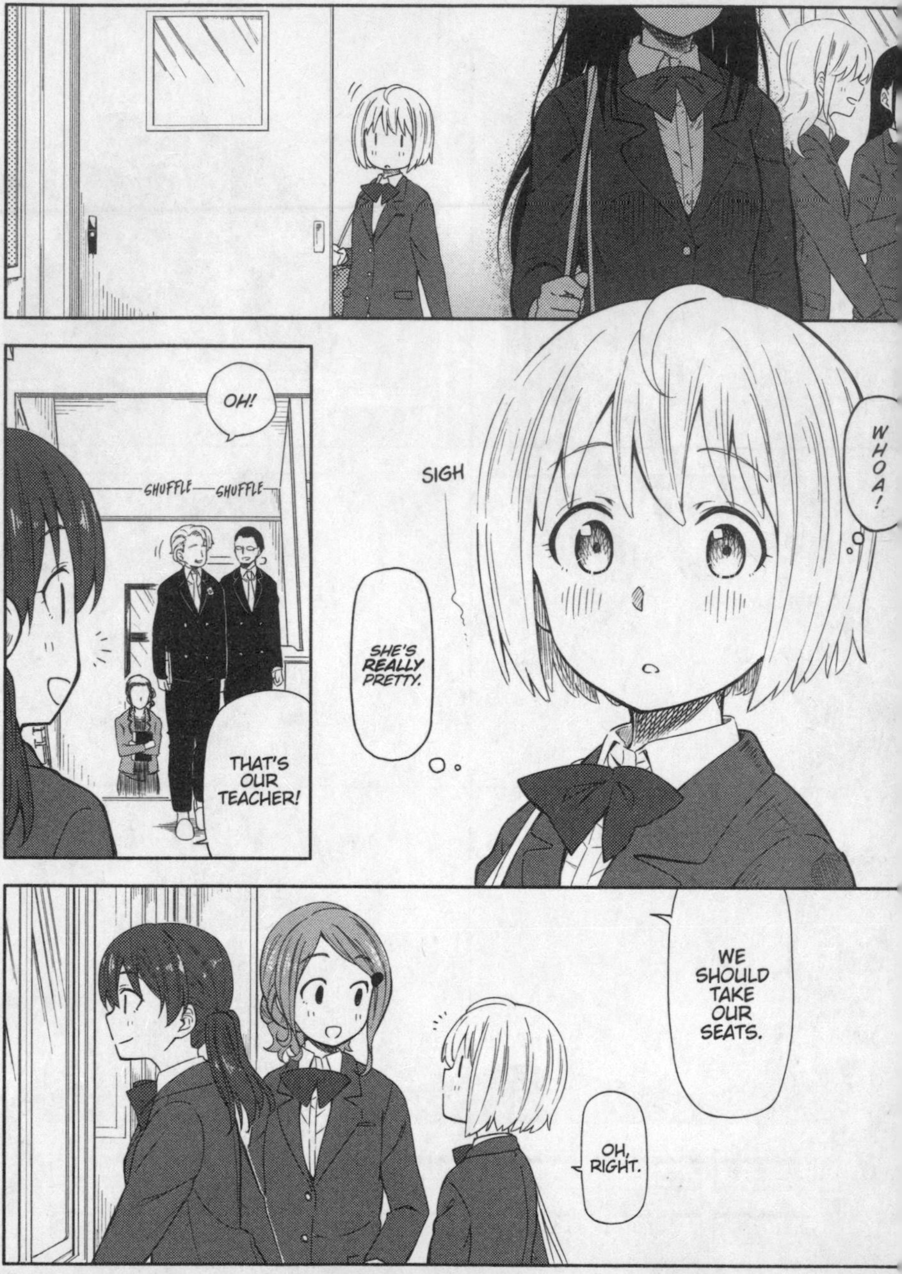
WHOA!
SIGH
SHE'S REALLY PRETTY.
OH!
SHUFFLE SHUFFLE
THAT'S OUR TEACHER!
WE SHOULD TAKE OUR SEATS.
OH, RIGHT.

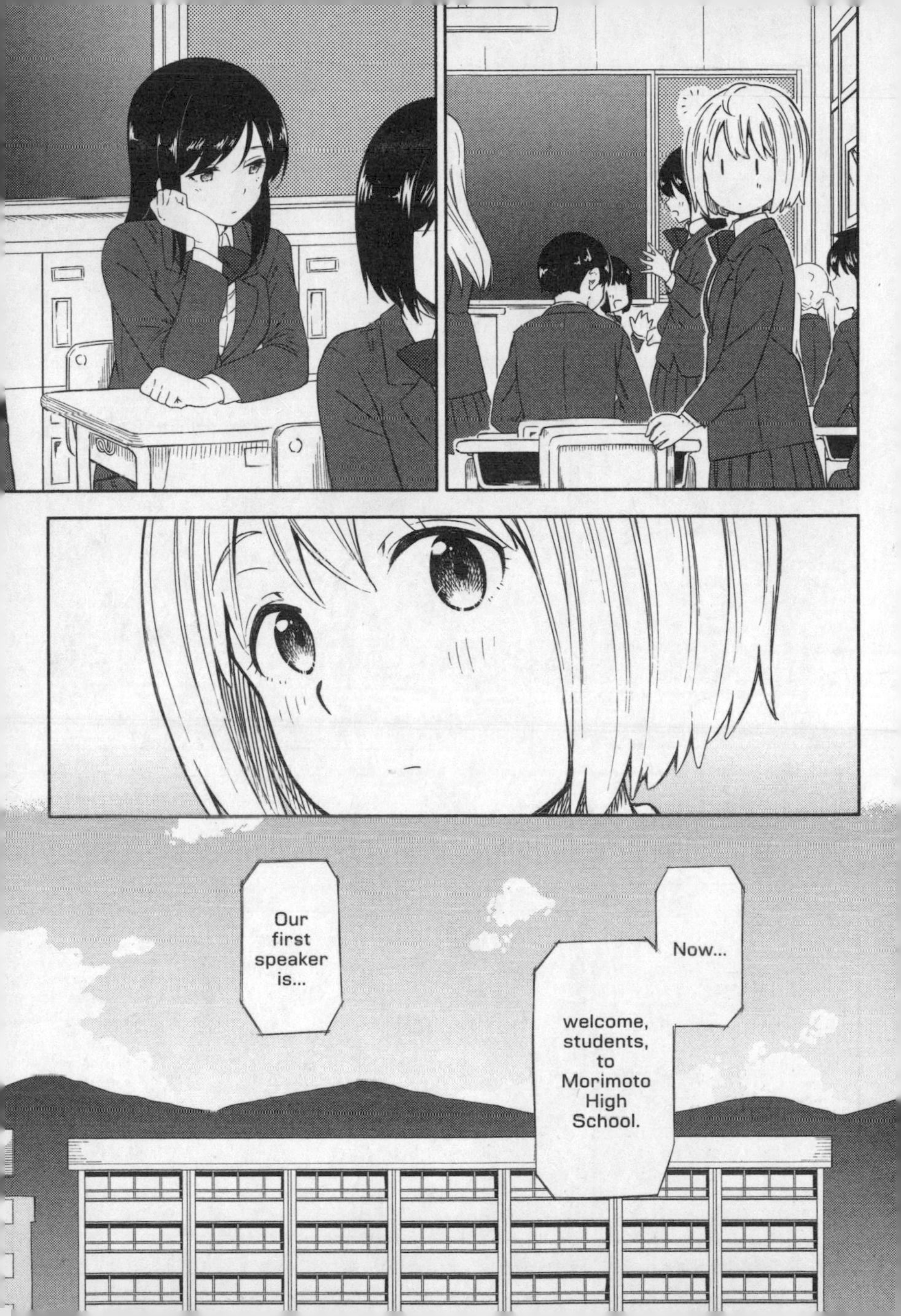
Now...
welcome, students, to Morimoto High School.
Our first speaker is...

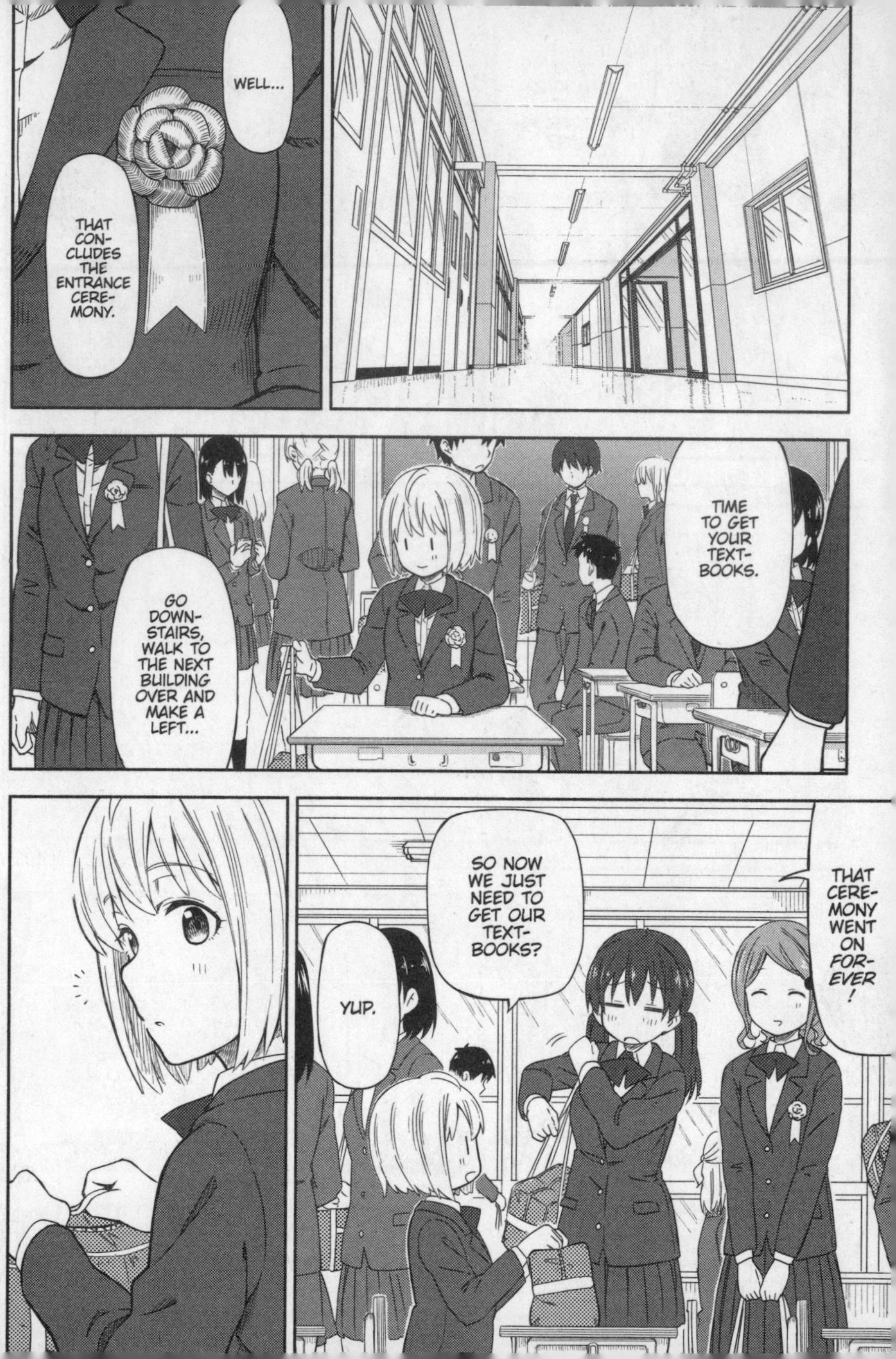
WELL...
THAT CONCLUDES THE ENTRANCE CEREMONY.
TIME TO GET YOUR TEXTBOOKS.
GO DOWNSTAIRS, WALK TO THE NEXT BUILDING OVER AND MAKE A LEFT...
THAT CEREMONY WENT ON FOREVER!
SO NOW WE JUST NEED TO GET OUR TEXTBOOKS?
YUP.

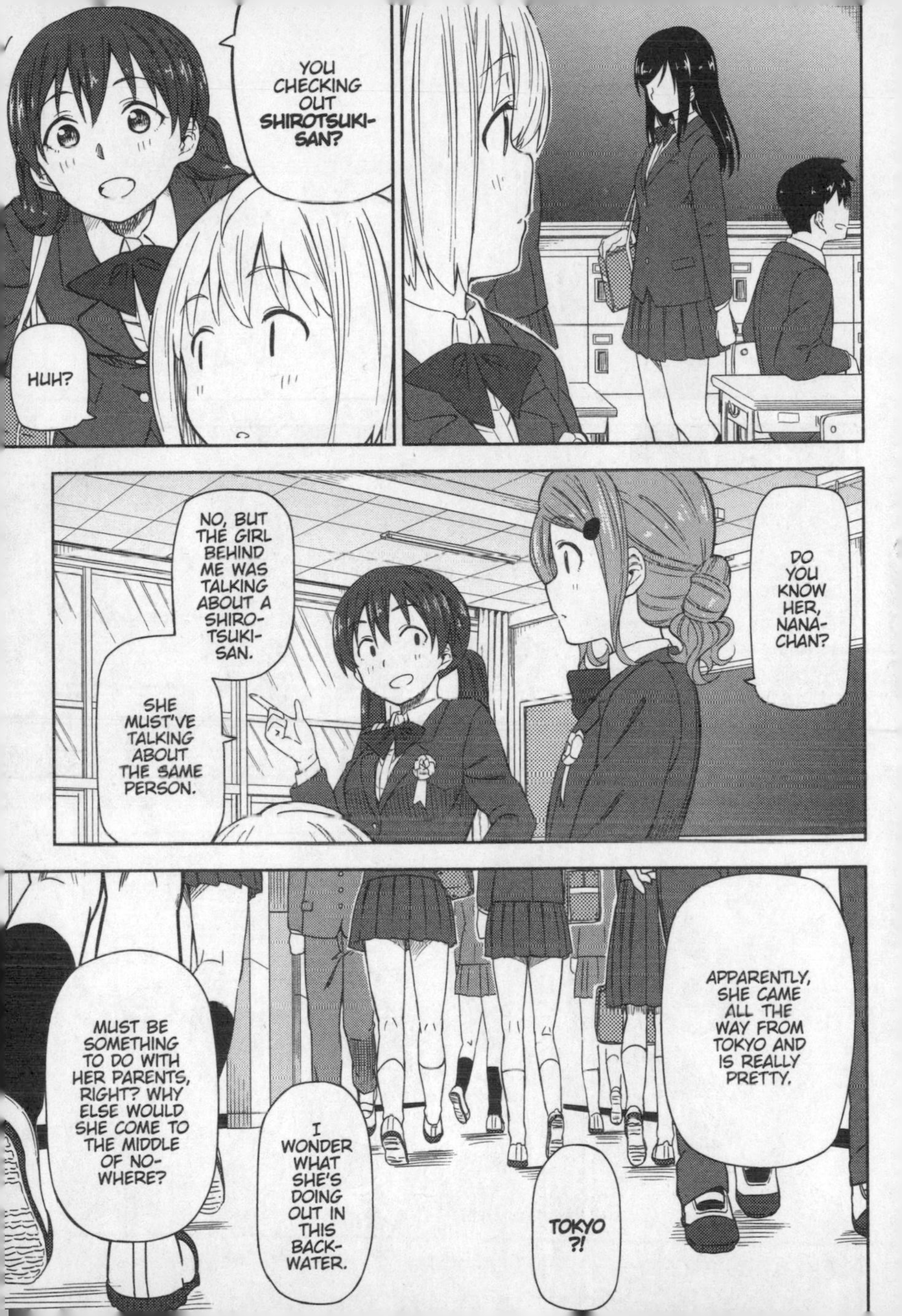
YOU CHECKING OUT SHIROTSUKI-SAN?
HUH?
DO YOU KNOW HER, NANA-CHAN?
NO, BUT THE GIRL BEHIND ME WAS TALKING ABOUT A SHIRO-TSUKI-SAN.
SHE MUST'VE TALKING ABOUT THE SAME PERSON.
APPARENTLY, SHE CAME ALL THE WAY FROM TOKYO AND IS REALLY PRETTY.
TOKYO ?!
I WONDER WHAT SHE'S DOING OUT IN THIS BACK-WATER.
MUST BE SOMETHING TO DO WITH HER PARENTS, RIGHT? WHY ELSE WOULD SHE COME TO THE MIDDLE OF NO-WHERE?

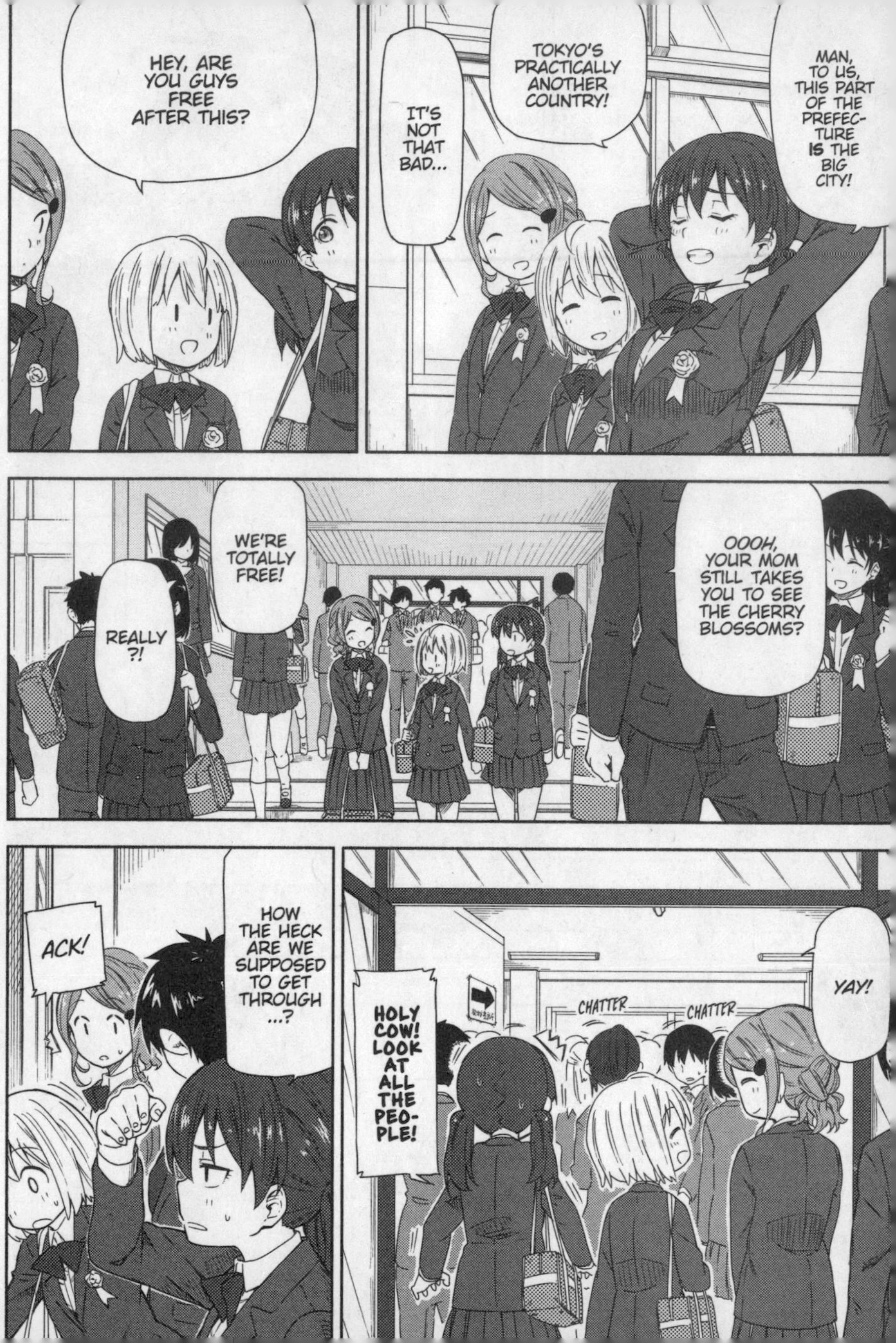
MAN, TO US, THIS PART OF THE PREFECTURE IS THE BIG CITY!
TOKYO'S PRACTICALLY ANOTHER COUNTRY!
IT'S NOT THAT BAD...
HEY, ARE YOU GUYS FREE AFTER THIS?
OOOH, YOUR MOM STILL TAKES YOU TO SEE THE CHERRY BLOSSOMS?
WE'RE TOTALLY FREE!
REALLY?!
YAY!
CHATTER
CHATTER
HOLY COW! LOOK AT ALL THE PEOPLE!
HOW THE HECK ARE WE SUPPOSED TO GET THROUGH ...?
ACK!

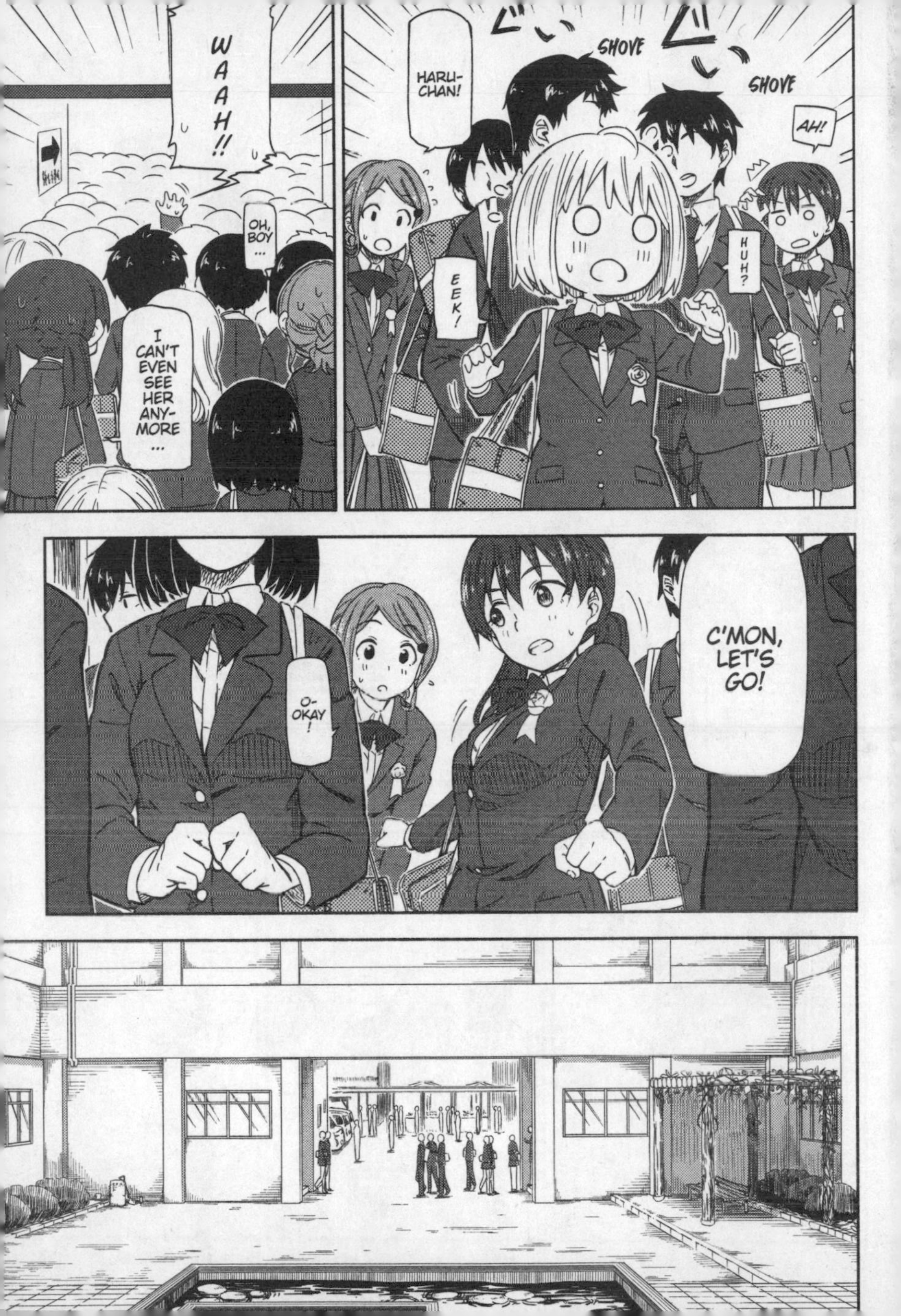
ぐい
SHOVE
ぐい
SHOVE
AH!
HARU-CHAN!
HUH?
EEK!
WAAAH!!
OH, BOY...
I CAN'T EVEN SEE HER ANYMORE...
C'MON, LET'S GO!
O-OKAY!

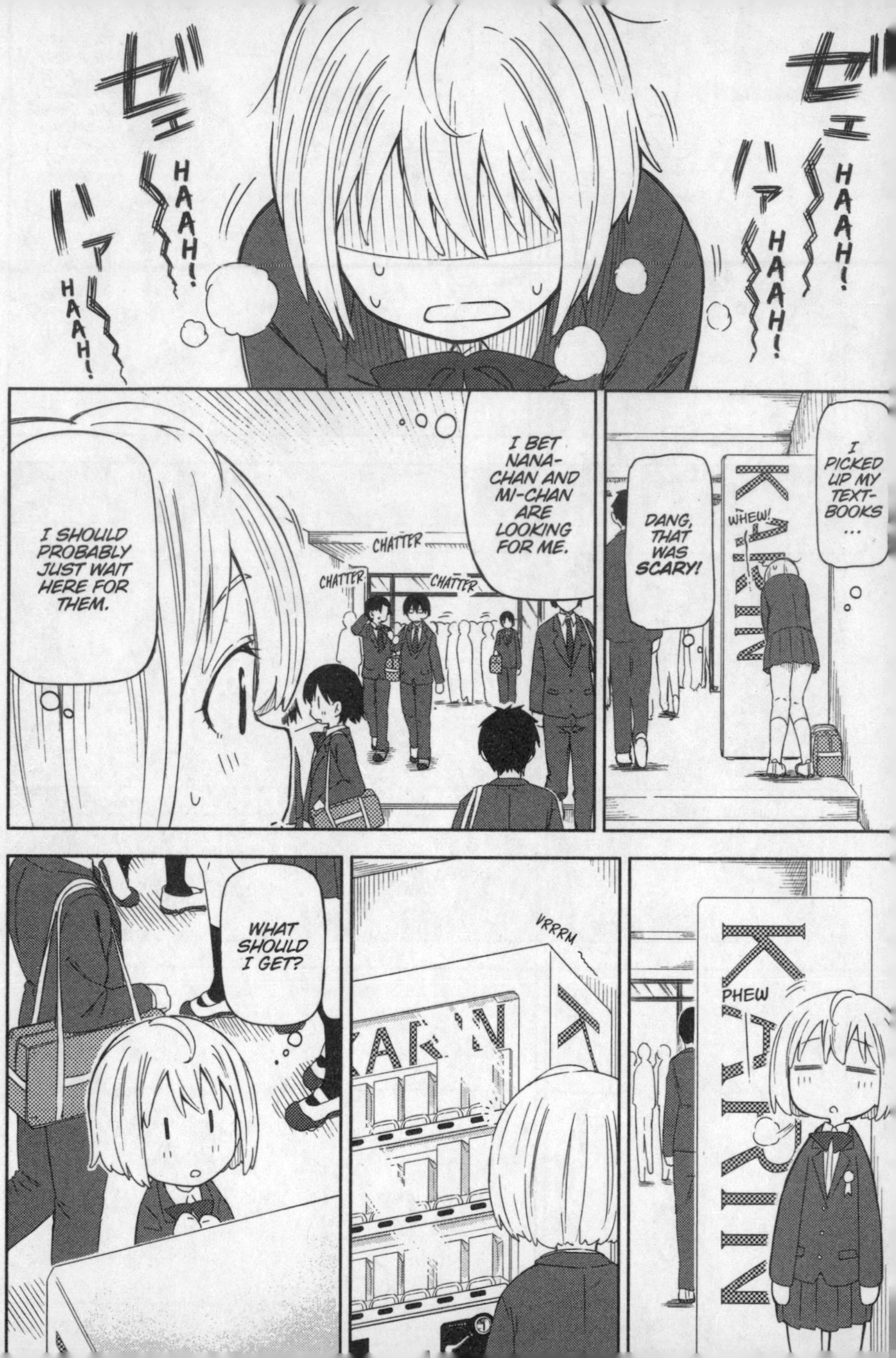

ゼェ
ハァ
HAAAH!
HAAAH!
ゼェ
ハァ
HAAAH!
HAAAH!
I PICKED UP MY TEXT-BOOKS ...
DANG, THAT WAS SCARY!
WHEW!
KARIN
I BET NANA-CHAN AND MI-CHAN ARE LOOKING FOR ME.
CHATTER
CHATTER
CHATTER
I SHOULD PROBABLY JUST WAIT HERE FOR THEM.
KARIN
PHEW
VRRRM
KARIN
WHAT SHOULD I GET?

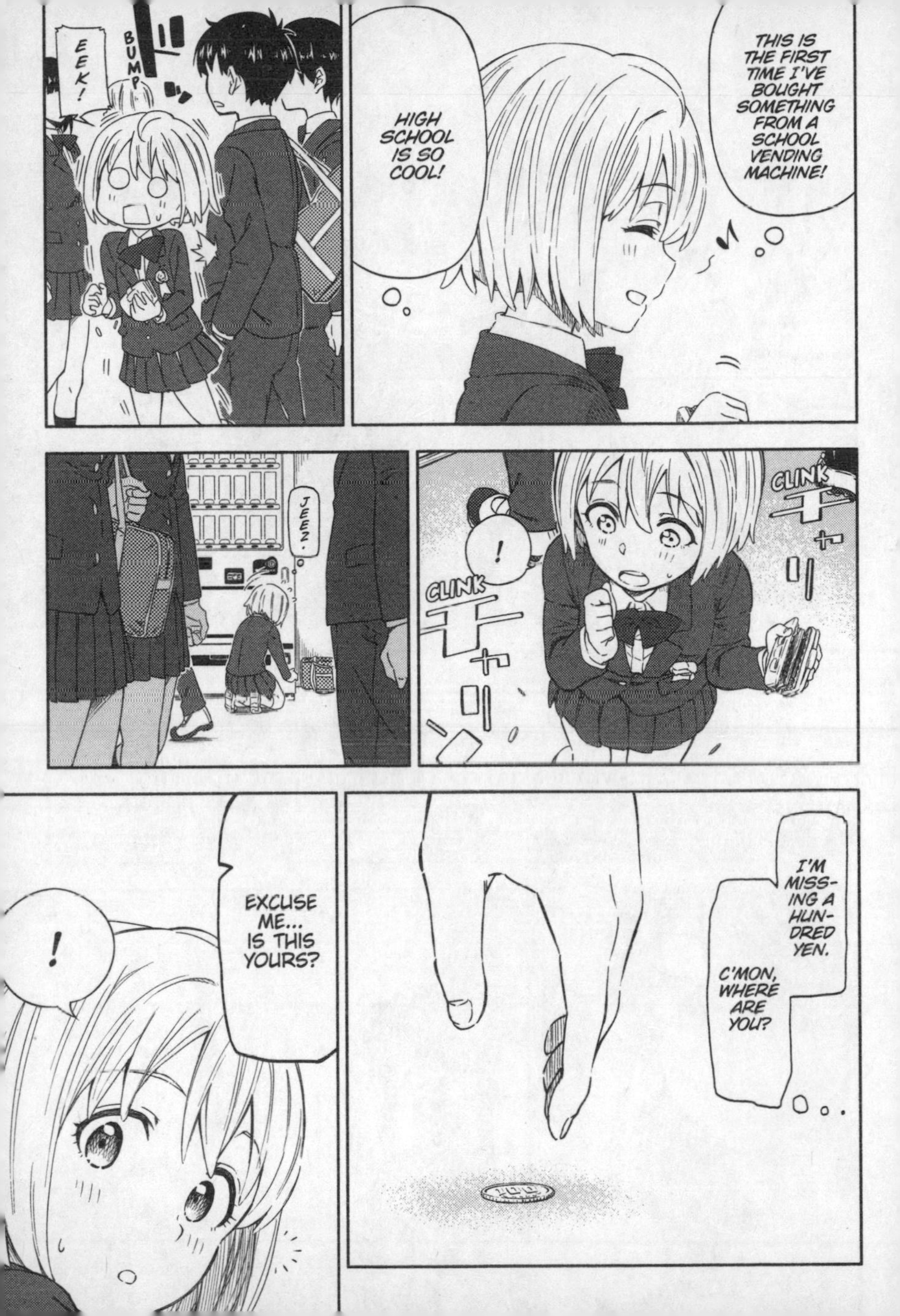
THIS IS THE FIRST TIME I'VE BOUGHT SOMETHING FROM A SCHOOL VENDING MACHINE!
HIGH SCHOOL IS SO COOL!
BUMP
EEK!
CLINK
!
CLINK
JEEZ.
I'M MISSING A HUNDRED YEN.
C'MON, WHERE ARE YOU?
EXCUSE ME... IS THIS YOURS?
!

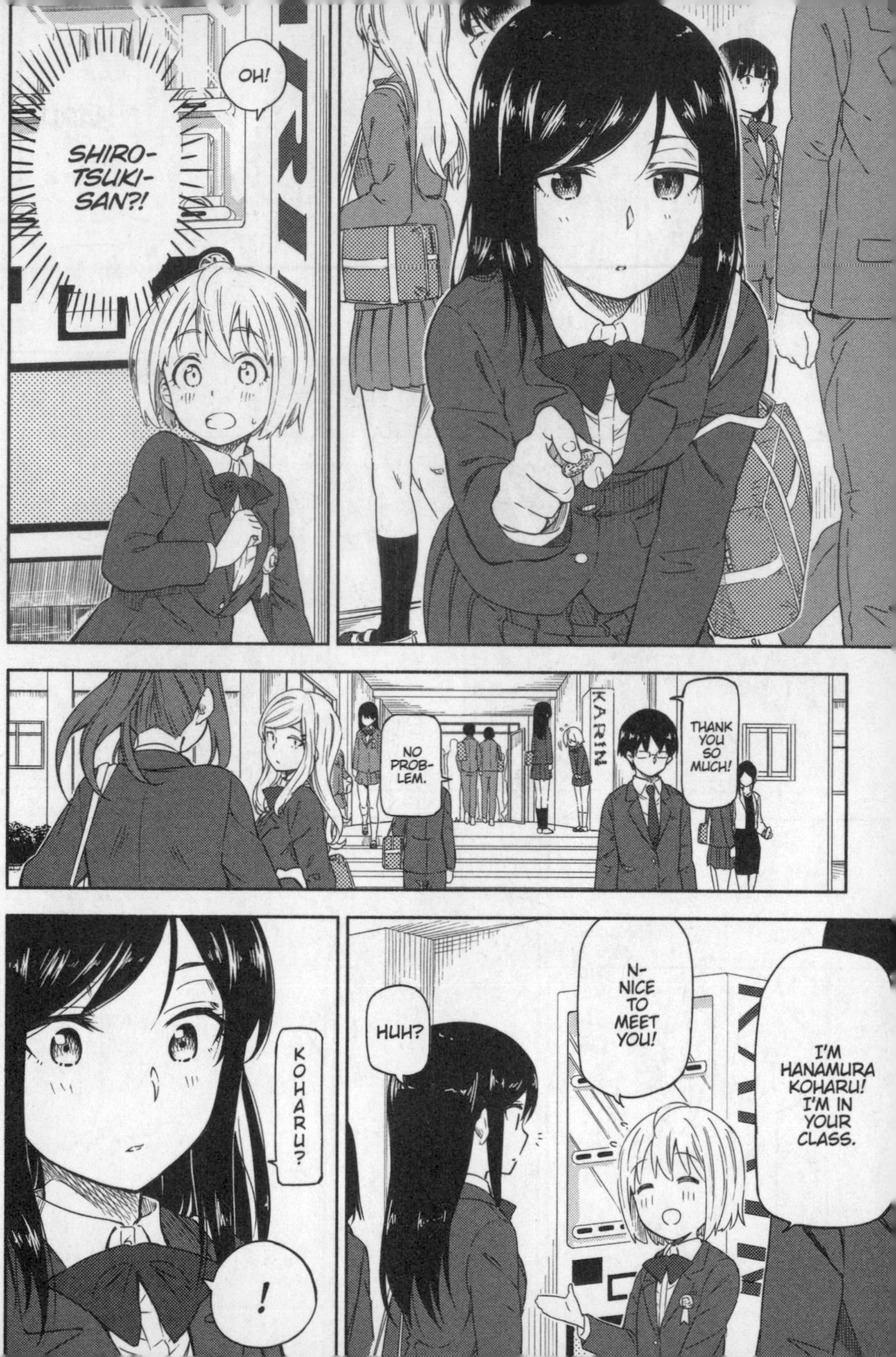
OH!
SHIRO-TSUKI-SAN?!
THANK YOU SO MUCH!
NO PROB-LEM.
KARIN
I'M HANAMURA KOHARU! I'M IN YOUR CLASS.
N-NICE TO MEET YOU!
HUH?
KOHARU?
!

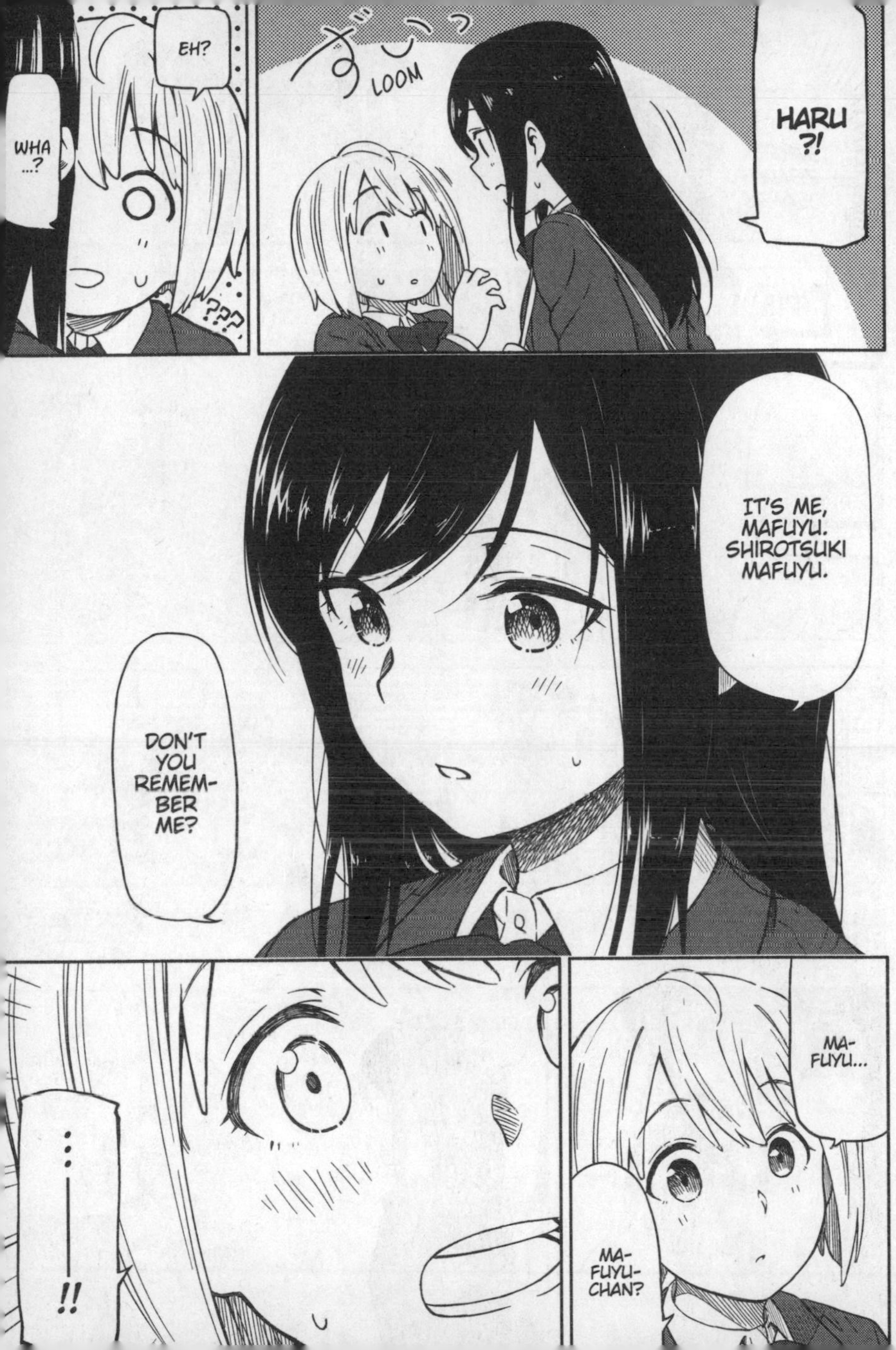
HARU ?!
LOOM
EH?
WHA ...?
???
IT'S ME, MAFUYU. SHIROTSUKI MAFUYU.
DON'T YOU REMEMBER ME?
MA-FUYU...
MA-FUYU-CHAN?
...!!

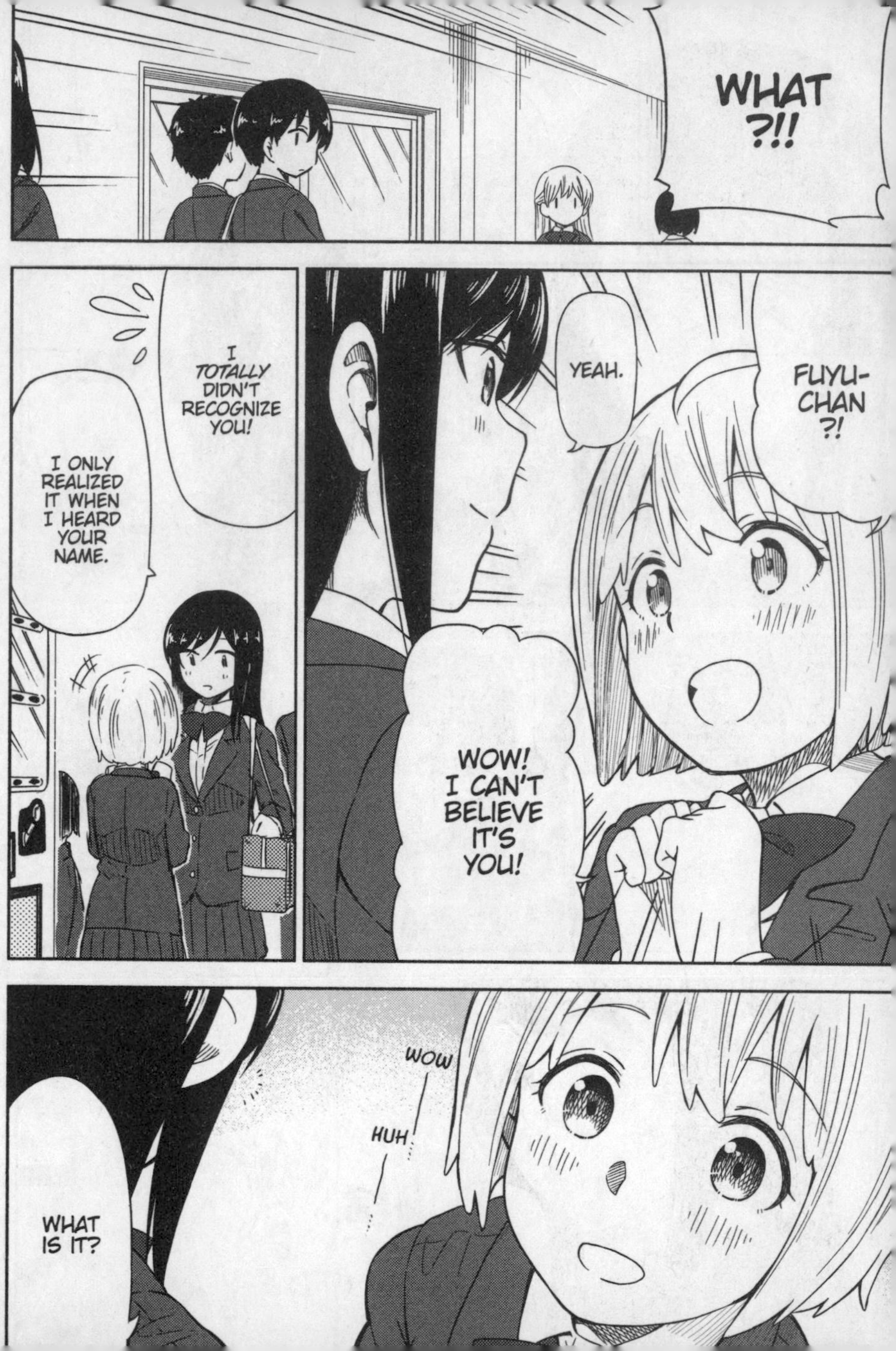
WHAT ?!!
FUYU-CHAN ?!
YEAH.
WOW! I CAN'T BELIEVE IT'S YOU!
I *TOTALLY* DIDN'T RECOGNIZE YOU!
I ONLY REALIZED IT WHEN I HEARD YOUR NAME.
WOW
HUH
WHAT IS IT?

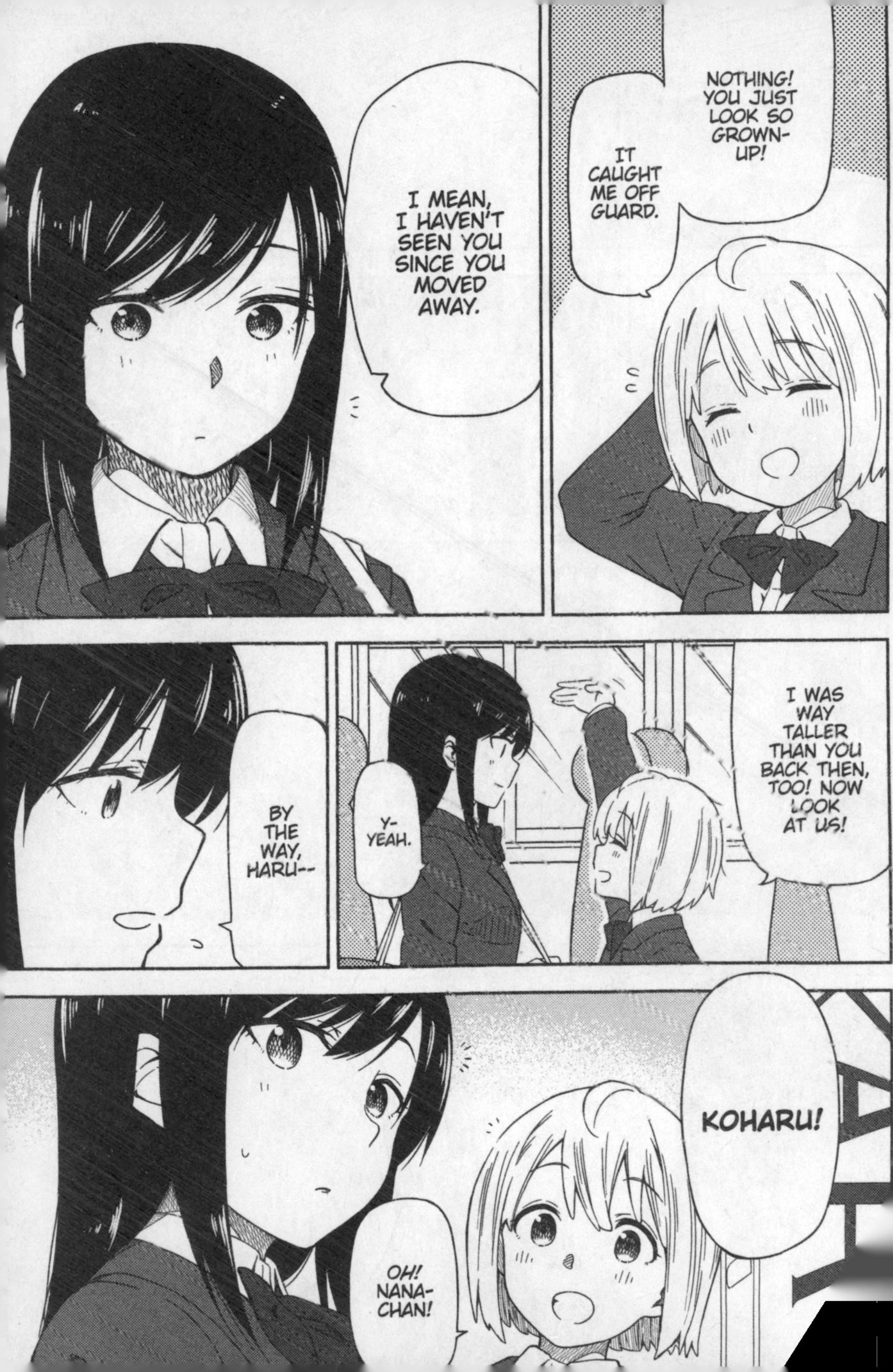
NOTHING! YOU JUST LOOK SO GROWN-UP!
IT CAUGHT ME OFF GUARD.
I MEAN, I HAVEN'T SEEN YOU SINCE YOU MOVED AWAY.
I WAS WAY TALLER THAN YOU BACK THEN, TOO! NOW LOOK AT US!
Y-YEAH.
BY THE WAY, HARU--
KOHARU!
OH! NANA-CHAN!

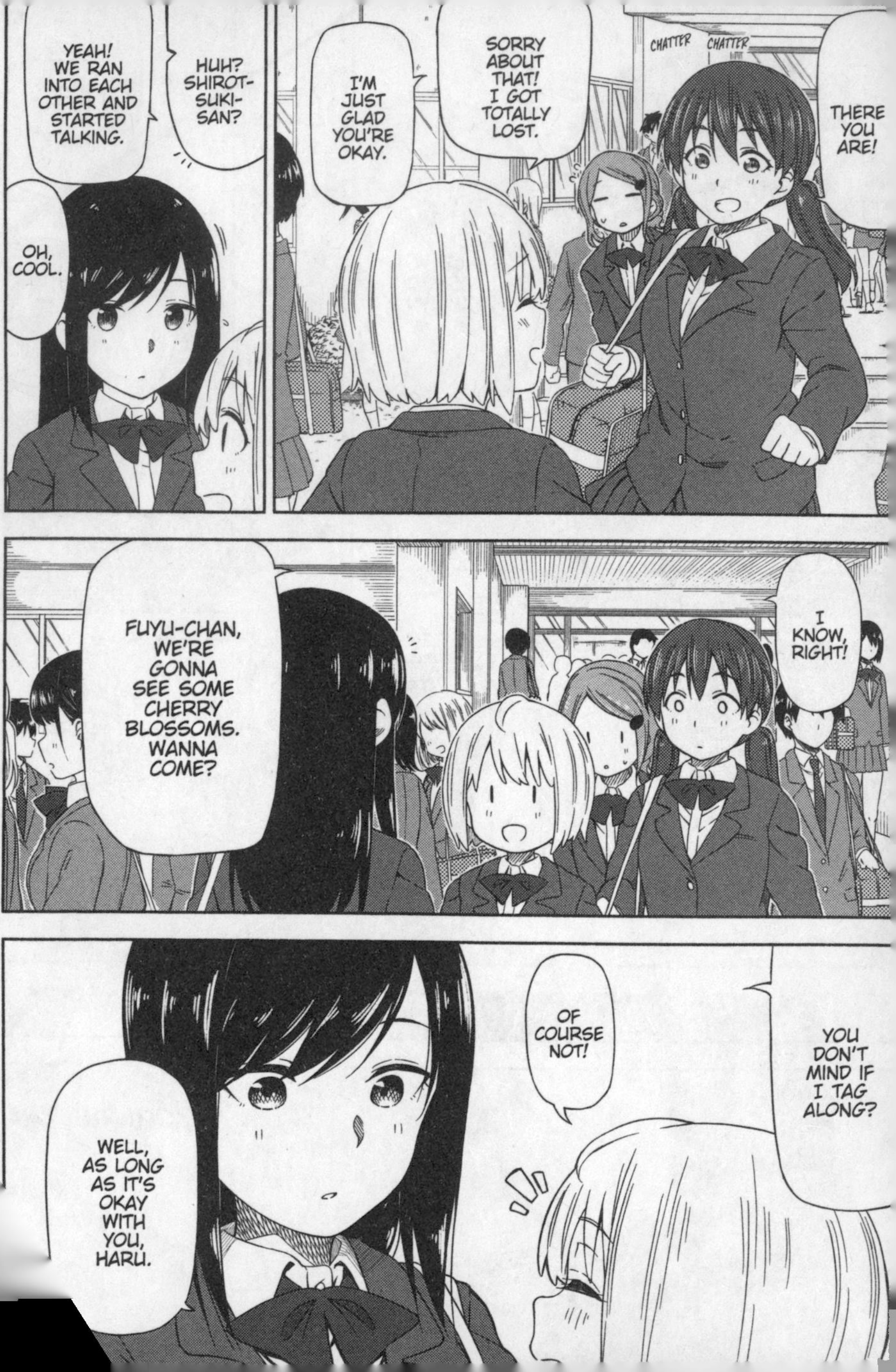
THERE YOU ARE!
CHATTER CHATTER
SORRY ABOUT THAT! I GOT TOTALLY LOST.
I'M JUST GLAD YOU'RE OKAY.
HUH? SHIROT-SUKI-SAN?
YEAH! WE RAN INTO EACH OTHER AND STARTED TALKING.
OH, COOL.
I KNOW, RIGHT!
FUYU-CHAN, WE'RE GONNA SEE SOME CHERRY BLOSSOMS. WANNA COME?
YOU DON'T MIND IF I TAG ALONG?
OF COURSE NOT!
WELL, AS LONG AS IT'S OKAY WITH YOU, HARU.

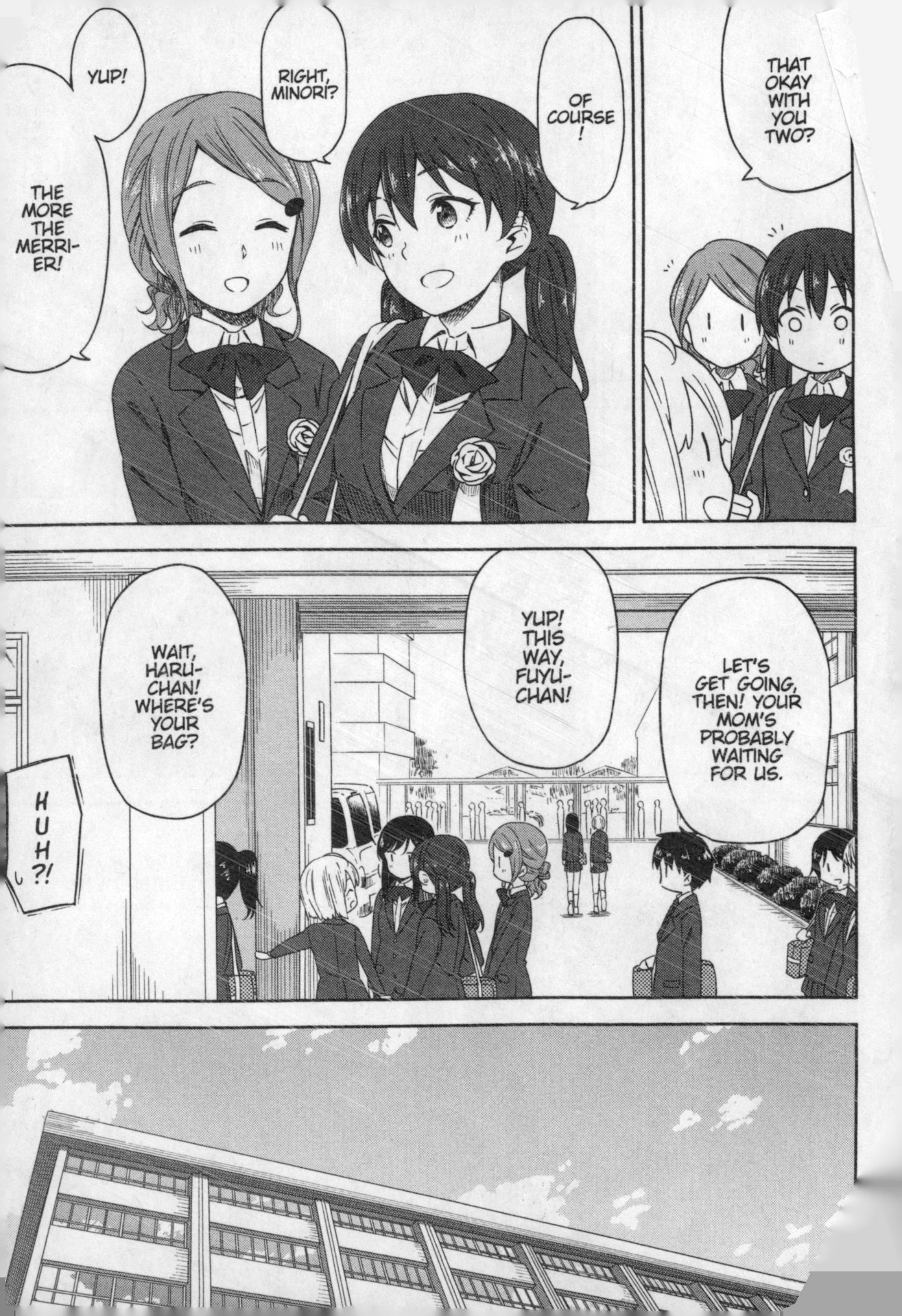
THAT OKAY WITH YOU TWO?
OF COURSE!
RIGHT, MINORI?
YUP!
THE MORE THE MERRIER!
LET'S GET GOING, THEN! YOUR MOM'S PROBABLY WAITING FOR US.
YUP! THIS WAY, FUYU-CHAN!
WAIT, HARU-CHAN! WHERE'S YOUR BAG?
HUH?!

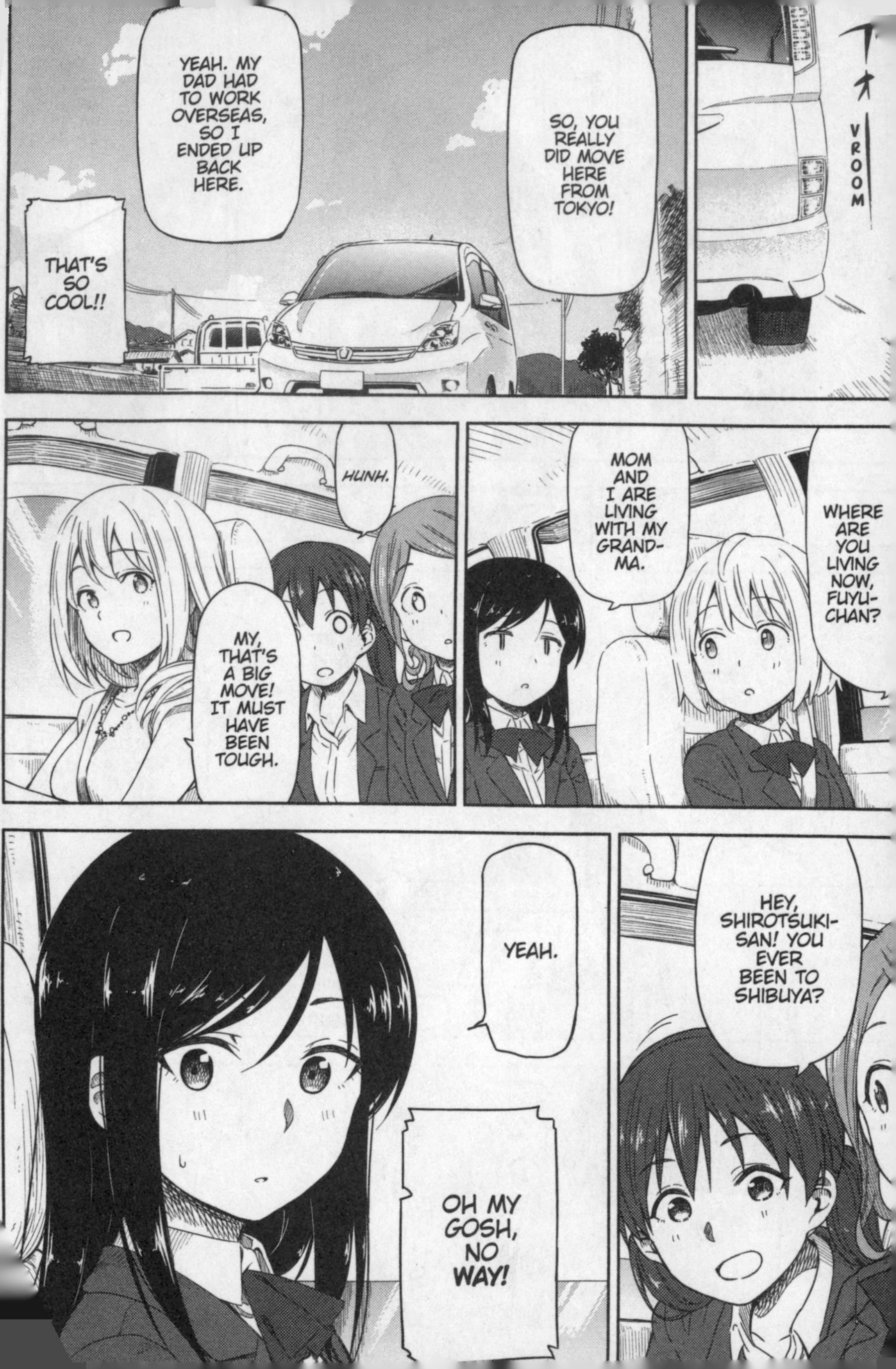
VROOM
SO, YOU REALLY DID MOVE HERE FROM TOKYO!
YEAH. MY DAD HAD TO WORK OVERSEAS, SO I ENDED UP BACK HERE.
THAT'S SO COOL!!
WHERE ARE YOU LIVING NOW, FUYU-CHAN?
MOM AND I ARE LIVING WITH MY GRAND-MA.
HUNH.
MY, THAT'S A BIG MOVE! IT MUST HAVE BEEN TOUGH.
HEY, SHIROTSUKI-SAN! YOU EVER BEEN TO SHIBUYA?
YEAH.
OH MY GOSH, NO WAY!

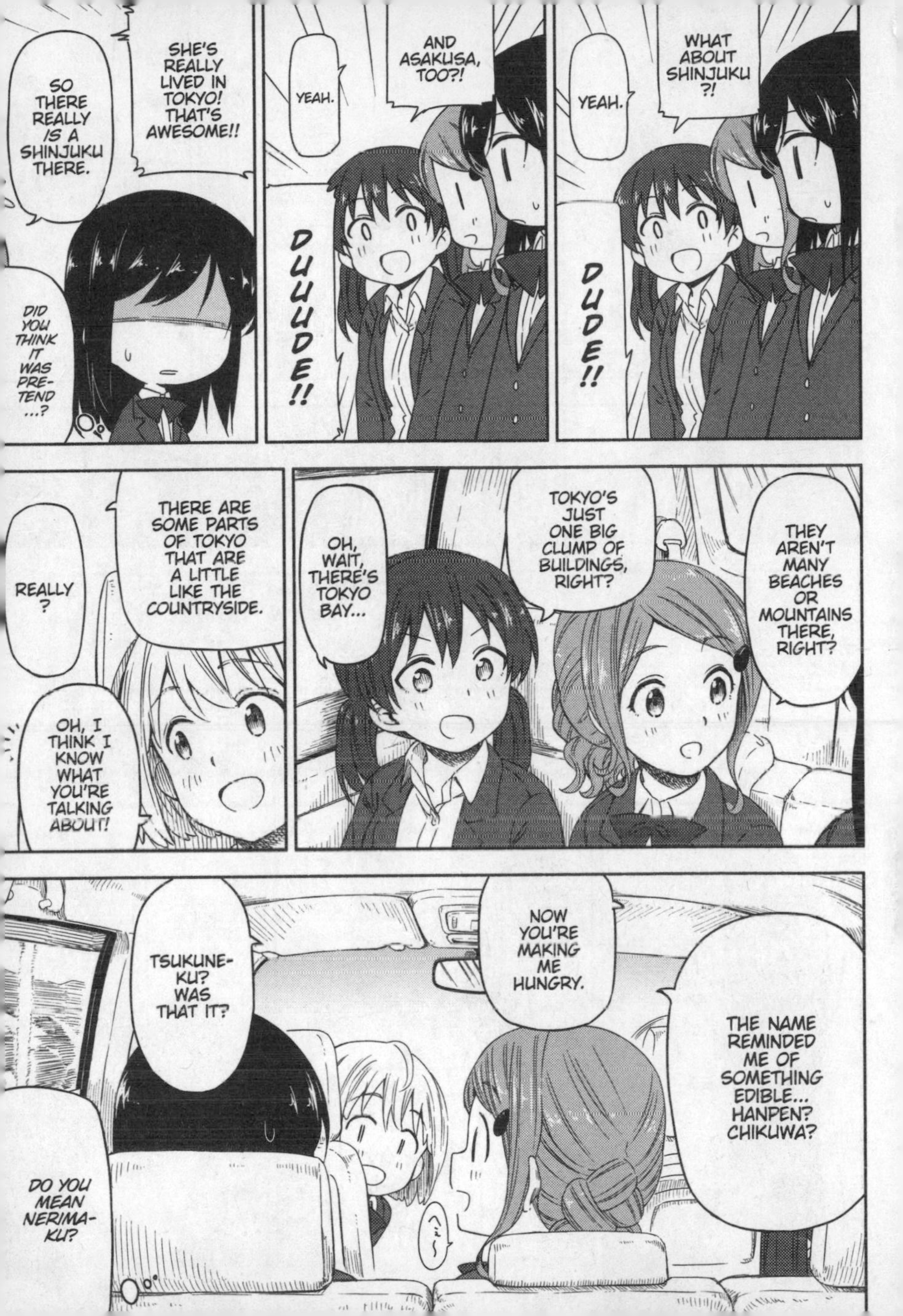
WHAT ABOUT SHINJUKU?!
YEAH.
DUDE!!
AND ASAKUSA, TOO?!
YEAH.
DUUUDE!!
SHE'S REALLY LIVED IN TOKYO! THAT'S AWESOME!!
SO THERE REALLY IS A SHINJUKU THERE.
DID YOU THINK IT WAS PRETEND...?
THEY AREN'T MANY BEACHES OR MOUNTAINS THERE, RIGHT?
TOKYO'S JUST ONE BIG CLUMP OF BUILDINGS, RIGHT?
OH, WAIT, THERE'S TOKYO BAY...
THERE ARE SOME PARTS OF TOKYO THAT ARE A LITTLE LIKE THE COUNTRYSIDE.
REALLY?
OH, I THINK I KNOW WHAT YOU'RE TALKING ABOUT!
THE NAME REMINDED ME OF SOMETHING EDIBLE... HANPEN? CHIKUWA?
NOW YOU'RE MAKING ME HUNGRY.
TSUKUNE-KU? WAS THAT IT?
DO YOU MEAN NERIMAKU?

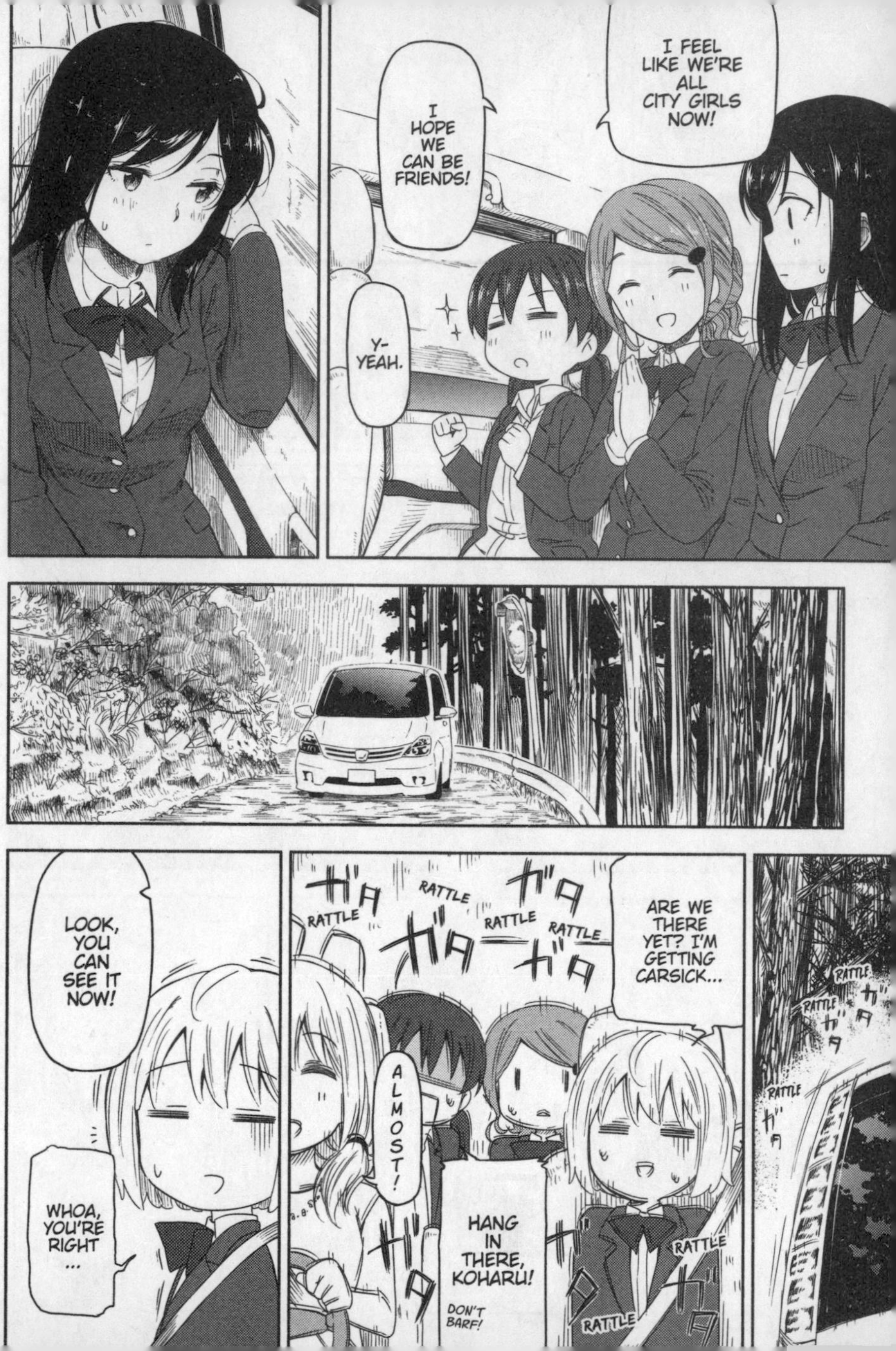
I FEEL LIKE WE'RE ALL CITY GIRLS NOW!
I HOPE WE CAN BE FRIENDS!
Y- YEAH.
RATTLE
ガタ
RATTLE
ガタ
RATTLE
ガタ
ARE WE THERE YET? I'M GETTING CARSICK...
RATTLE
ガタ
RATTLE
ガタ
RATTLE
RATTLE
ガタ
ガタ
ALMOST!
HANG IN THERE, KOHARU!
DON'T BARF!
RATTLE
RATTLE
ガタ
LOOK, YOU CAN SEE IT NOW!
WHOA, YOU'RE RIGHT...

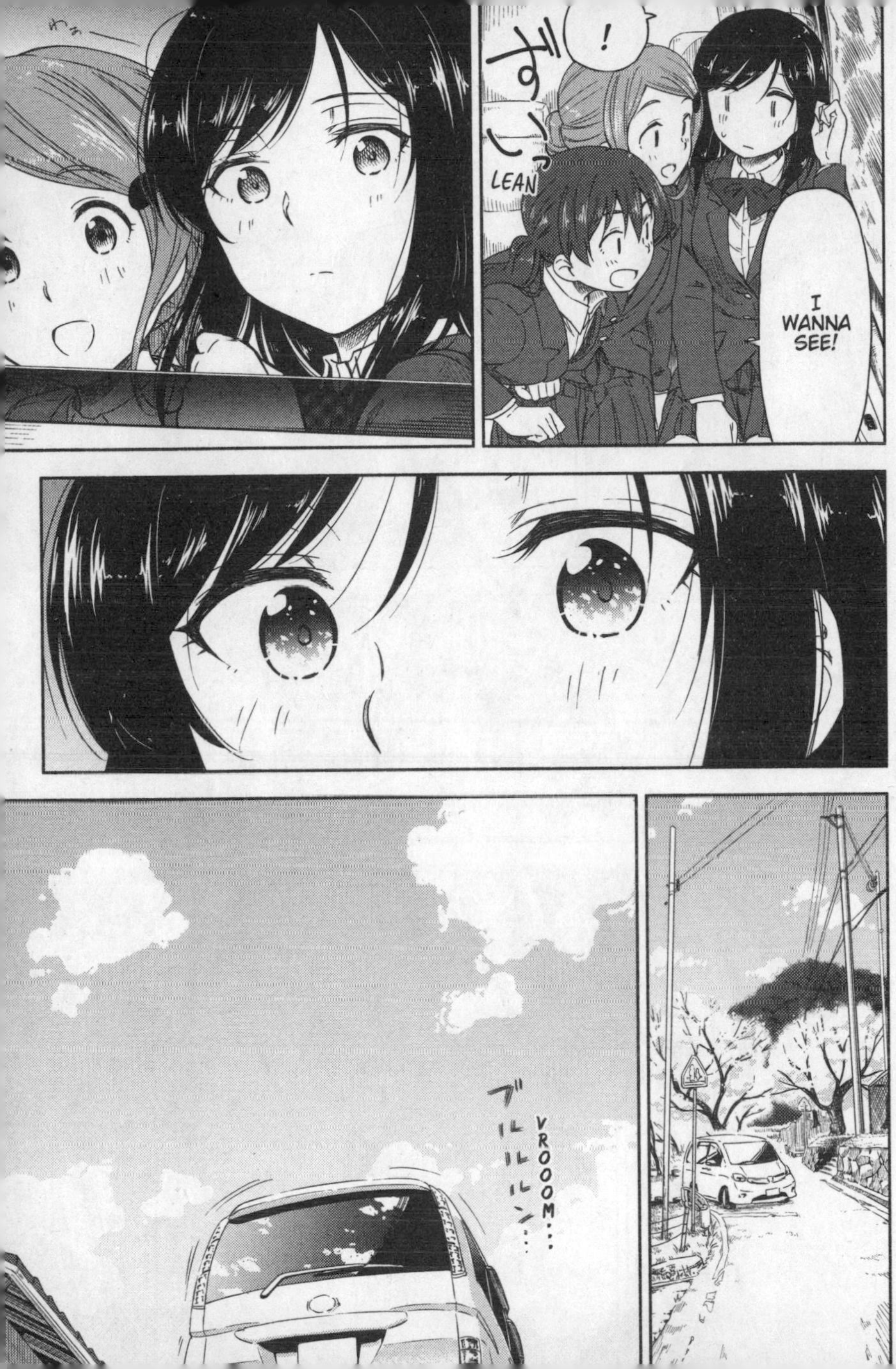
!
ずいっ
LEAN
I WANNA SEE!
わぁー
ブルルルン…
VROOOM...

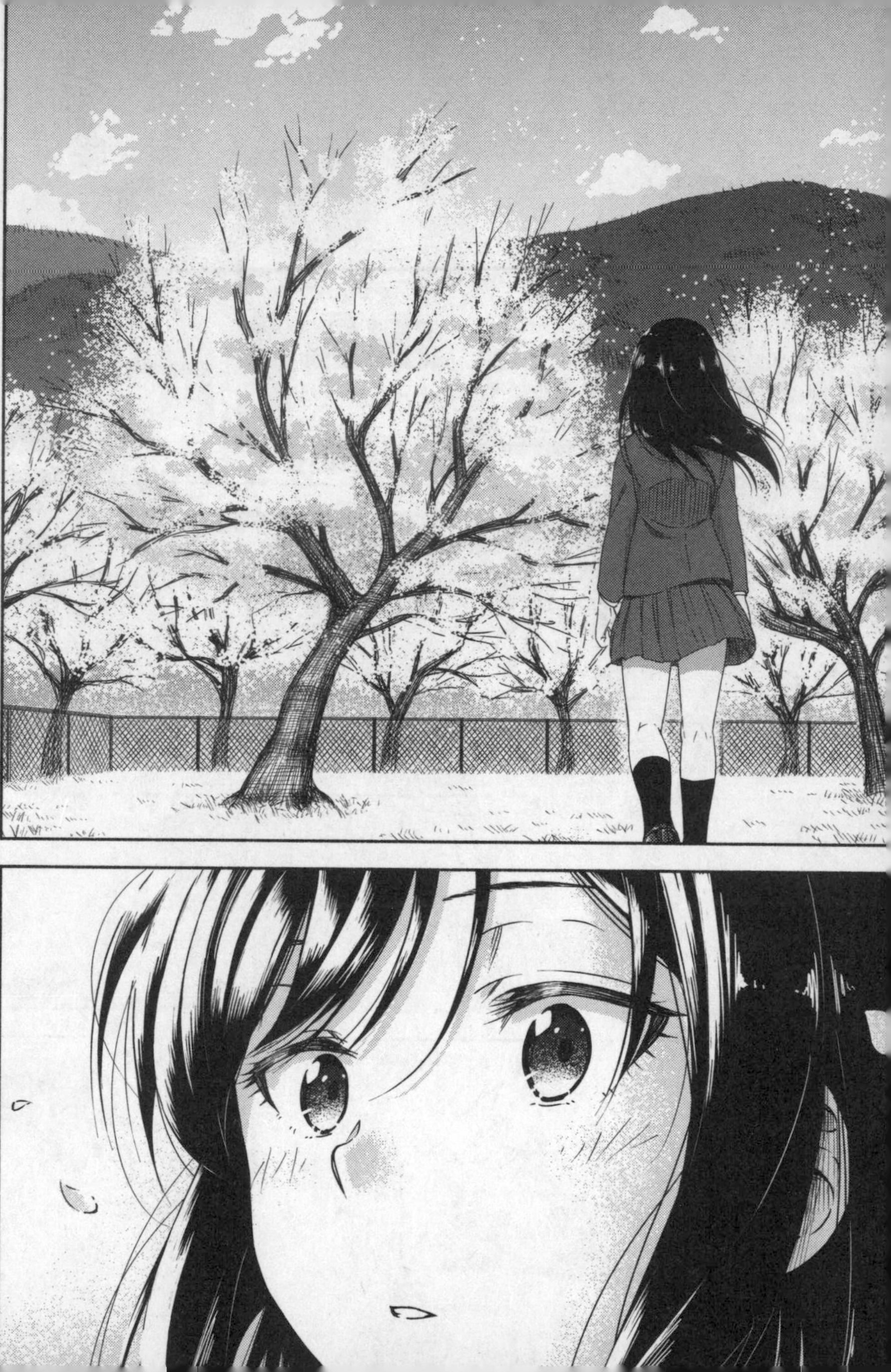

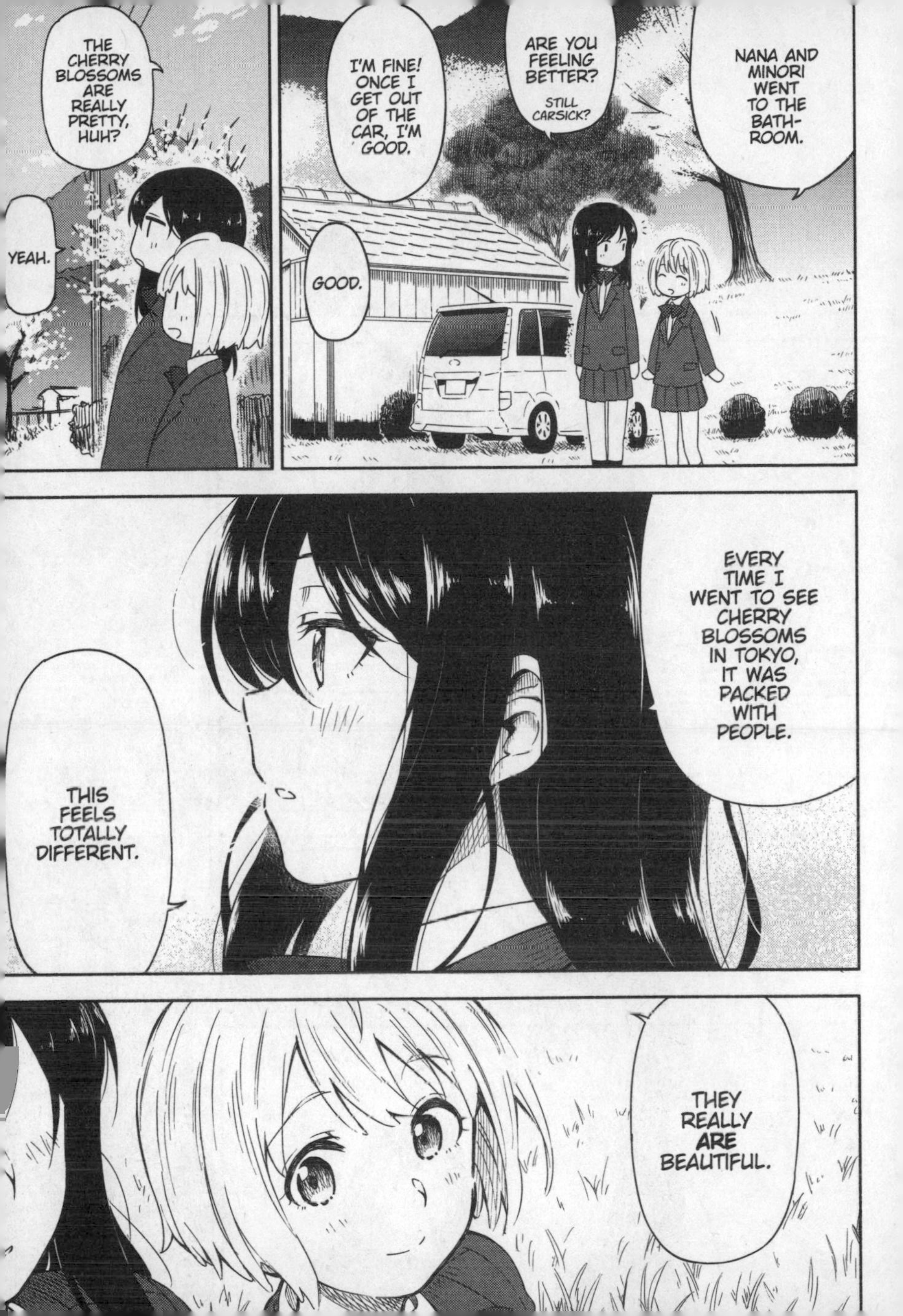
NANA AND MINORI WENT TO THE BATH-ROOM.
ARE YOU FEELING BETTER?
STILL CARSICK?
I'M FINE! ONCE I GET OUT OF THE CAR, I'M GOOD.
GOOD.
THE CHERRY BLOSSOMS ARE REALLY PRETTY, HUH?
YEAH.
EVERY TIME I WENT TO SEE CHERRY BLOSSOMS IN TOKYO, IT WAS PACKED WITH PEOPLE.
THIS FEELS TOTALLY DIFFERENT.
THEY REALLY ARE BEAUTIFUL.

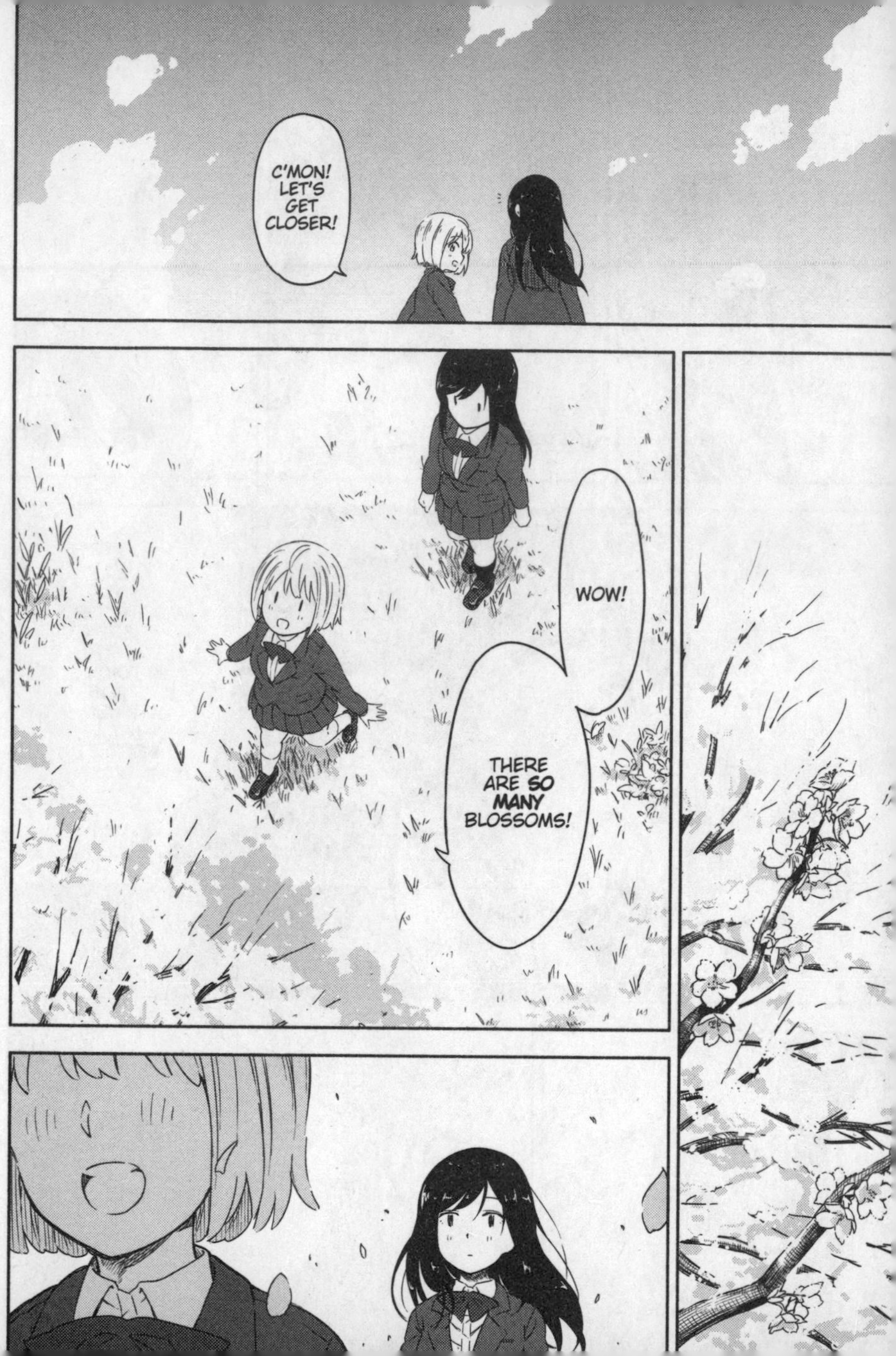
C'MON! LET'S GET CLOSER!
WOW!
THERE ARE SO MANY BLOSSOMS!

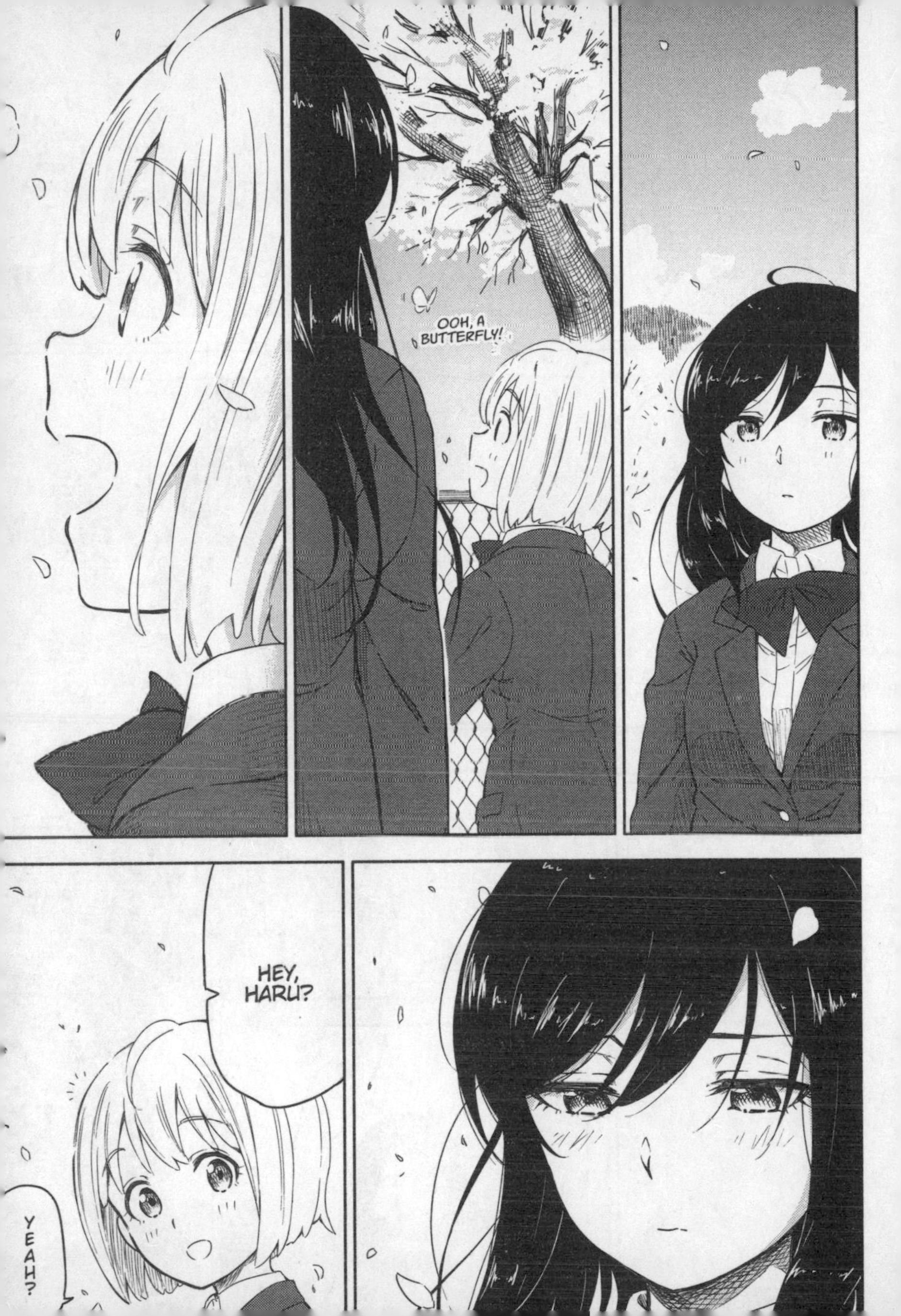
OOH, A BUTTERFLY!
HEY, HARU?
YEAH?

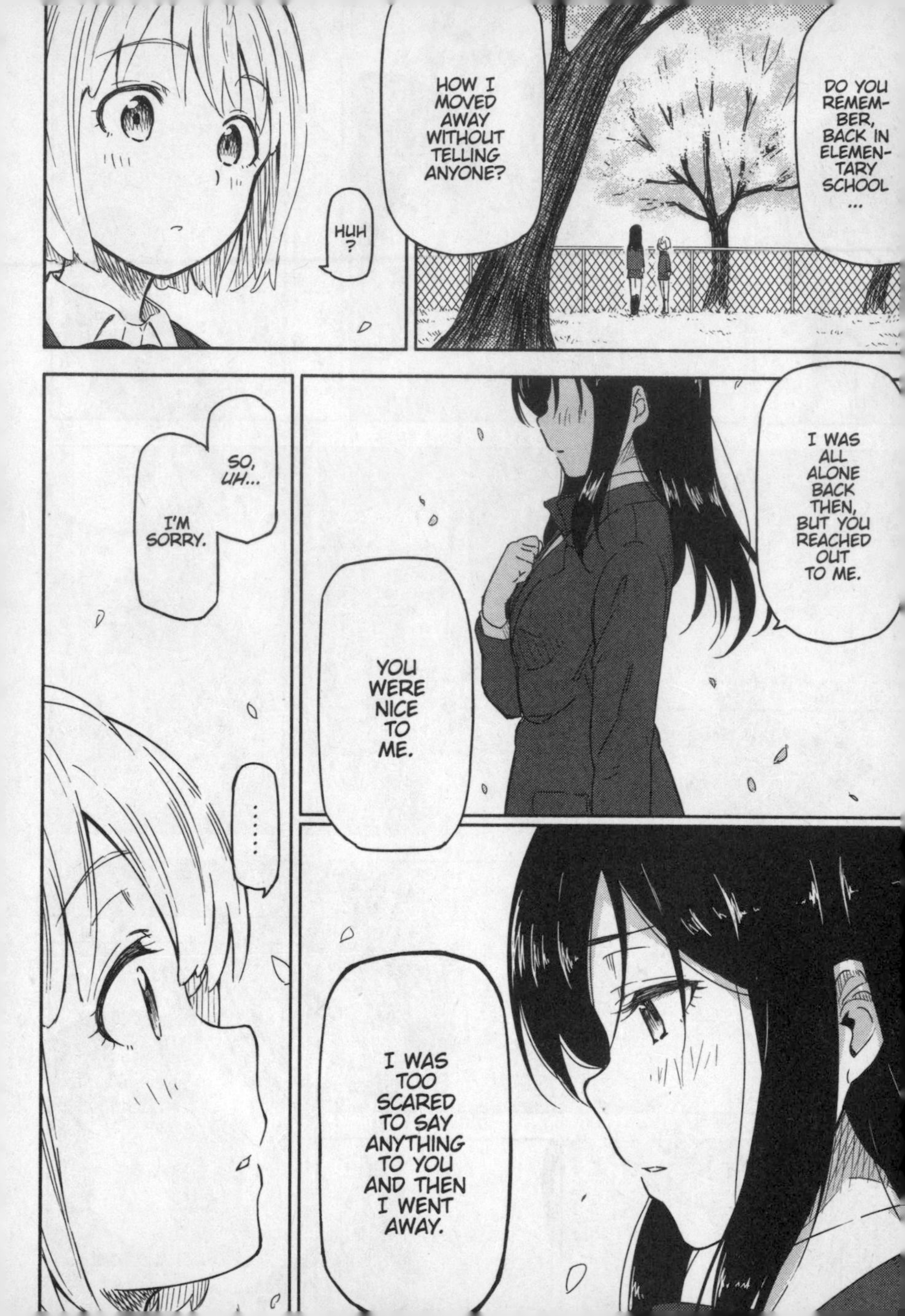
DO YOU REMEMBER, BACK IN ELEMENTARY SCHOOL...
HOW I MOVED AWAY WITHOUT TELLING ANYONE?
HUH?
I WAS ALL ALONE BACK THEN, BUT YOU REACHED OUT TO ME.
YOU WERE NICE TO ME.
I WAS TOO SCARED TO SAY ANYTHING TO YOU AND THEN I WENT AWAY.
SO, UH... I'M SORRY.
......

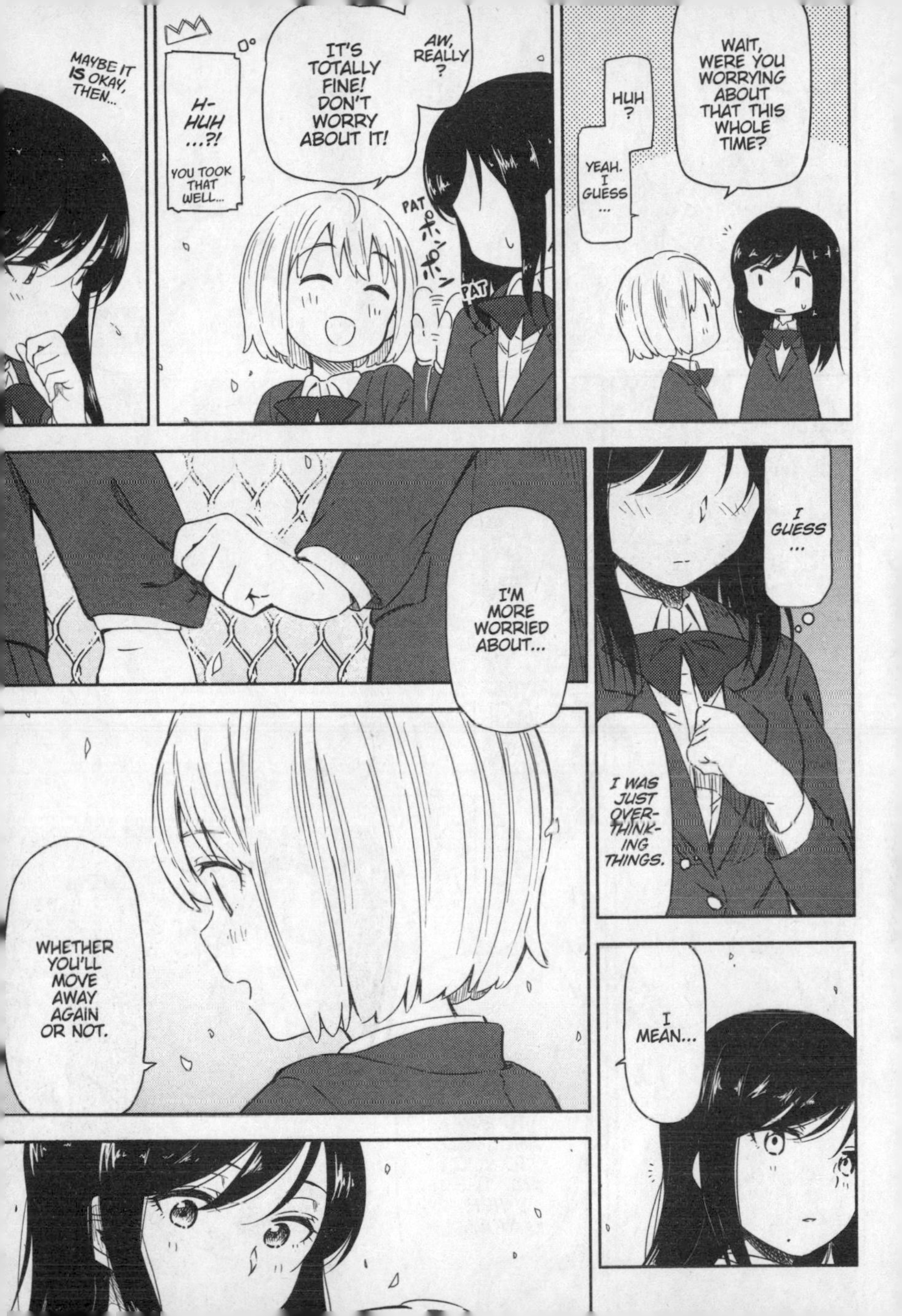
WAIT, WERE YOU WORRYING ABOUT THAT THIS WHOLE TIME?
HUH?
YEAH. I GUESS...
AW, REALLY?
IT'S TOTALLY FINE! DON'T WORRY ABOUT IT!
PAT
PAT
H-HUH...?!
YOU TOOK THAT WELL...
MAYBE IT IS OKAY, THEN...
I GUESS...
I WAS JUST OVER-THINKING THINGS.
I'M MORE WORRIED ABOUT...
WHETHER YOU'LL MOVE AWAY AGAIN OR NOT.
I MEAN...

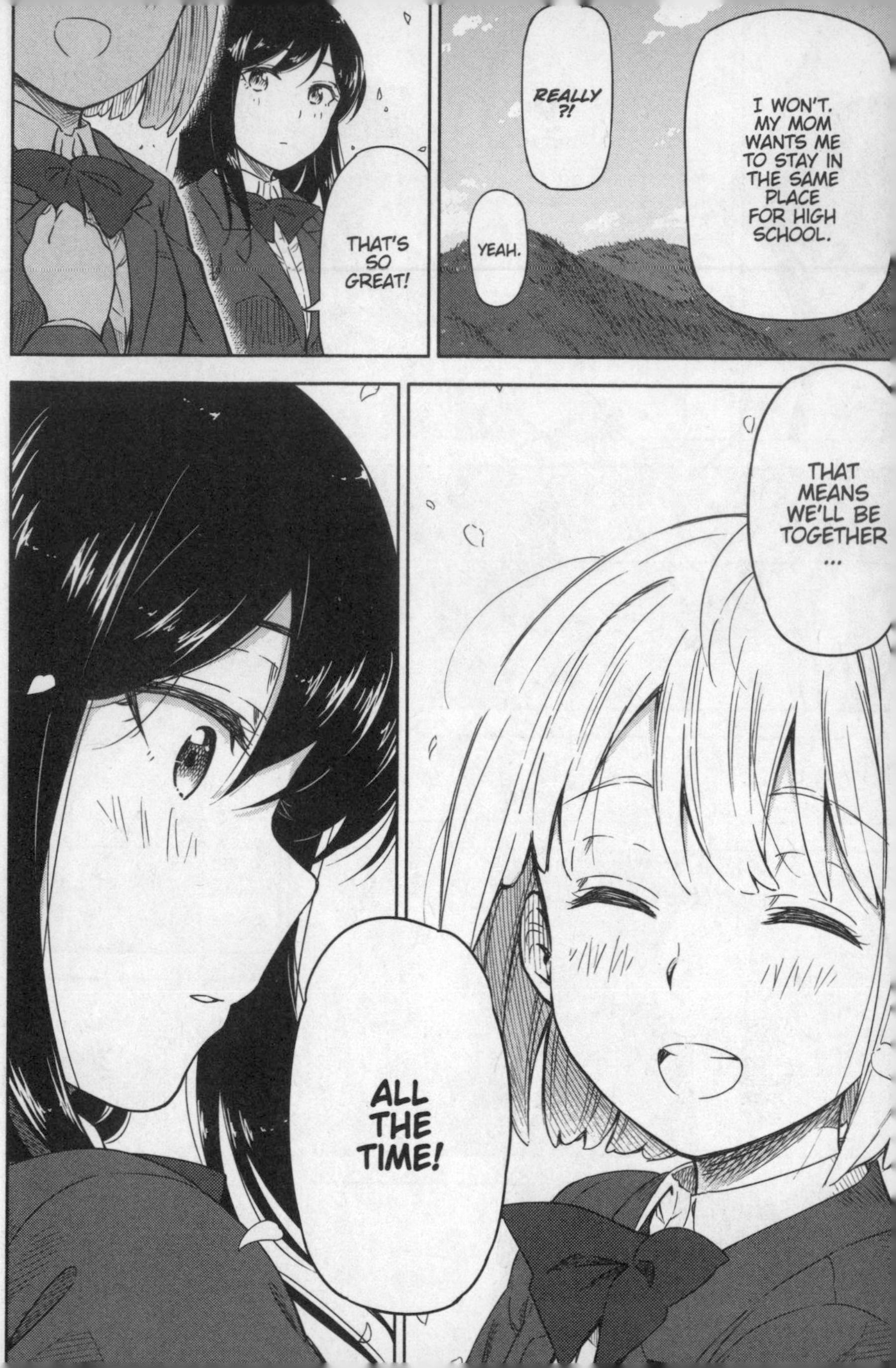
I WON'T. MY MOM WANTS ME TO STAY IN THE SAME PLACE FOR HIGH SCHOOL.
REALLY?!
YEAH.
THAT'S SO GREAT!
THAT MEANS WE'LL BE TOGETHER...
ALL THE TIME!

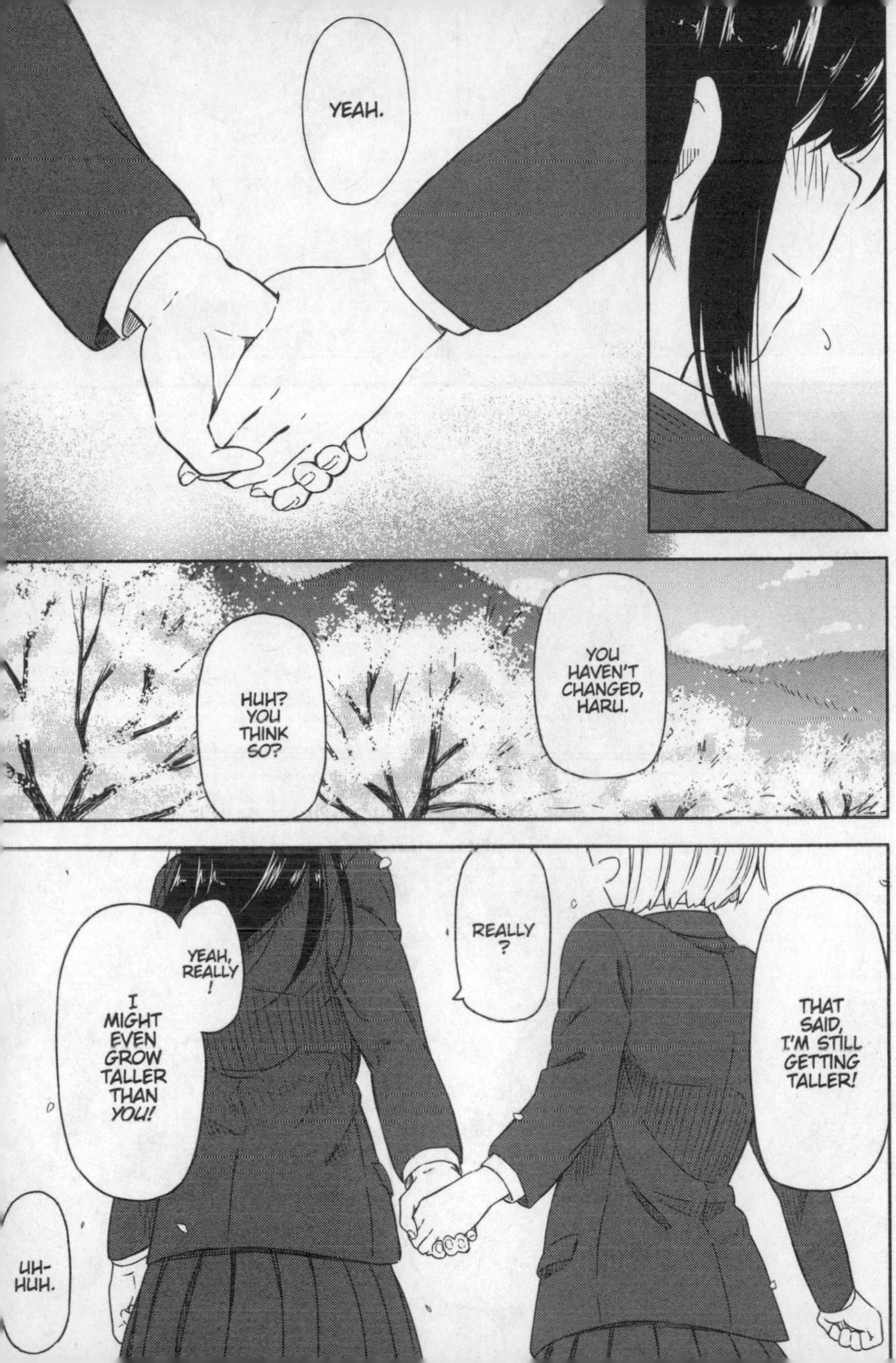
YEAH.
YOU HAVEN'T CHANGED, HARU.
HUH? YOU THINK SO?
THAT SAID, I'M STILL GETTING TALLER!
REALLY?
YEAH, REALLY!
I MIGHT EVEN GROW TALLER THAN YOU!
UH-HUH.

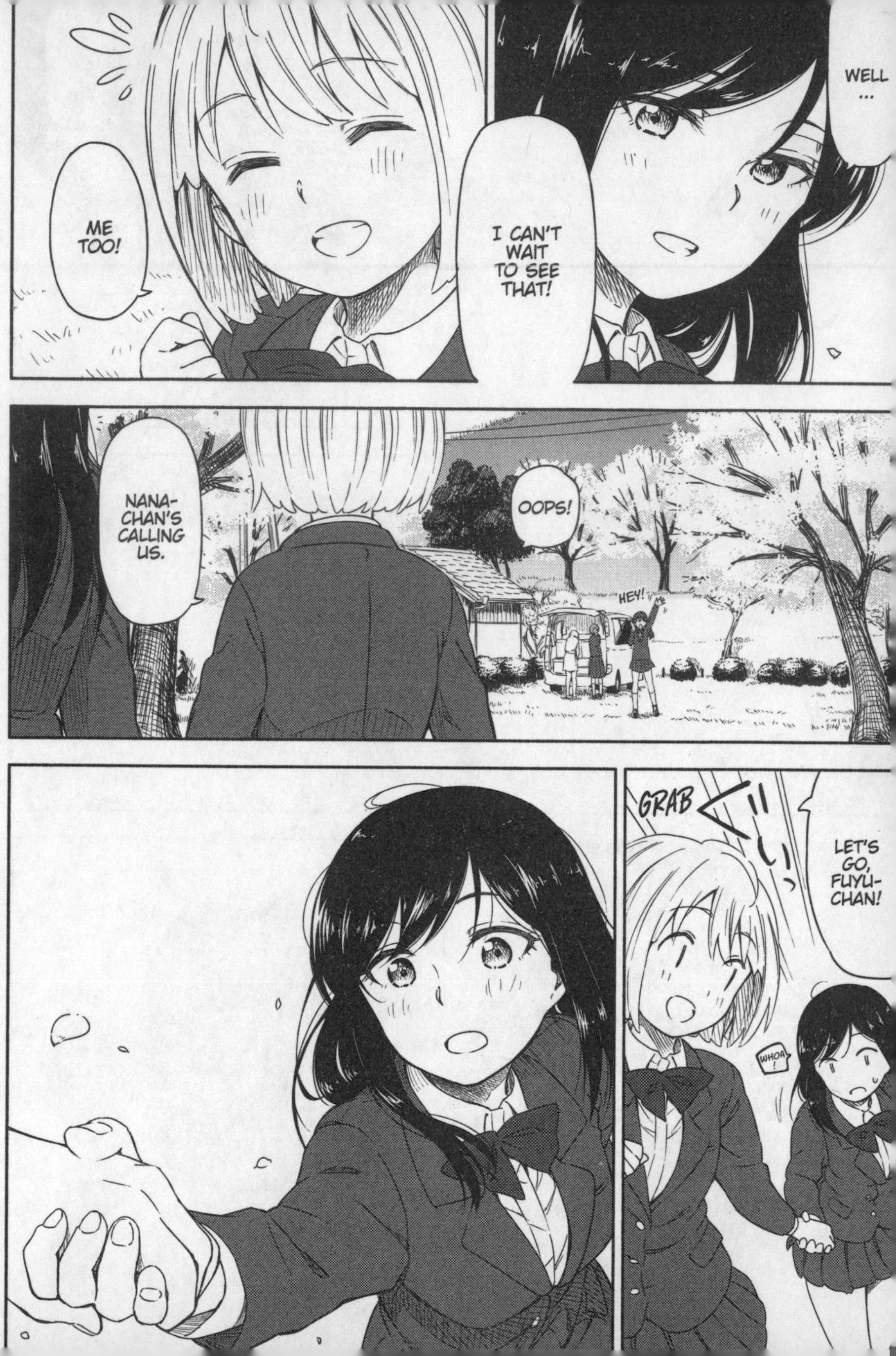
WELL ...
I CAN'T WAIT TO SEE THAT!
ME TOO!
OOPS!
HEY!
NANA-CHAN'S CALLING US.
GRAB
LET'S GO, FUYU-CHAN!
WHOA!

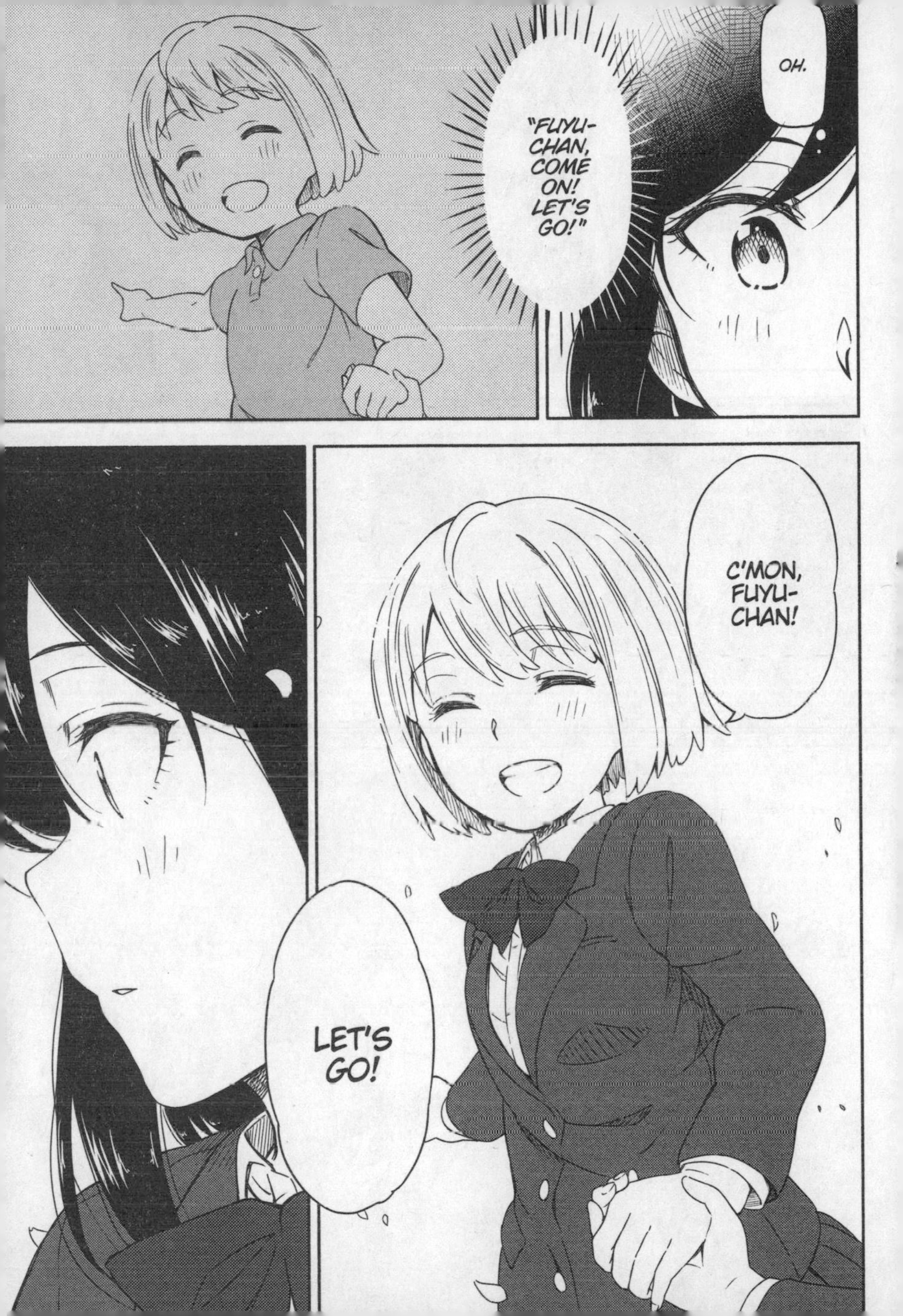
OH.
"FUYU-CHAN, COME ON! LET'S GO!"
C'MON, FUYU-CHAN!
LET'S GO!

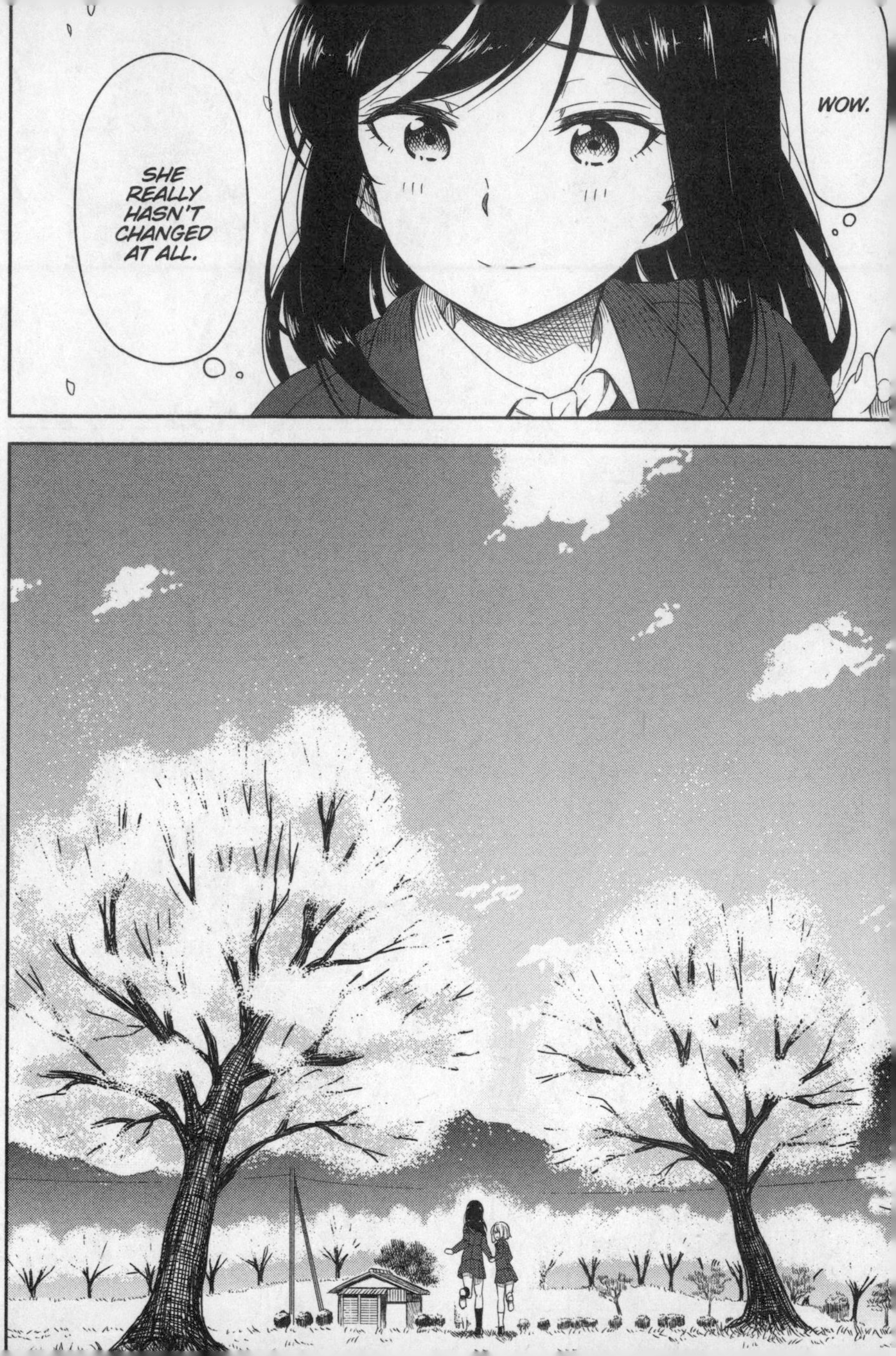
WOW.
SHE REALLY HASN'T CHANGED AT ALL.

Our Wonderful Days

story & art by Kei Hamuro

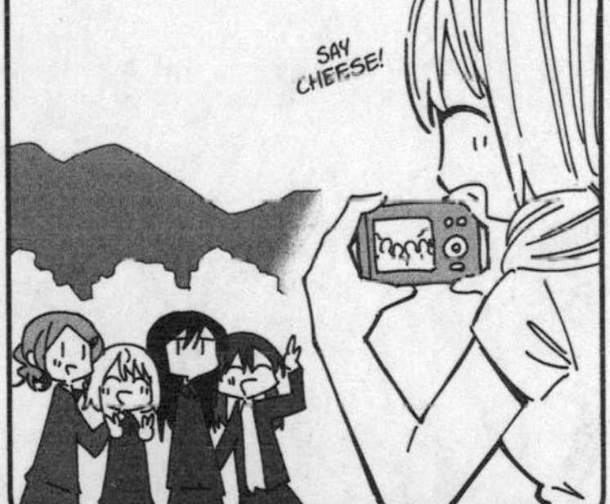
SAY CHEESE!

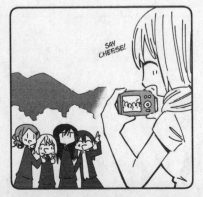

Our Wonderful Days
Tsurezure Biyori

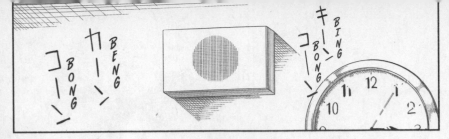

コ BONG サ BENG コ BONG キ BING

FUYU-CHAN, LET'S WALK HOME TOGE-THER!

OKAY.

UH...

OH.

MAN, I'M POOPED!

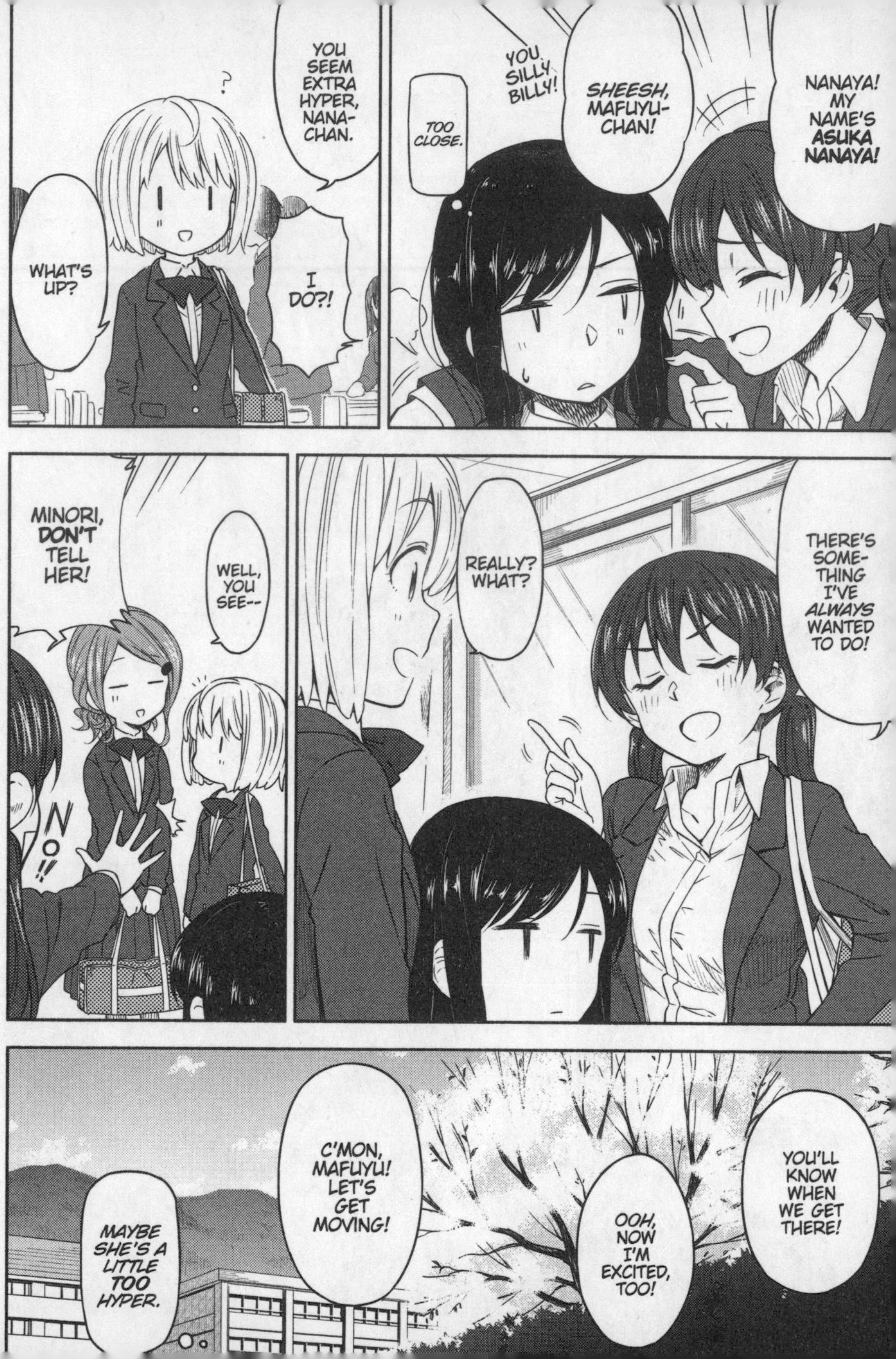
NANAYA! MY NAME'S ASUKA NANAYA!
SHEESH, MAFUYU-CHAN!
YOU SILLY BILLY!
TOO CLOSE.
YOU SEEM EXTRA HYPER, NANA-CHAN.
?
I DO?!
WHAT'S UP?
THERE'S SOME-THING I'VE ALWAYS WANTED TO DO!
REALLY? WHAT?
WELL, YOU SEE--
MINORI, DON'T TELL HER!
NO!!
YOU'LL KNOW WHEN WE GET THERE!
OOH, NOW I'M EXCITED, TOO!
C'MON, MAFUYU! LET'S GET MOVING!
MAYBE SHE'S A LITTLE TOO HYPER.

Chapter 2
Their Home Life

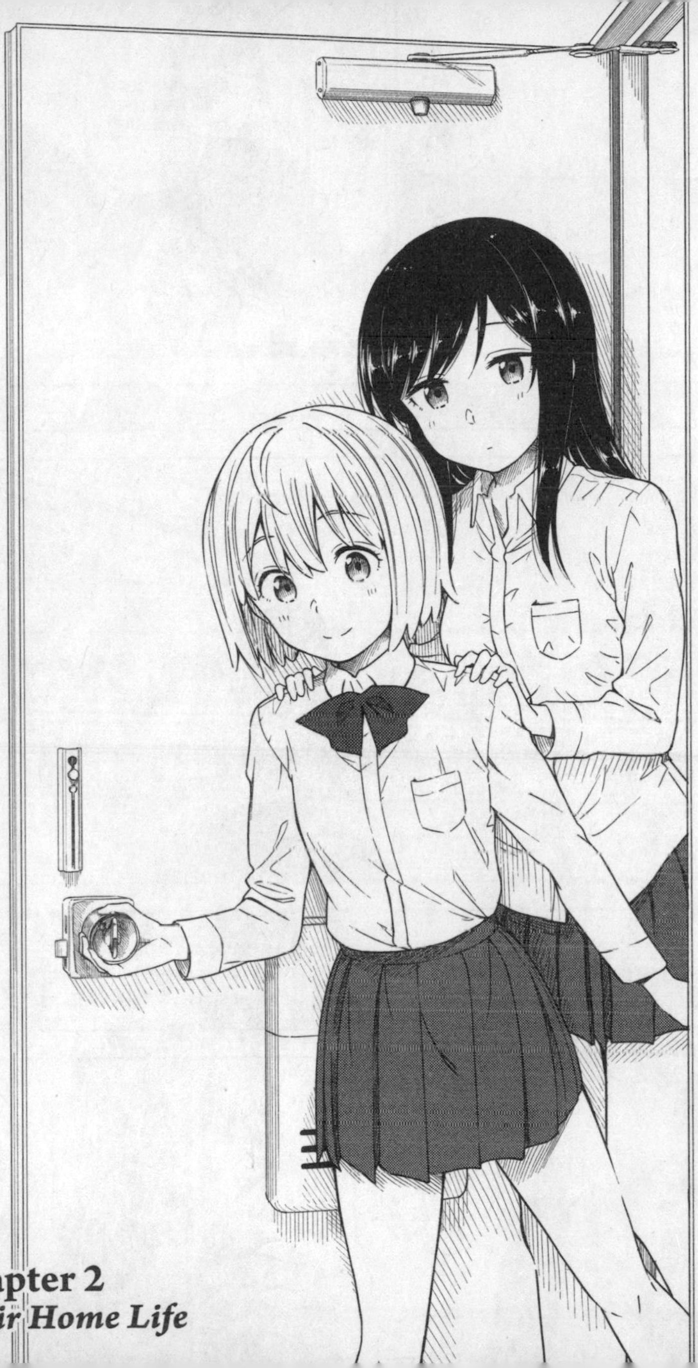

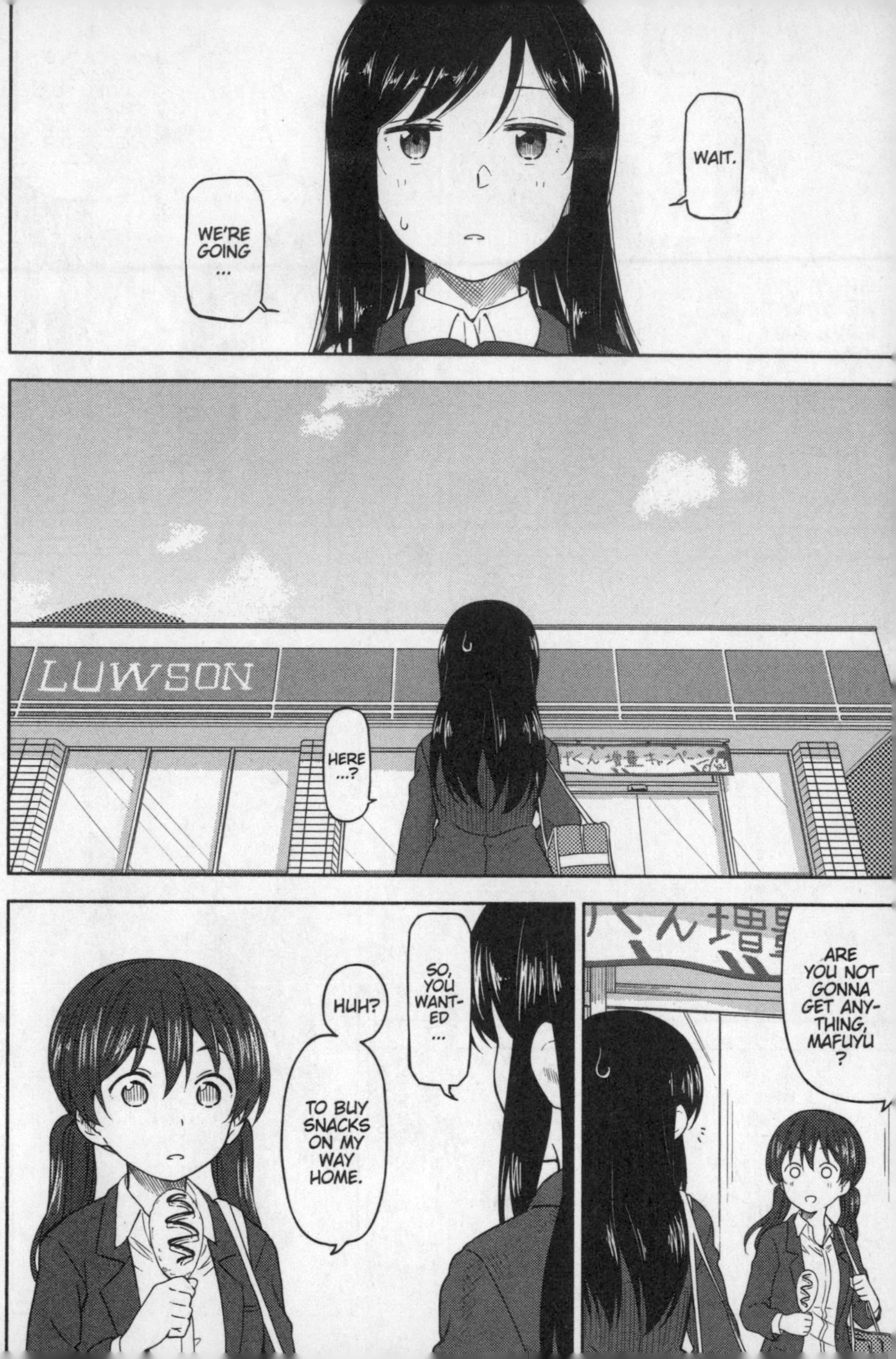
WAIT.
WE'RE GOING ...
LUWSON
HERE ...?
ARE YOU NOT GONNA GET ANY-THING, MAFUYU?
SO, YOU WANT-ED ...
HUH?
TO BUY SNACKS ON MY WAY HOME.

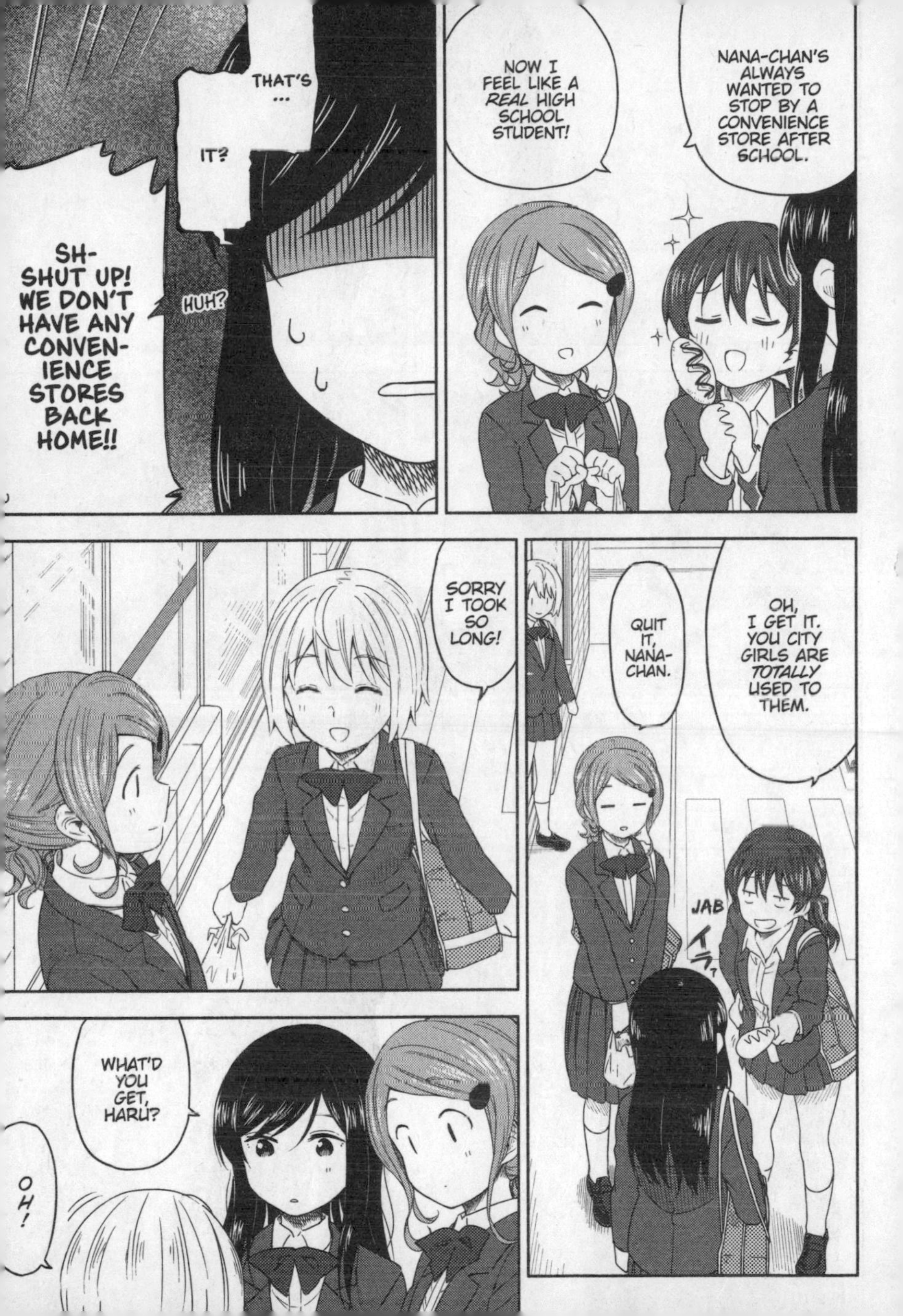
NANA-CHAN'S ALWAYS WANTED TO STOP BY A CONVENIENCE STORE AFTER SCHOOL.
NOW I FEEL LIKE A *REAL* HIGH SCHOOL STUDENT!
THAT'S ... IT?
HUH?
SH- SHUT UP! WE DON'T HAVE ANY CONVENIENCE STORES BACK HOME!!
OH, I GET IT. YOU CITY GIRLS ARE *TOTALLY* USED TO THEM.
QUIT IT, NANA-CHAN.
JAB
SORRY I TOOK SO LONG!
WHAT'D YOU GET, HARU?
OH!

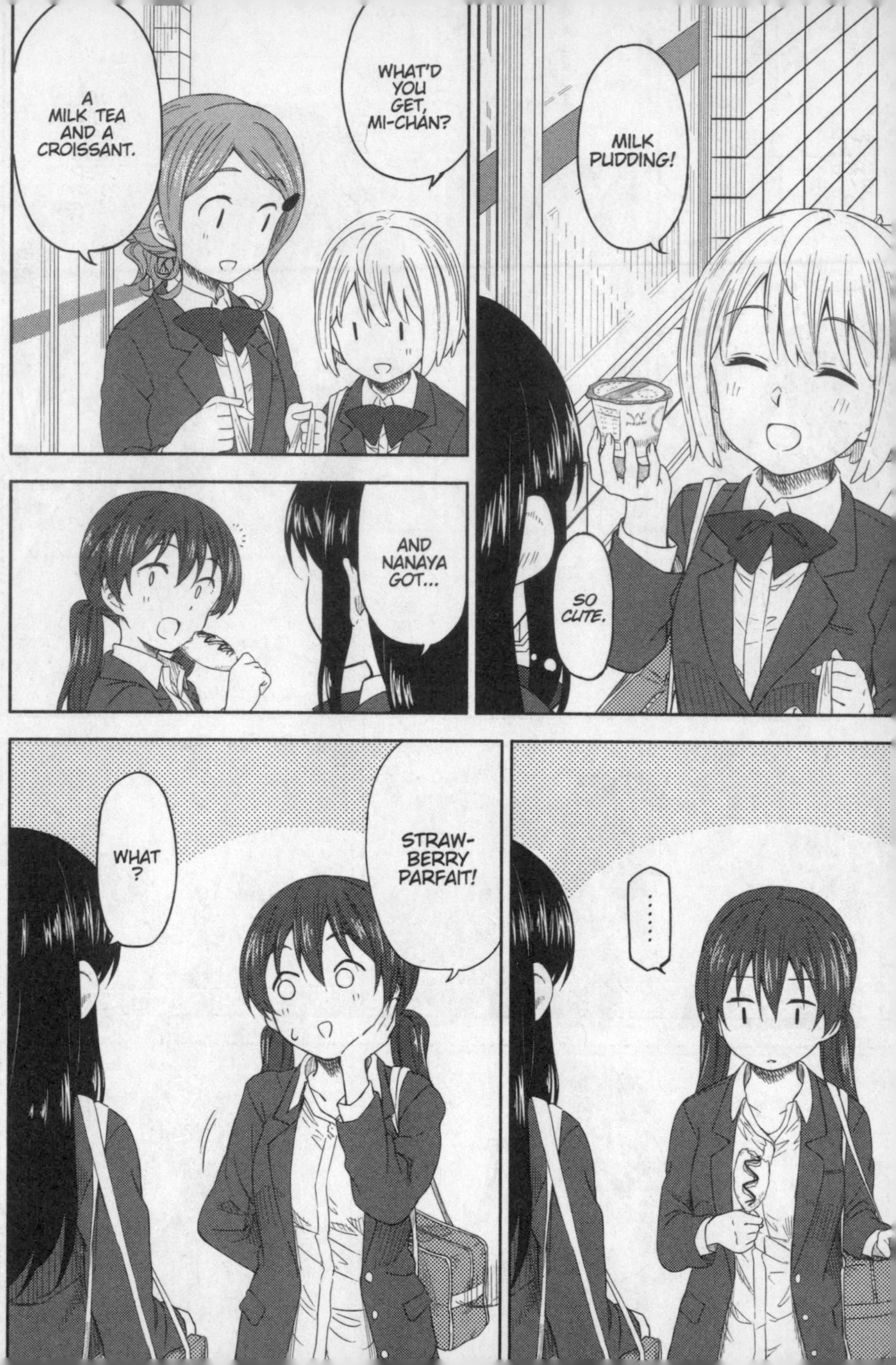
A MILK TEA AND A CROISSANT.
WHAT'D YOU GET, MI-CHAN?
MILK PUDDING!
SO CUTE.
AND NANAYA GOT...
WHAT?
STRAW-BERRY PARFAIT!
......

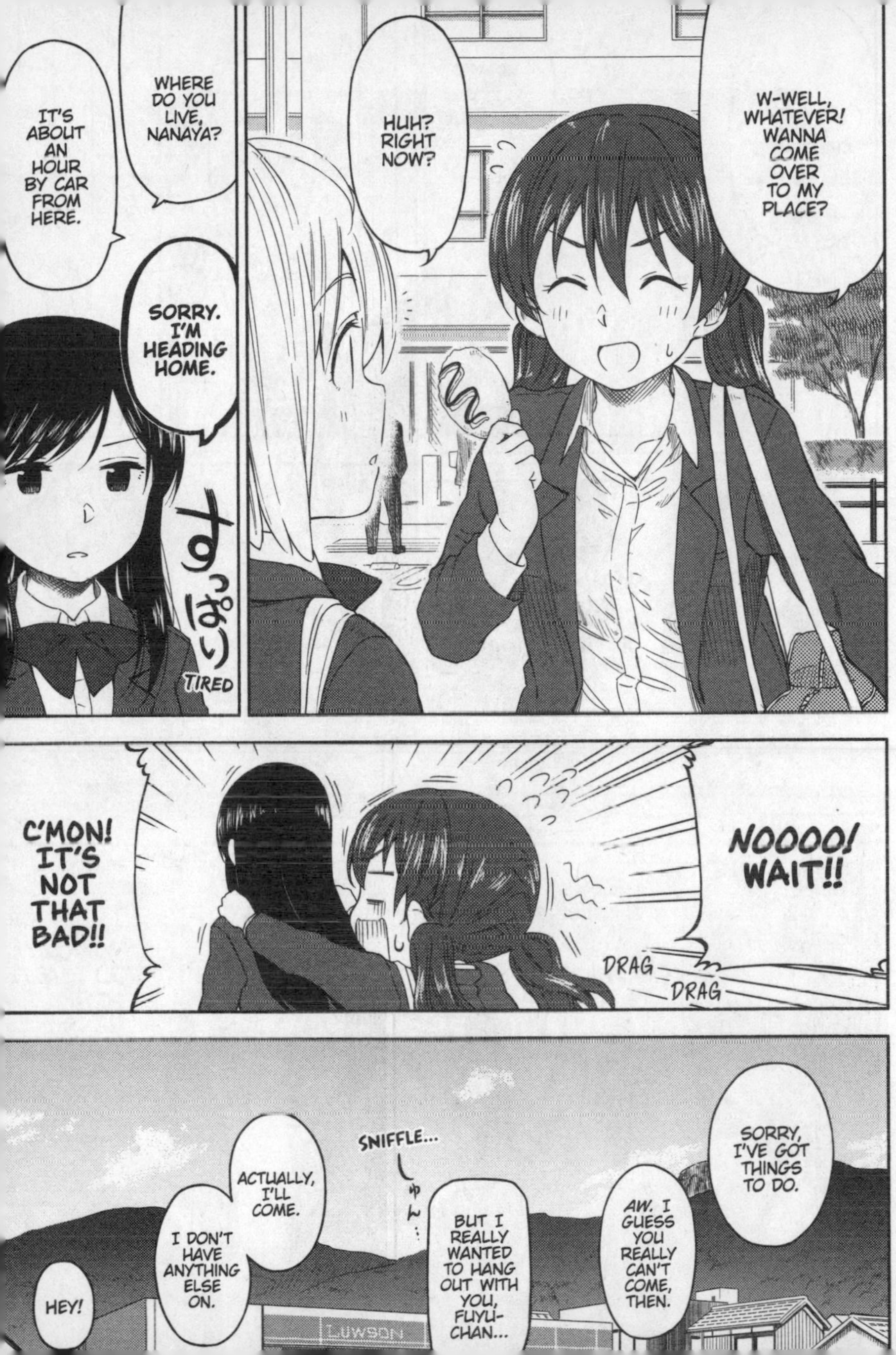
W-WELL, WHATEVER! WANNA COME OVER TO MY PLACE?
HUH? RIGHT NOW?
WHERE DO YOU LIVE, NANAYA?
IT'S ABOUT AN HOUR BY CAR FROM HERE.
SORRY. I'M HEADING HOME.
すっぱり
TIRED
NOOOO! WAIT!!
C'MON! IT'S NOT THAT BAD!!
DRAG
DRAG
SORRY, I'VE GOT THINGS TO DO.
AW. I GUESS YOU REALLY CAN'T COME, THEN.
BUT I REALLY WANTED TO HANG OUT WITH YOU, FUYU-CHAN...
SNIFFLE...
しゅん…
ACTUALLY, I'LL COME.
I DON'T HAVE ANYTHING ELSE ON.
HEY!
LUWSON

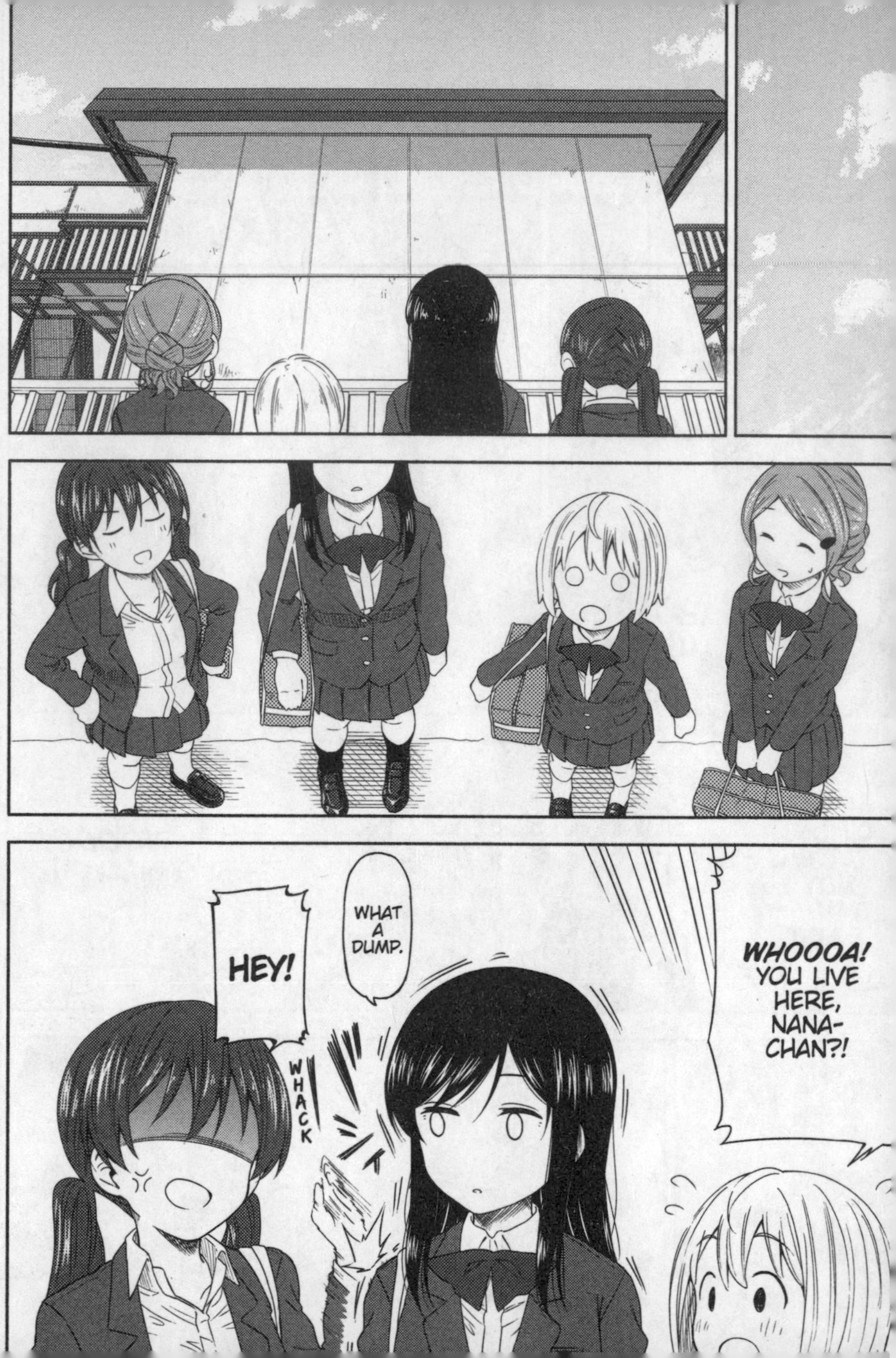
WHOOOA! YOU LIVE HERE, NANA-CHAN?!
WHAT A DUMP.
HEY!
WHACK

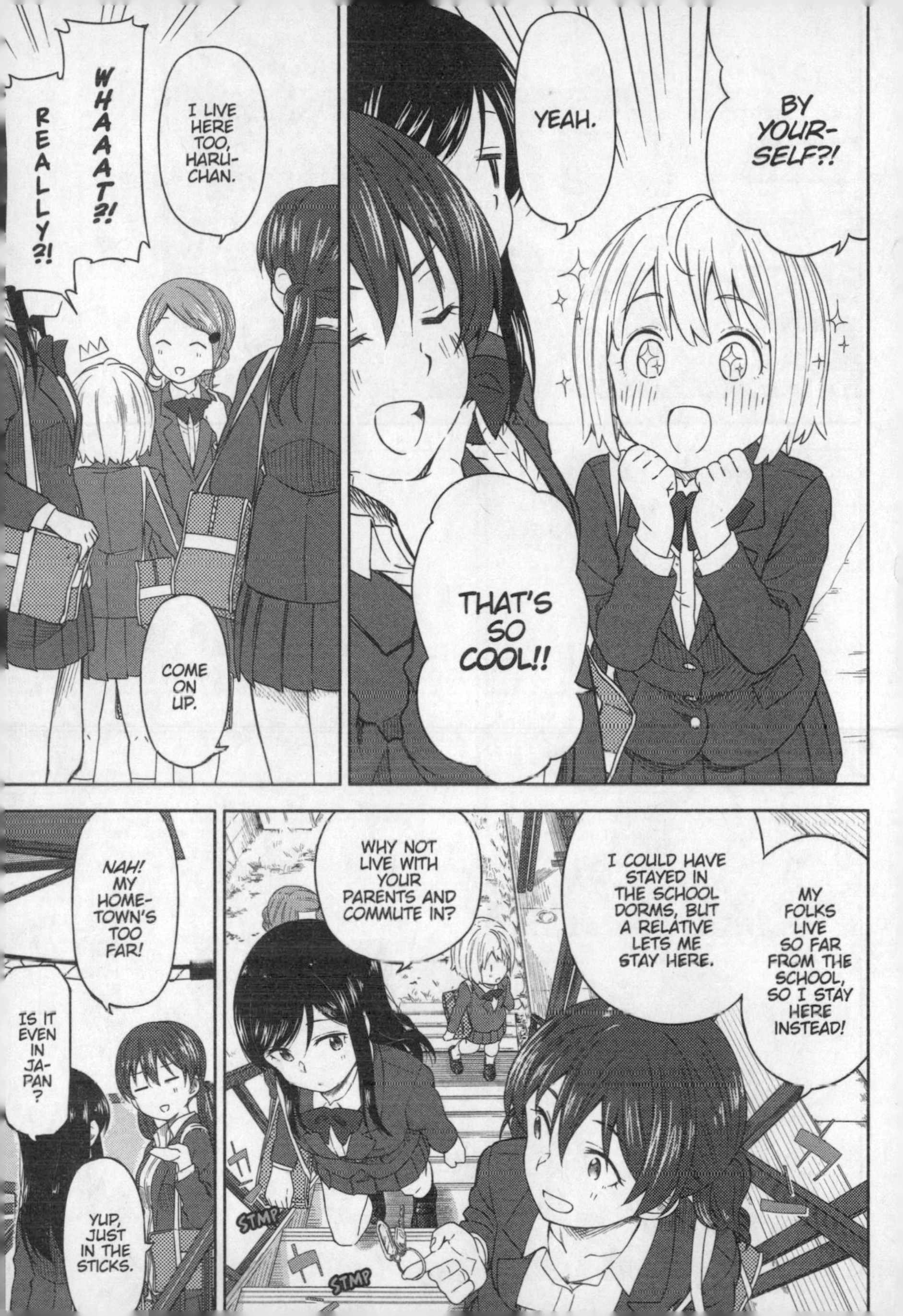
BY YOURSELF?!
YEAH.
THAT'S SO COOL!!
I LIVE HERE TOO, HARU-CHAN.
WHAAAAT?!
REALLY?!
COME ON UP.
MY FOLKS LIVE SO FAR FROM THE SCHOOL, SO I STAY HERE INSTEAD!
I COULD HAVE STAYED IN THE SCHOOL DORMS, BUT A RELATIVE LETS ME STAY HERE.
WHY NOT LIVE WITH YOUR PARENTS AND COMMUTE IN?
STMP
STMP
NAH! MY HOMETOWN'S TOO FAR!
IS IT EVEN IN JAPAN?
YUP, JUST IN THE STICKS.

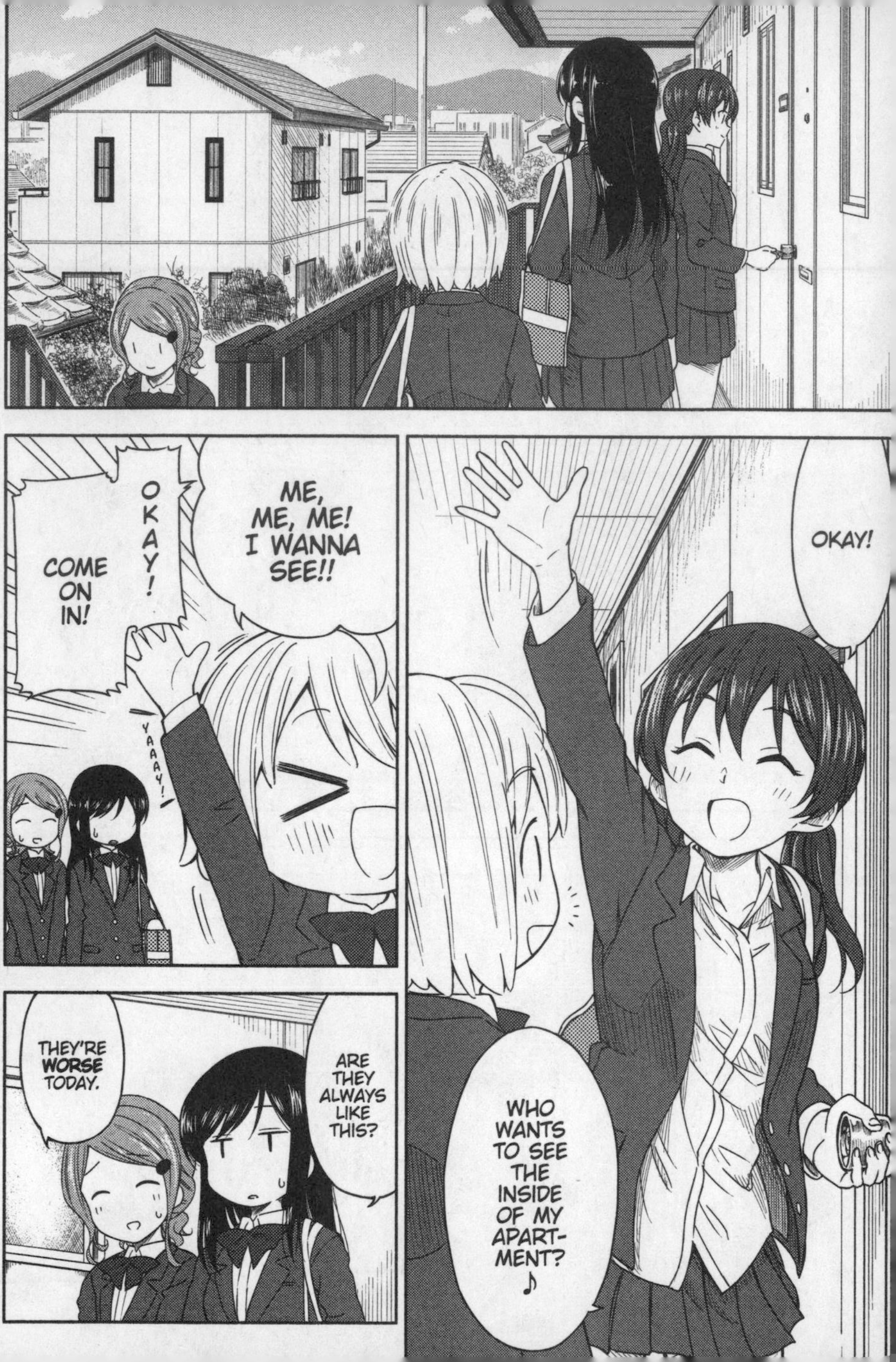
OKAY!
WHO WANTS TO SEE THE INSIDE OF MY APART-MENT? ♪
ME, ME, ME! I WANNA SEE!!
OKAY! COME ON IN!
YAAAAY!
ARE THEY ALWAYS LIKE THIS?
THEY'RE **WORSE** TODAY.

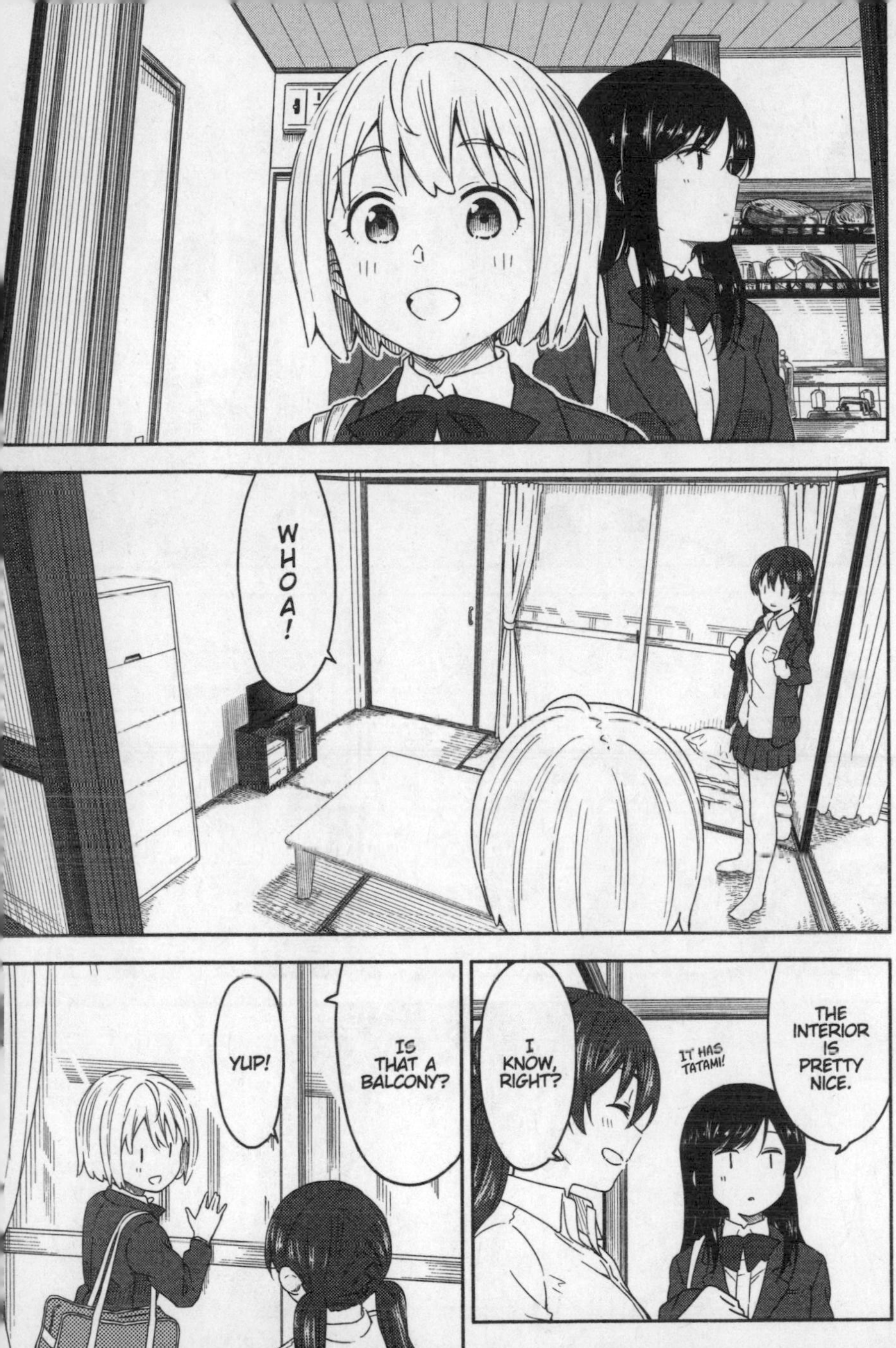

WHOA!
THE INTERIOR IS PRETTY NICE.
IT HAS TATAMI!
I KNOW, RIGHT?
IS THAT A BALCONY?
YUP!

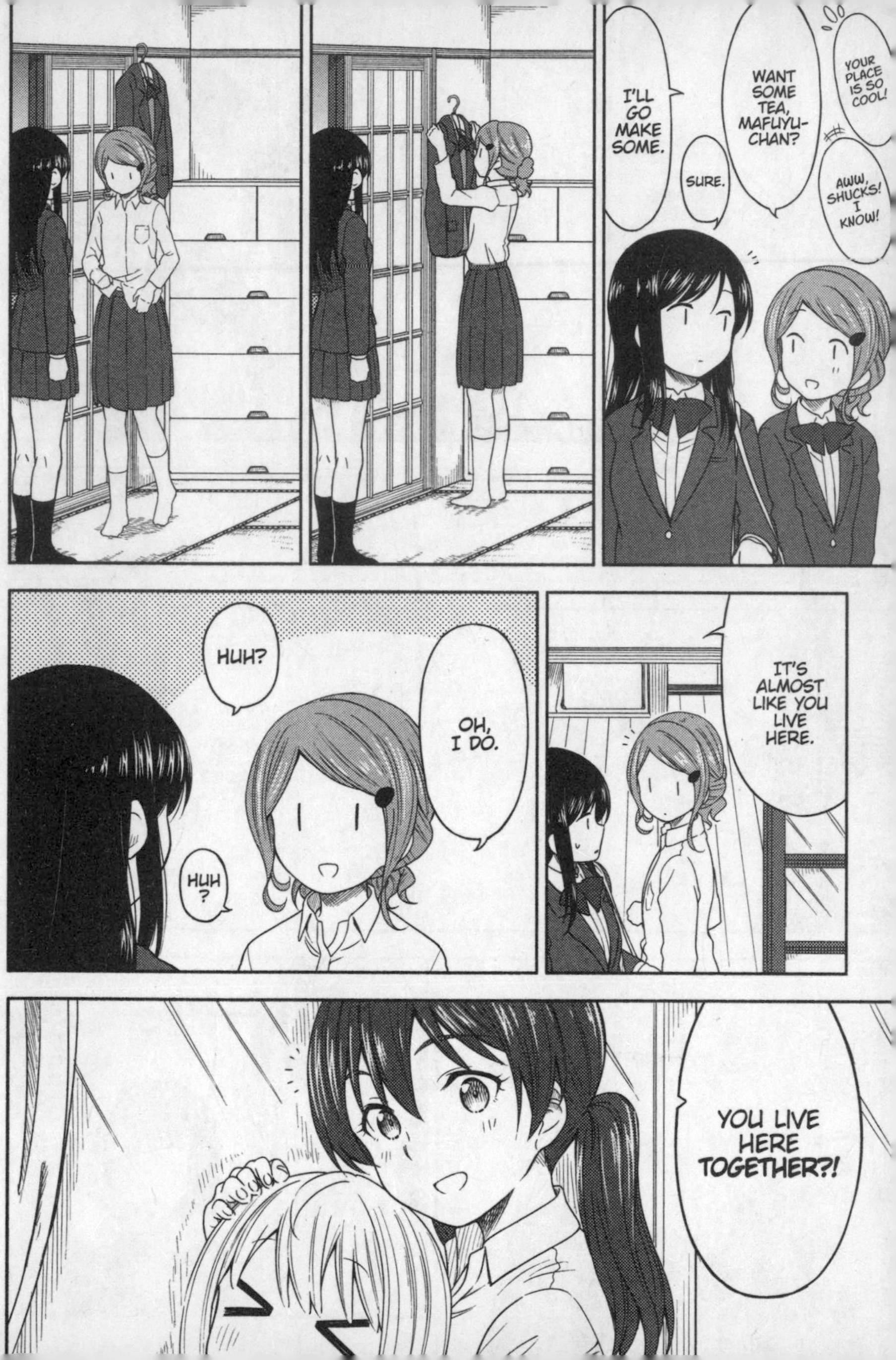

YOUR PLACE IS SO COOL!
AWW, SHUCKS! I KNOW!
WANT SOME TEA, MAFUYU-CHAN?
SURE.
I'LL GO MAKE SOME.
IT'S ALMOST LIKE YOU LIVE HERE.
HUH?
OH, I DO.
HUH?
YOU LIVE HERE TOGETHER?!

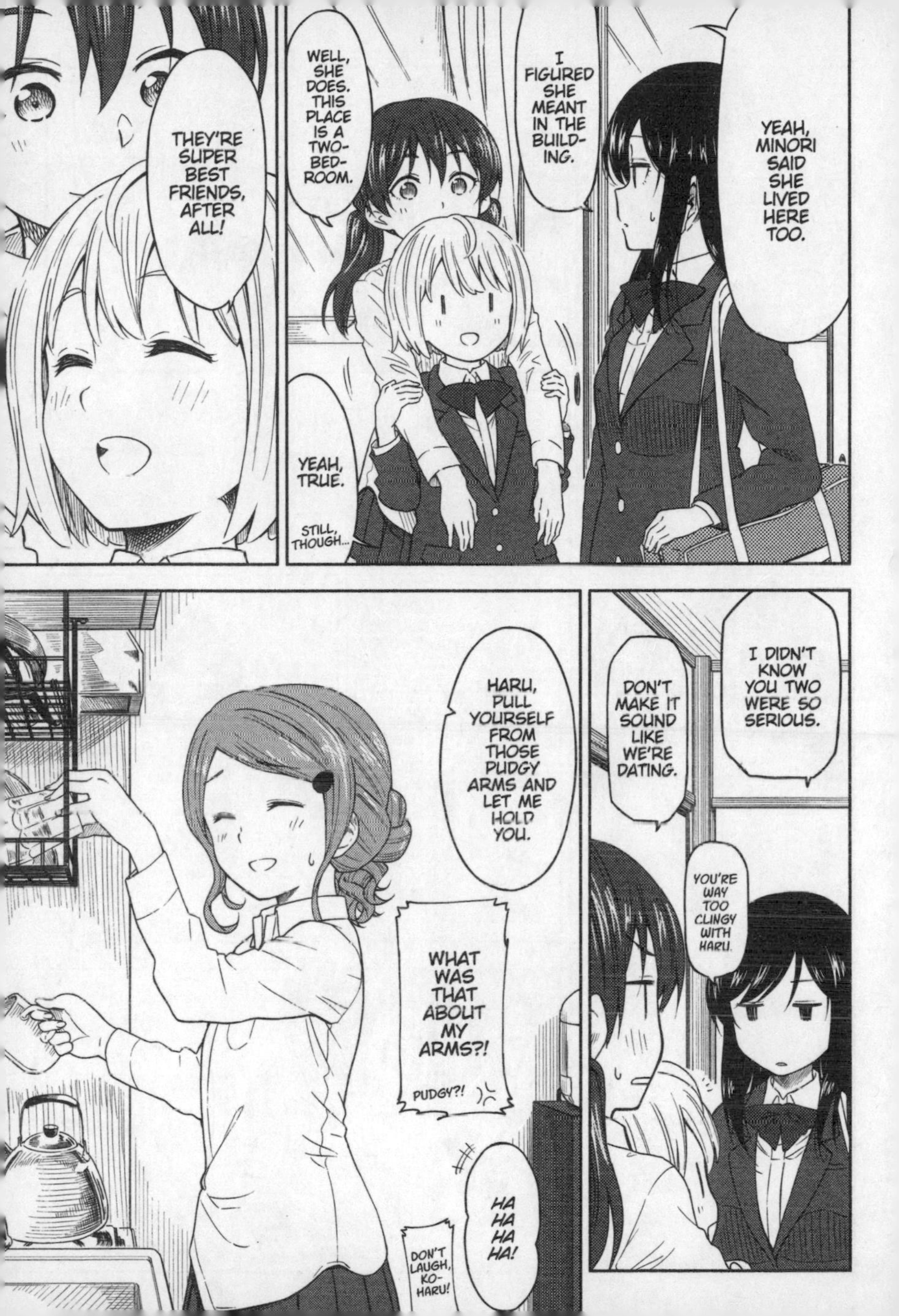
YEAH, MINORI SAID SHE LIVED HERE TOO.
I FIGURED SHE MEANT IN THE BUILD-ING.
WELL, SHE DOES. THIS PLACE IS A TWO-BED-ROOM.
YEAH, TRUE.
STILL, THOUGH...
THEY'RE SUPER BEST FRIENDS, AFTER ALL!
I DIDN'T KNOW YOU TWO WERE SO SERIOUS.
DON'T MAKE IT SOUND LIKE WE'RE DATING.
YOU'RE WAY TOO CLINGY WITH HARU.
HARU, PULL YOURSELF FROM THOSE PUDGY ARMS AND LET ME HOLD YOU.
WHAT WAS THAT ABOUT MY ARMS?!
PUDGY?!
HA HA HA HA HA!
DON'T LAUGH, KO-HARU!

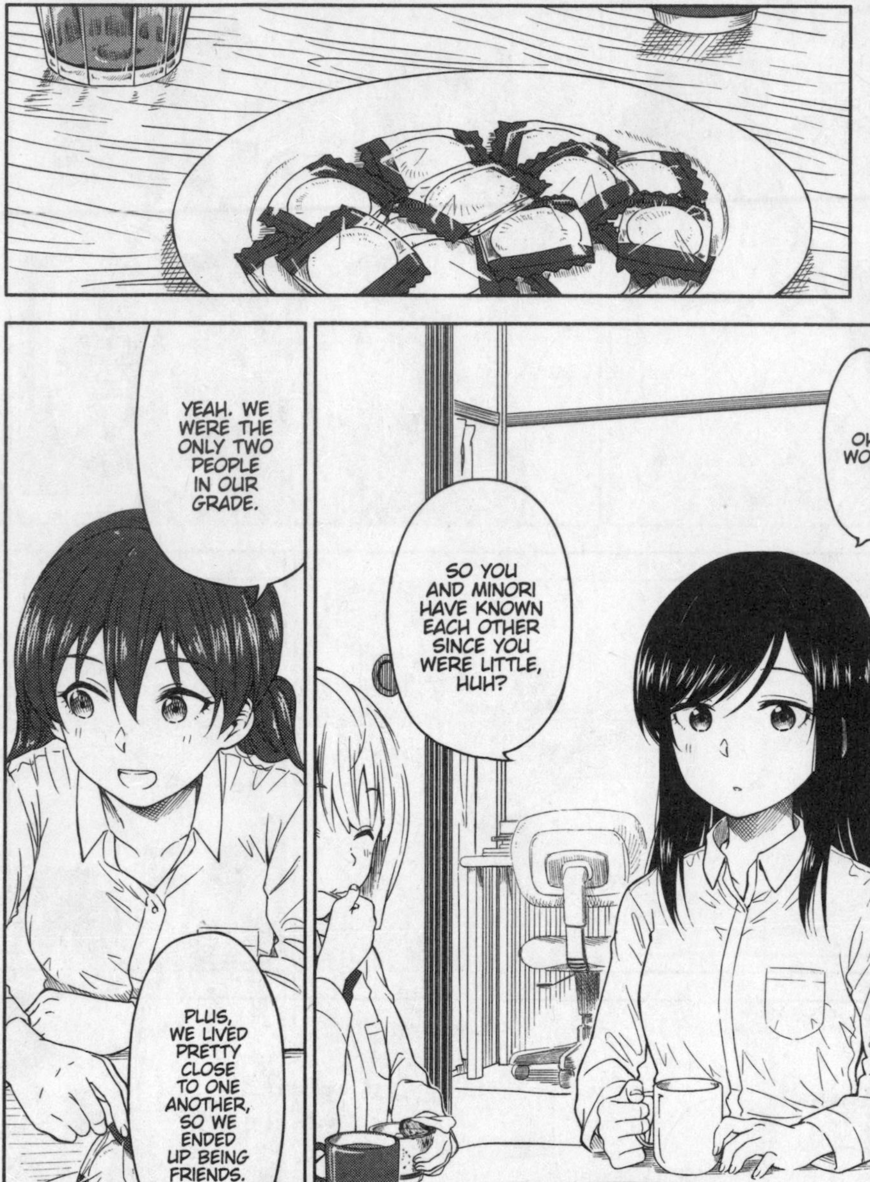
OH, WOW.
SO YOU AND MINORI HAVE KNOWN EACH OTHER SINCE YOU WERE LITTLE, HUH?
YEAH. WE WERE THE ONLY TWO PEOPLE IN OUR GRADE.
PLUS, WE LIVED PRETTY CLOSE TO ONE ANOTHER, SO WE ENDED UP BEING FRIENDS.

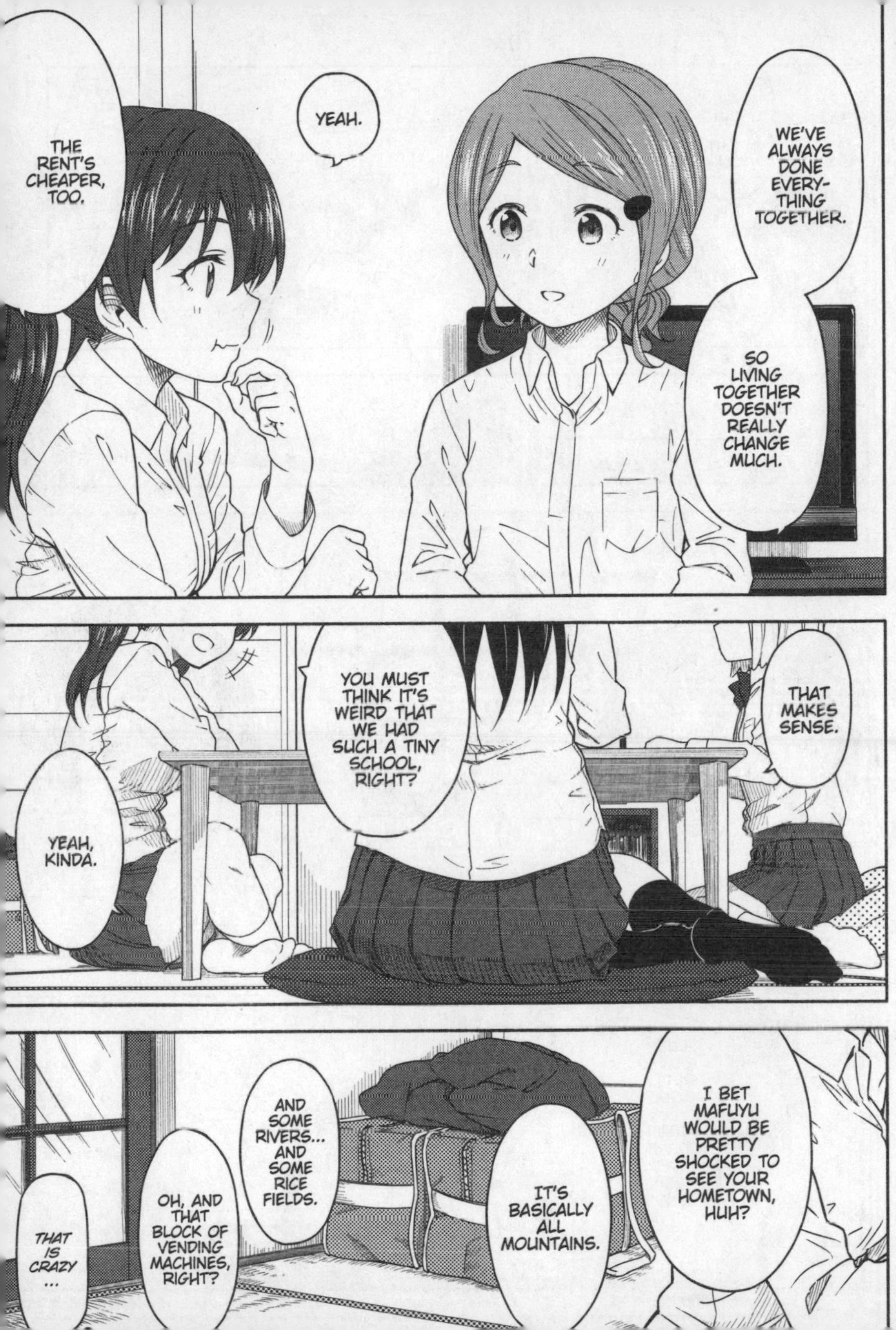
WE'VE ALWAYS DONE EVERY-THING TOGETHER.
SO LIVING TOGETHER DOESN'T REALLY CHANGE MUCH.
YEAH.
THE RENT'S CHEAPER, TOO.
THAT MAKES SENSE.
YOU MUST THINK IT'S WEIRD THAT WE HAD SUCH A TINY SCHOOL, RIGHT?
YEAH, KINDA.
I BET MAFUYU WOULD BE PRETTY SHOCKED TO SEE YOUR HOMETOWN, HUH?
IT'S BASICALLY ALL MOUNTAINS.
AND SOME RIVERS... AND SOME RICE FIELDS.
OH, AND THAT BLOCK OF VENDING MACHINES, RIGHT?
THAT IS CRAZY...

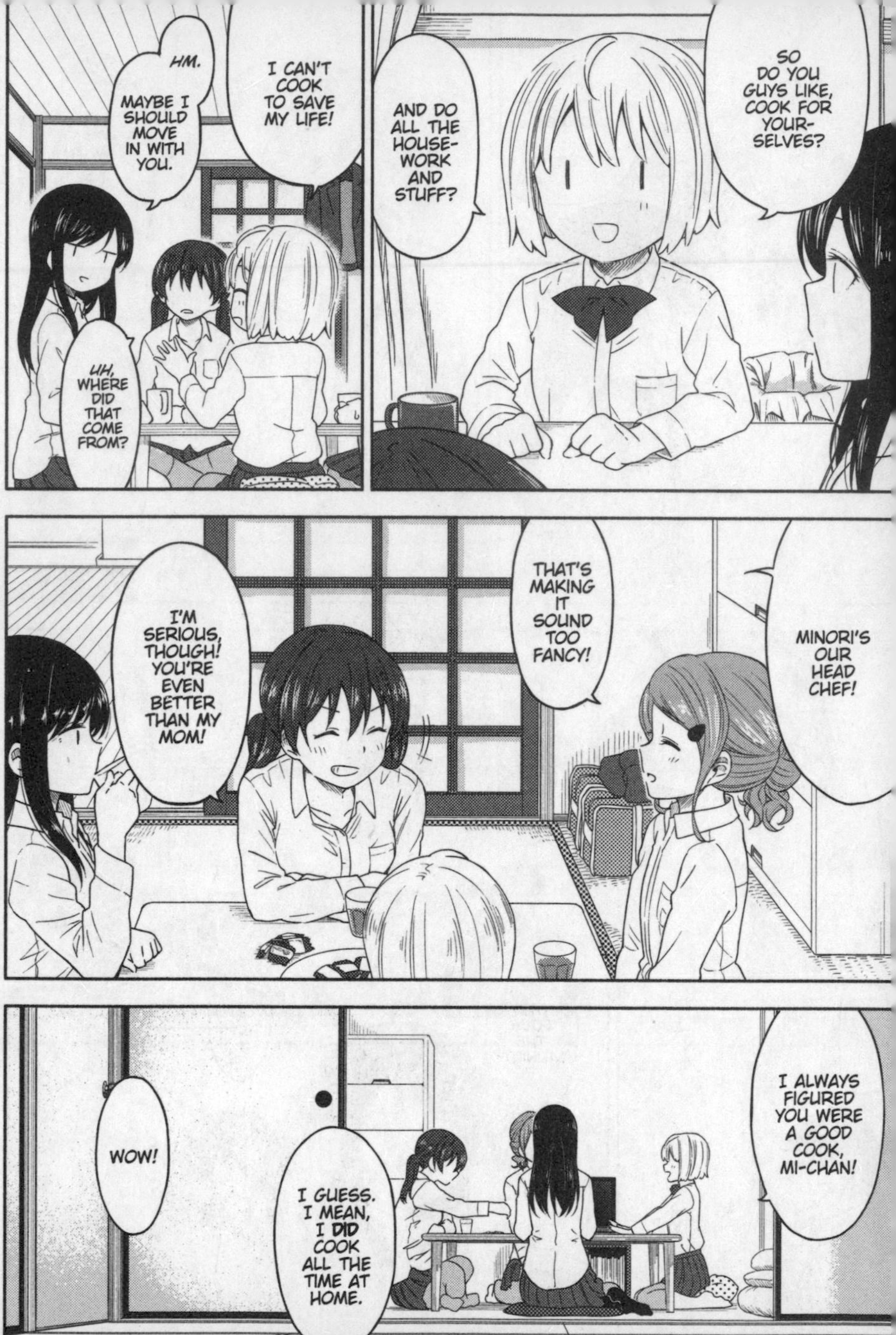
SO DO YOU GUYS LIKE, COOK FOR YOUR-SELVES?
AND DO ALL THE HOUSE-WORK AND STUFF?
I CAN'T COOK TO SAVE MY LIFE!
HM. MAYBE I SHOULD MOVE IN WITH YOU.
UH, WHERE DID THAT COME FROM?
MINORI'S OUR HEAD CHEF!
THAT'S MAKING IT SOUND TOO FANCY!
I'M SERIOUS, THOUGH! YOU'RE EVEN BETTER THAN MY MOM!
I ALWAYS FIGURED YOU WERE A GOOD COOK, MI-CHAN!
I GUESS. I MEAN, I **DID** COOK ALL THE TIME AT HOME.
WOW!

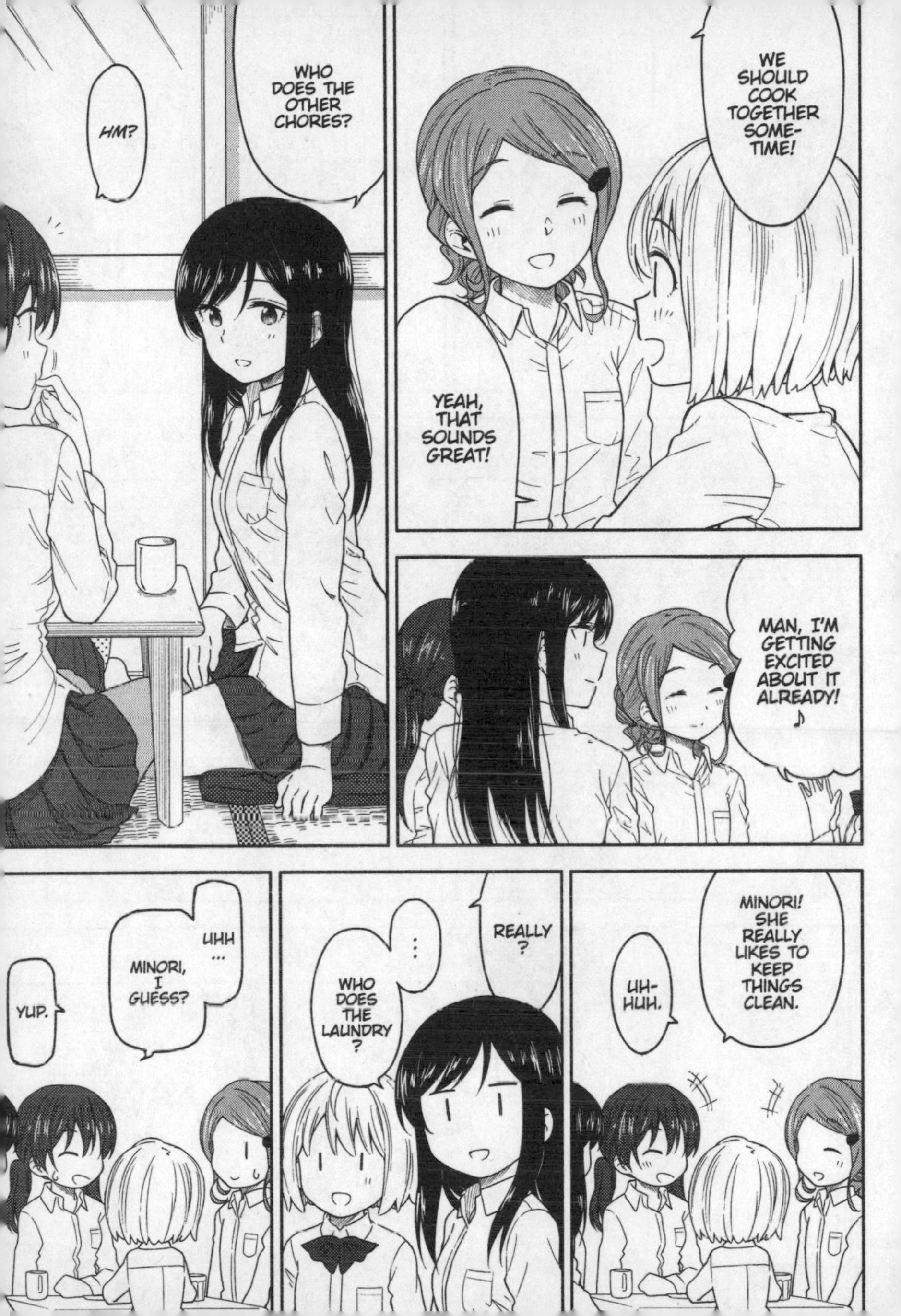
WE SHOULD COOK TOGETHER SOME-TIME!
YEAH, THAT SOUNDS GREAT!
MAN, I'M GETTING EXCITED ABOUT IT ALREADY! ♪
WHO DOES THE OTHER CHORES?
HM?
MINORI! SHE REALLY LIKES TO KEEP THINGS CLEAN.
UH-HUH.
REALLY?
...
WHO DOES THE LAUNDRY?
UHH...
MINORI, I GUESS?
YUP.

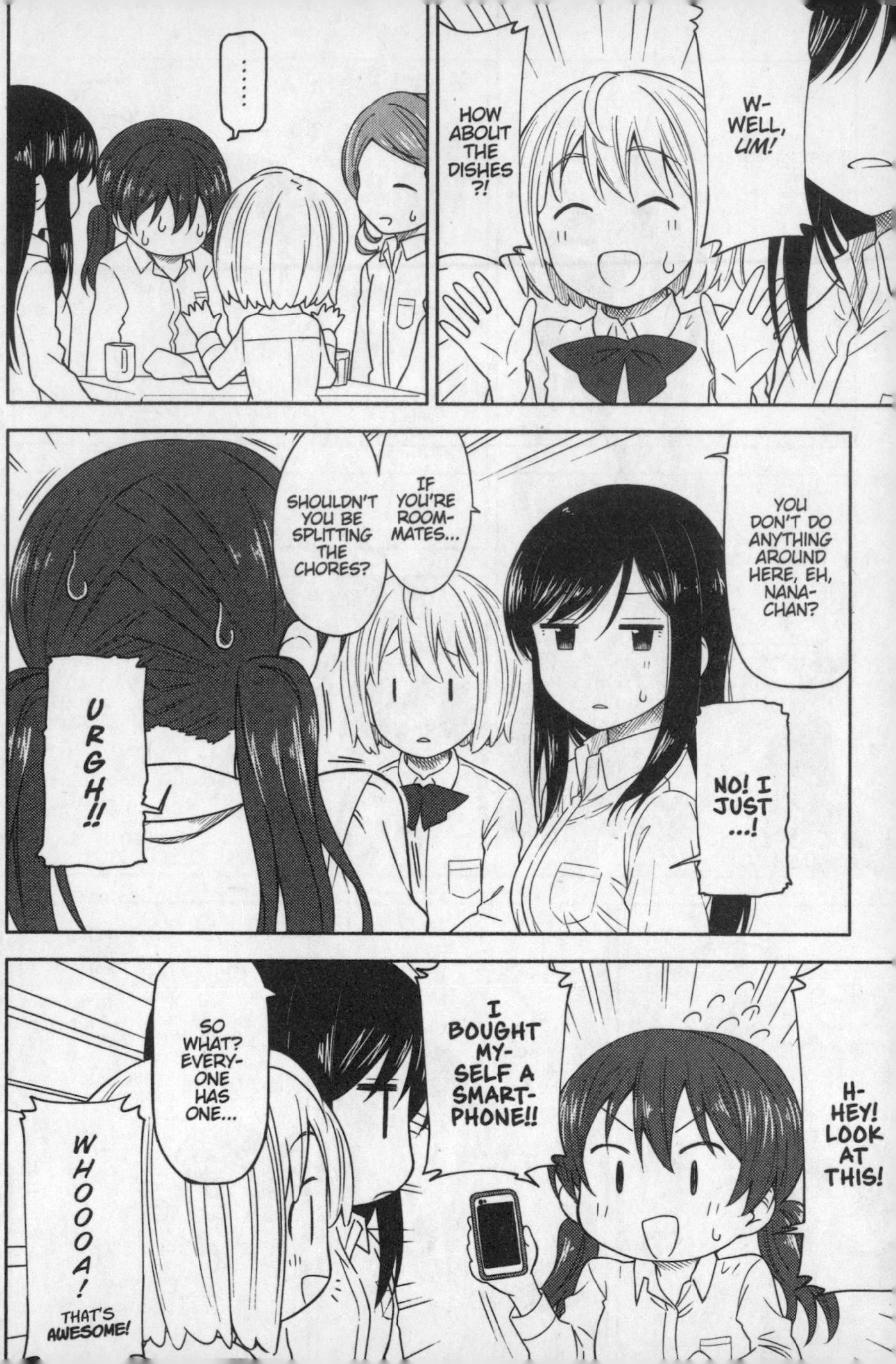
W-WELL, UM!
HOW ABOUT THE DISHES?!
......
YOU DON'T DO ANYTHING AROUND HERE, EH, NANA-CHAN?
NO! I JUST ...!
IF YOU'RE ROOM-MATES...
SHOULDN'T YOU BE SPLITTING THE CHORES?
URGH!!
H-HEY! LOOK AT THIS!
I BOUGHT MY-SELF A SMART-PHONE!!
SO WHAT? EVERY-ONE HAS ONE...
WHOOOOA!
THAT'S AWESOME!

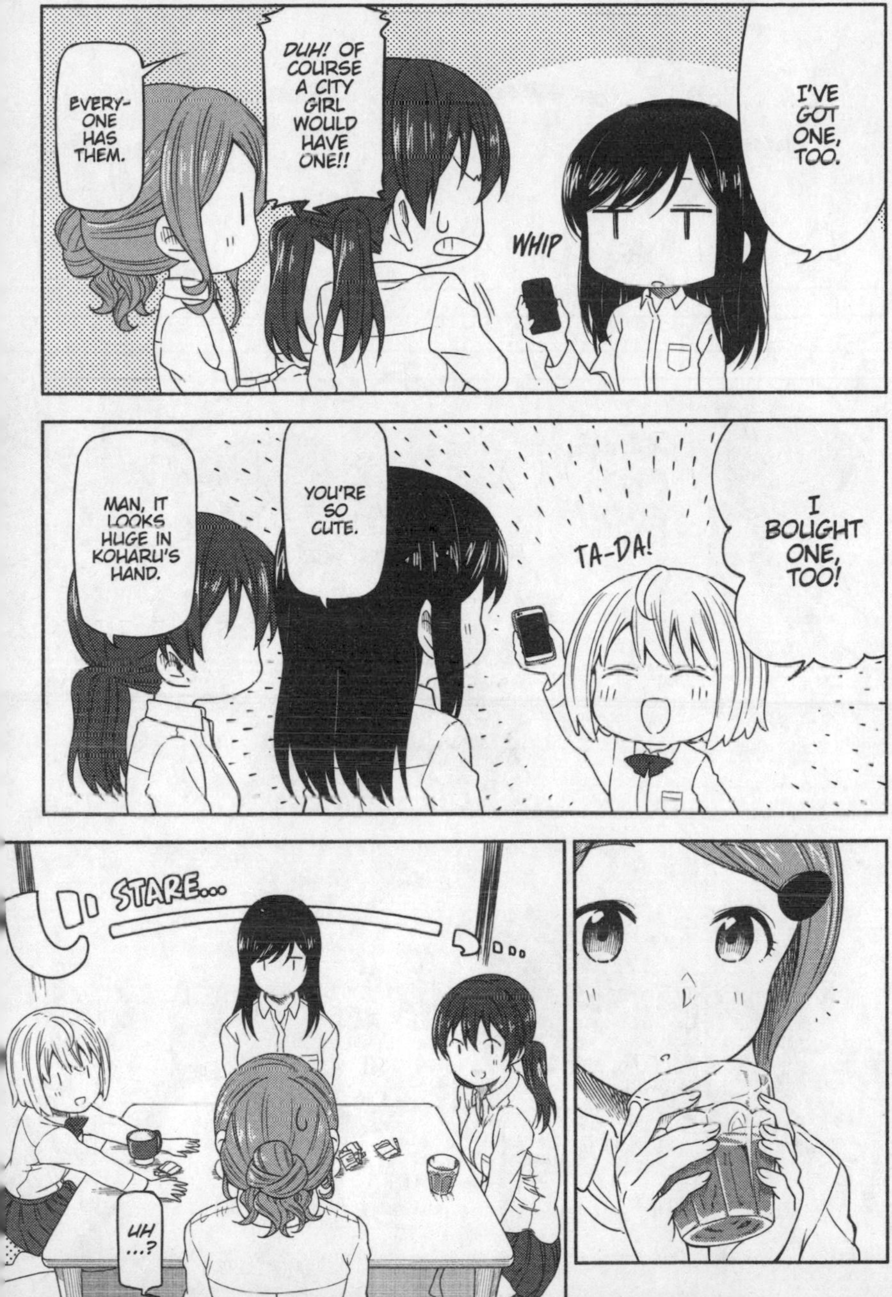
I'VE GOT ONE, TOO.
WHIP
DUH! OF COURSE A CITY GIRL WOULD HAVE ONE!!
EVERY-ONE HAS THEM.
I BOUGHT ONE, TOO!
TA-DA!
YOU'RE SO CUTE.
MAN, IT LOOKS HUGE IN KOHARU'S HAND.
STARE...
UH ...?

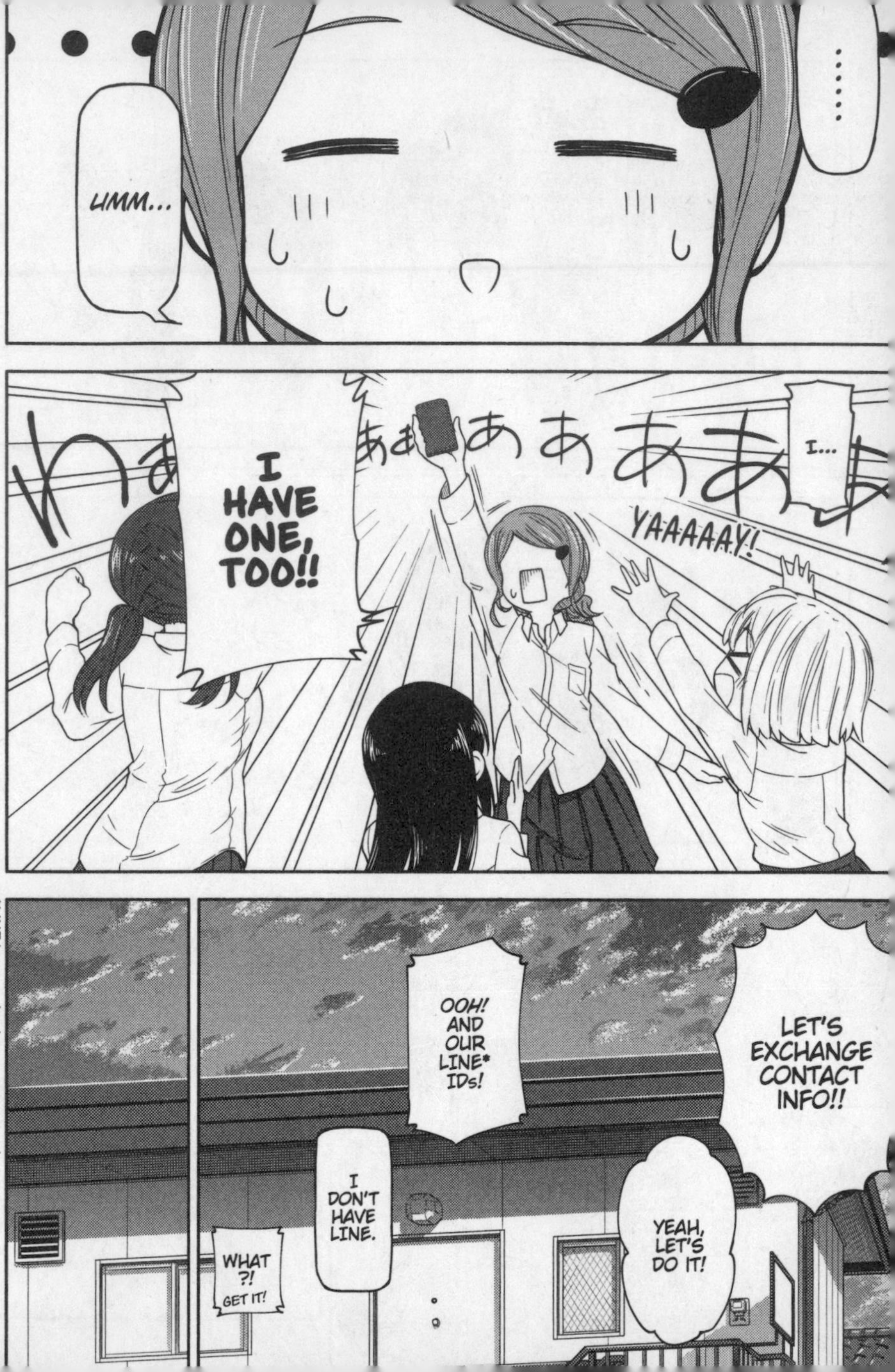
......
UMM...
I...
わああああああ
YAAAAAY!
I HAVE ONE, TOO!!
LET'S EXCHANGE CONTACT INFO!!
OOH! AND OUR LINE* IDs!
YEAH, LET'S DO IT!
I DON'T HAVE LINE.
WHAT?!
GET IT!

*LINE is a popular Japanese messaging app.

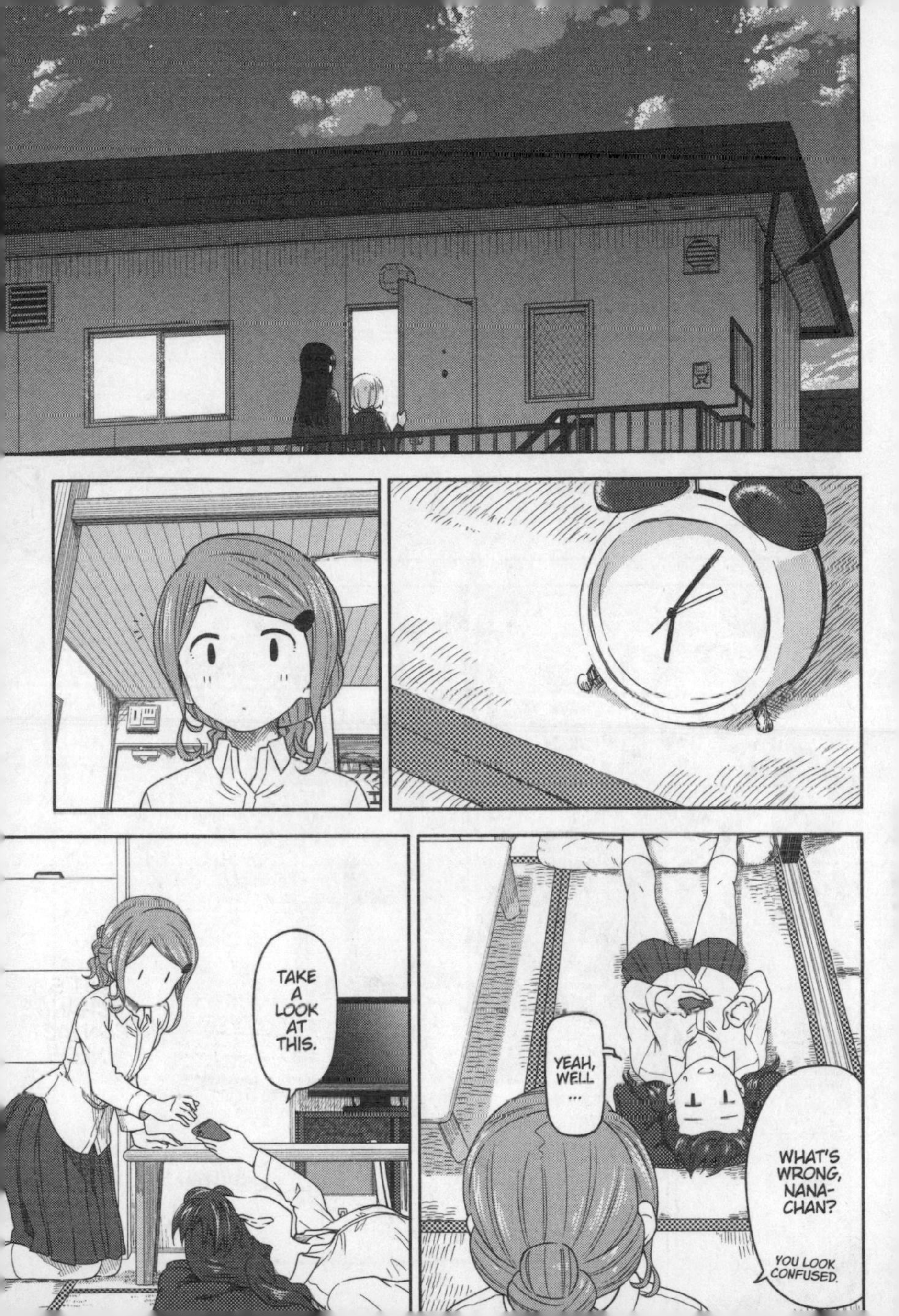
WHAT'S WRONG, NANA-CHAN?
YOU LOOK CONFUSED.
YEAH, WELL ...
TAKE A LOOK AT THIS.

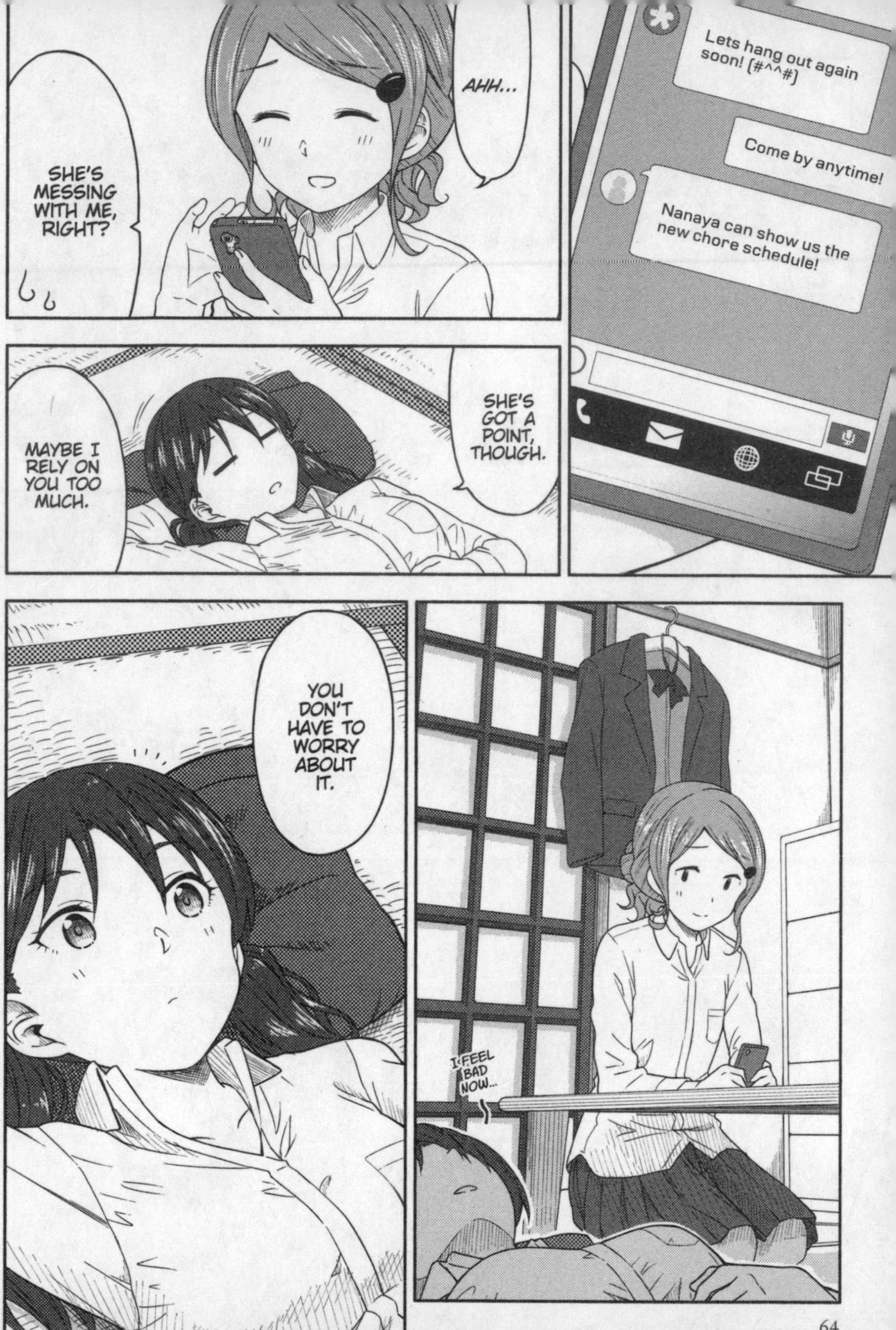
Lets hang out again soon! (#^^#)
Come by anytime!
Nanaya can show us the new chore schedule!
AHH...
SHE'S MESSING WITH ME, RIGHT?
SHE'S GOT A POINT, THOUGH.
MAYBE I RELY ON YOU TOO MUCH.
I FEEL BAD NOW...
YOU DON'T HAVE TO WORRY ABOUT IT.

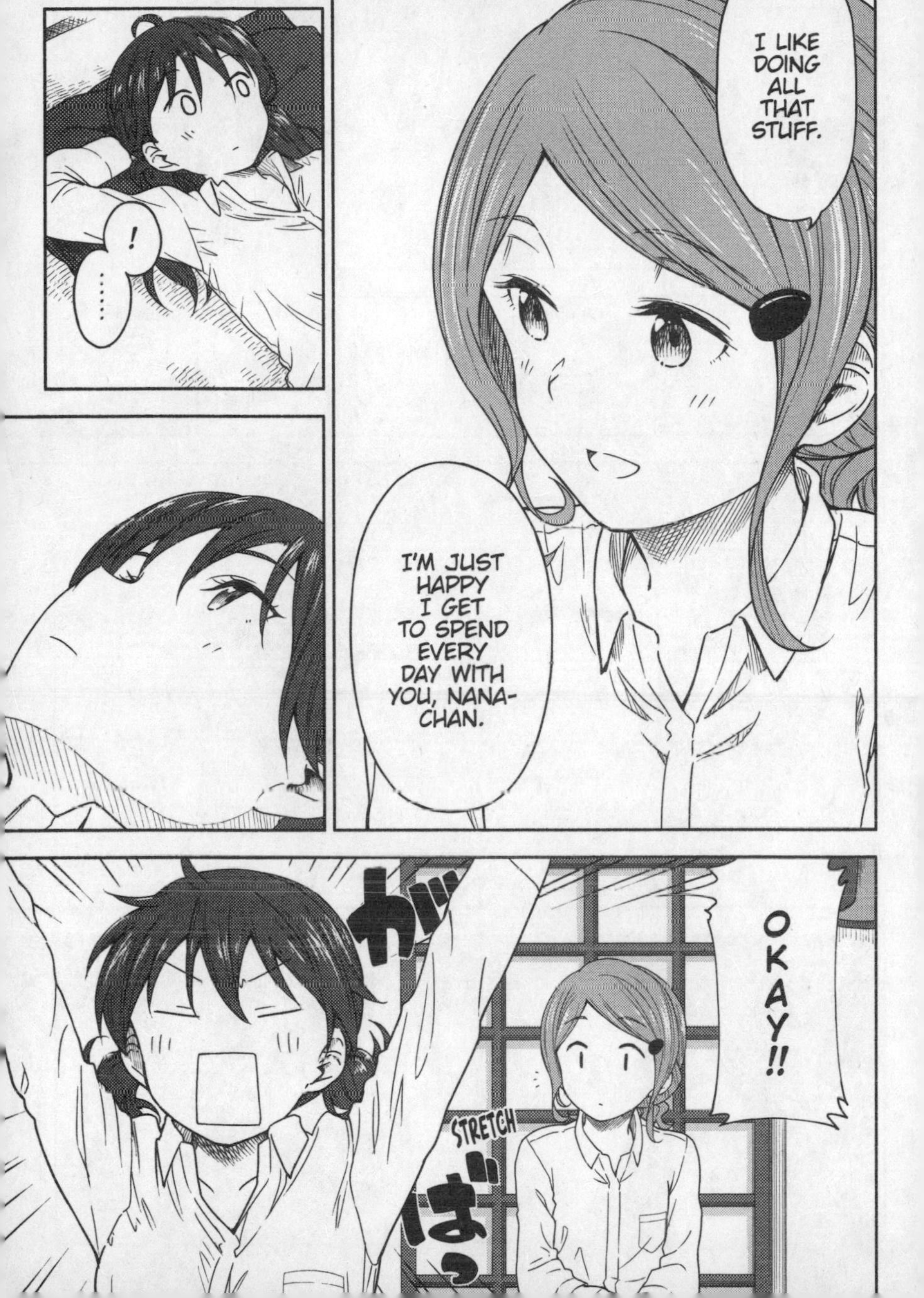
I LIKE DOING ALL THAT STUFF.
I'M JUST HAPPY I GET TO SPEND EVERY DAY WITH YOU, NANA-CHAN.
!
......
OKAY!!
が
STRETCH
ばっ

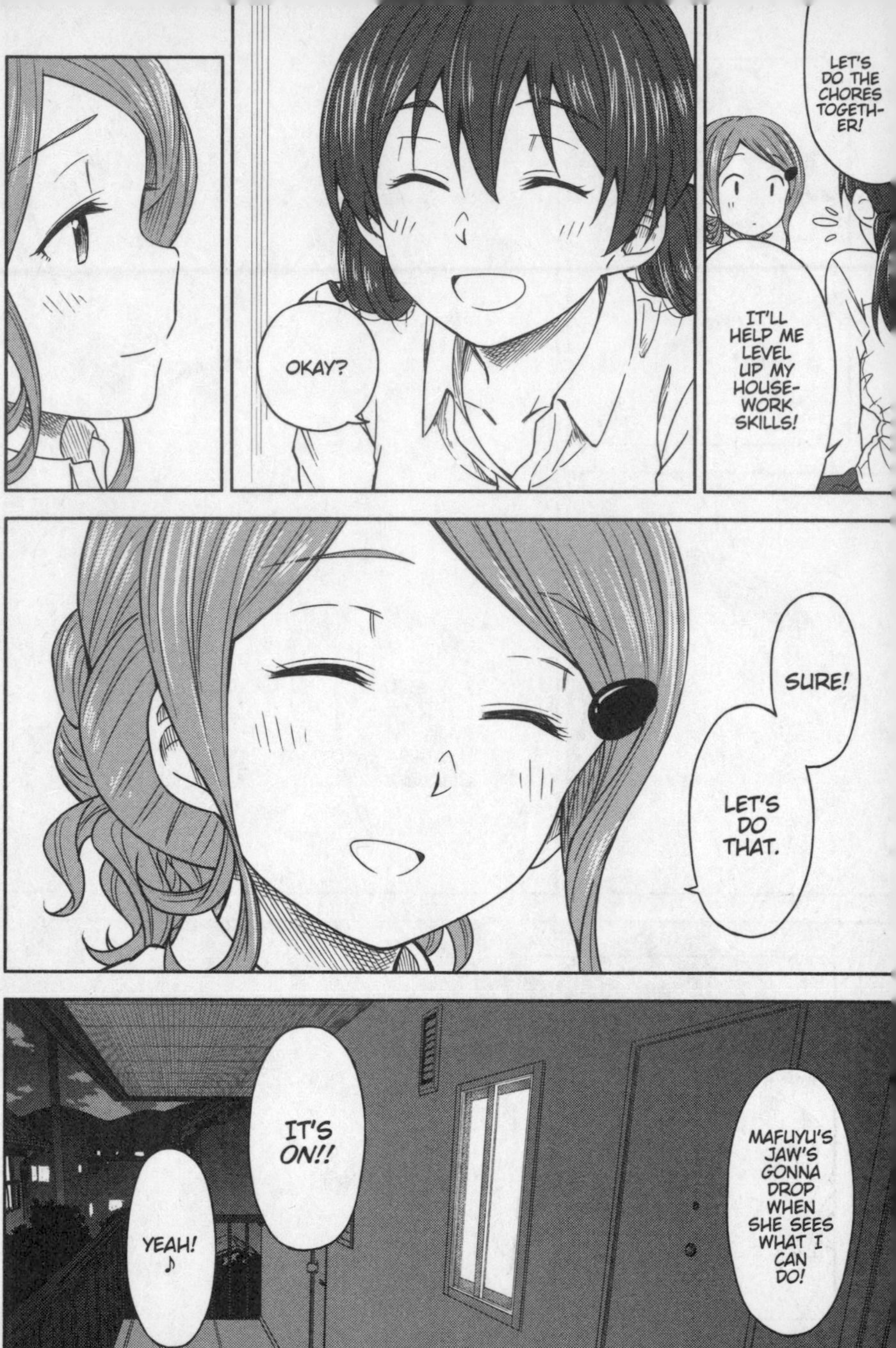
LET'S DO THE CHORES TOGETH-ER!
IT'LL HELP ME LEVEL UP MY HOUSE-WORK SKILLS!
OKAY?
SURE!
LET'S DO THAT.
MAFUYU'S JAW'S GONNA DROP WHEN SHE SEES WHAT I CAN DO!
IT'S ON!!
YEAH! ♪

Our Wonderful Days

story & art by Kei Hamuro

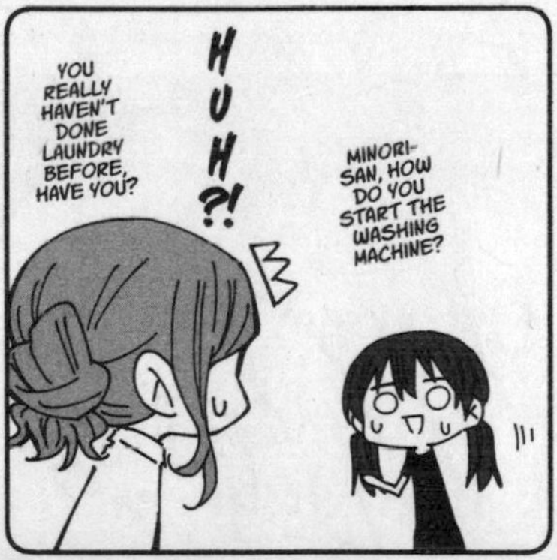
MINORI-SAN, HOW DO YOU START THE WASHING MACHINE?
HUH?!
YOU REALLY HAVEN'T DONE LAUNDRY BEFORE, HAVE YOU?

Our
Wonderful
Days

Tsurezure
Biyori

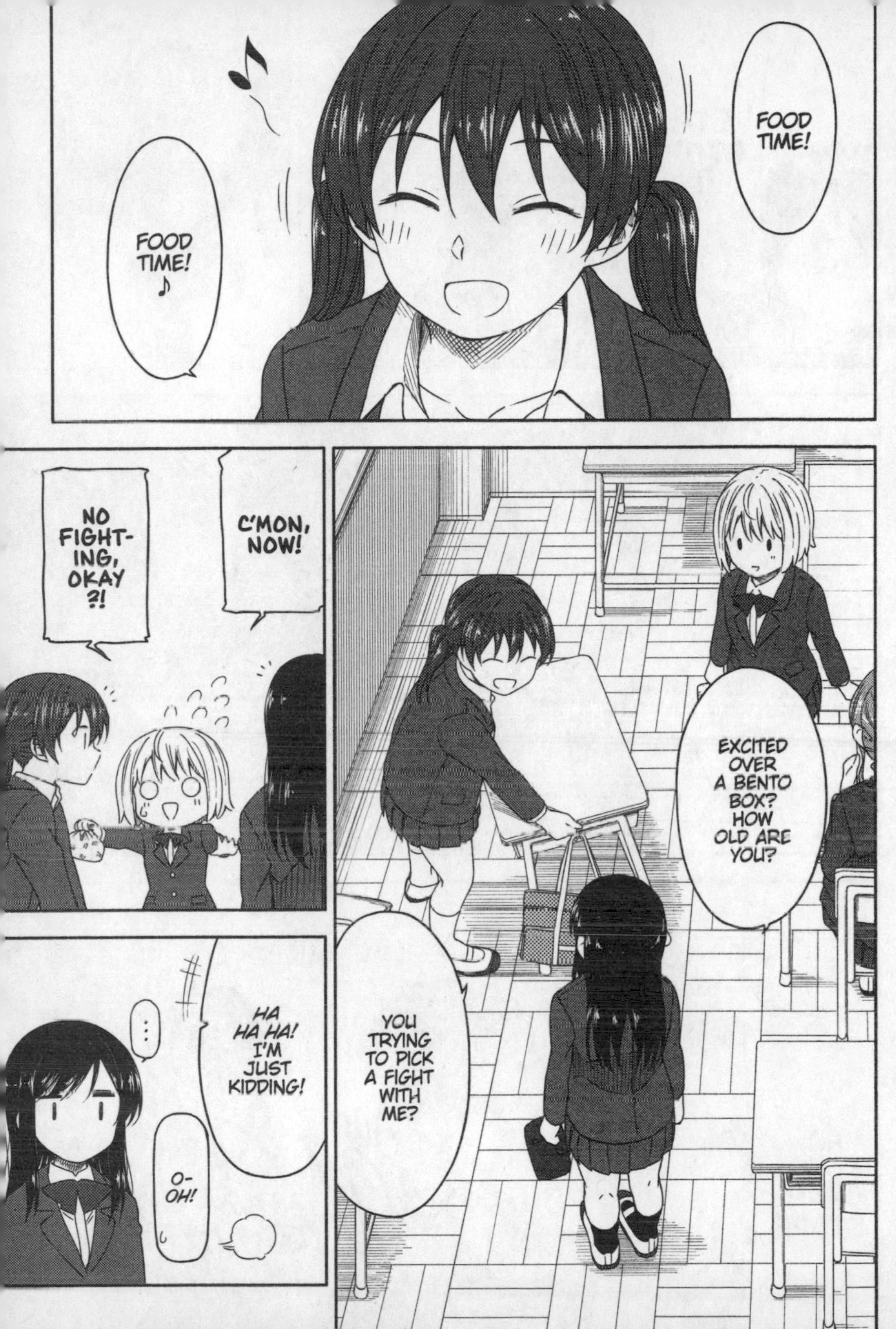
FOOD TIME!
FOOD TIME! ♪
EXCITED OVER A BENTO BOX? HOW OLD ARE YOU?
YOU TRYING TO PICK A FIGHT WITH ME?
C'MON, NOW!
NO FIGHT-ING, OKAY?!
HA HA HA! I'M JUST KIDDING!
...
O-OH!

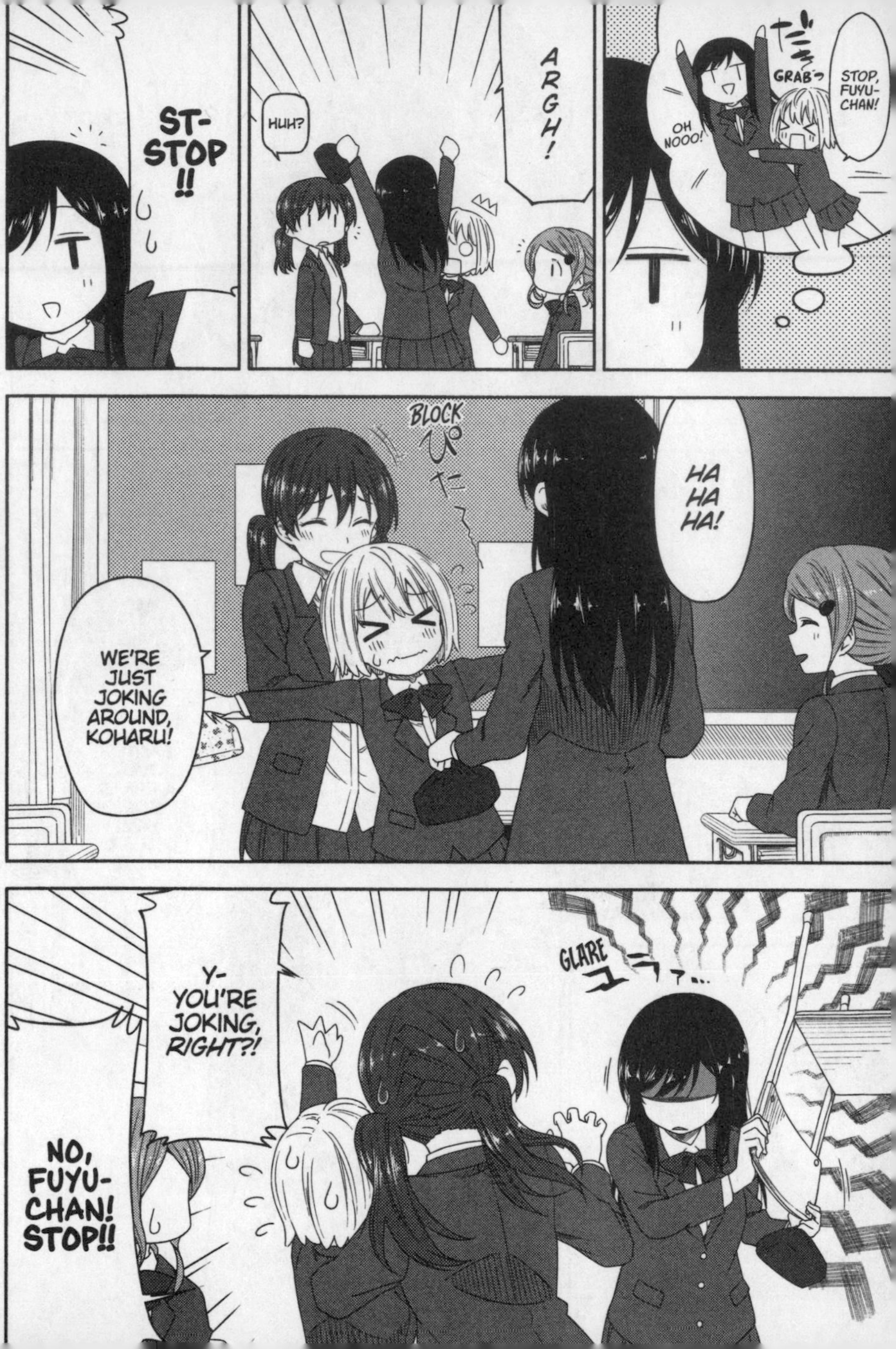
STOP, FUYU-CHAN!
GRAB
OH NOOO!
ARGH!
HUH?
ST-STOP!!
HA HA HA!
BLOCK
WE'RE JUST JOKING AROUND, KOHARU!
GLARE
Y-YOU'RE JOKING, RIGHT?!
NO, FUYU-CHAN! STOP!!

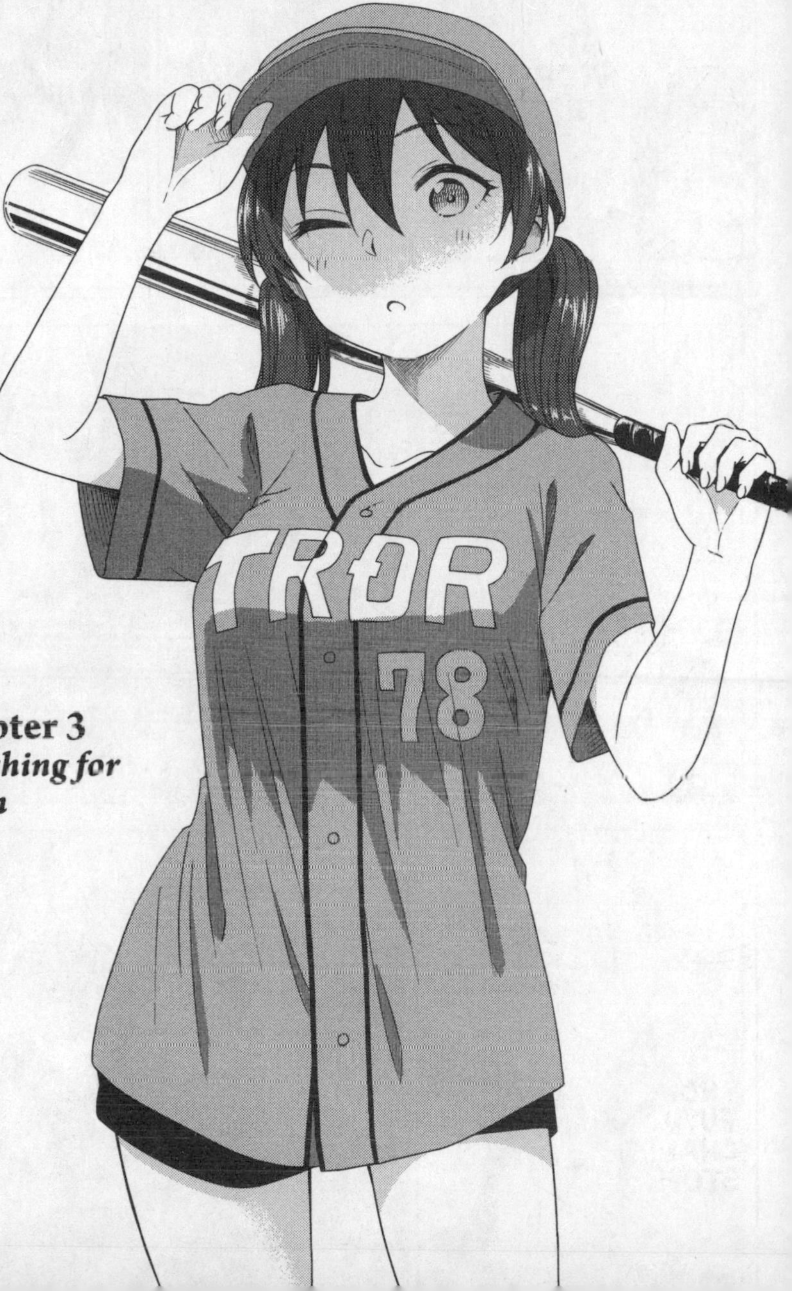
78

Chapter 3
Searching for Youth

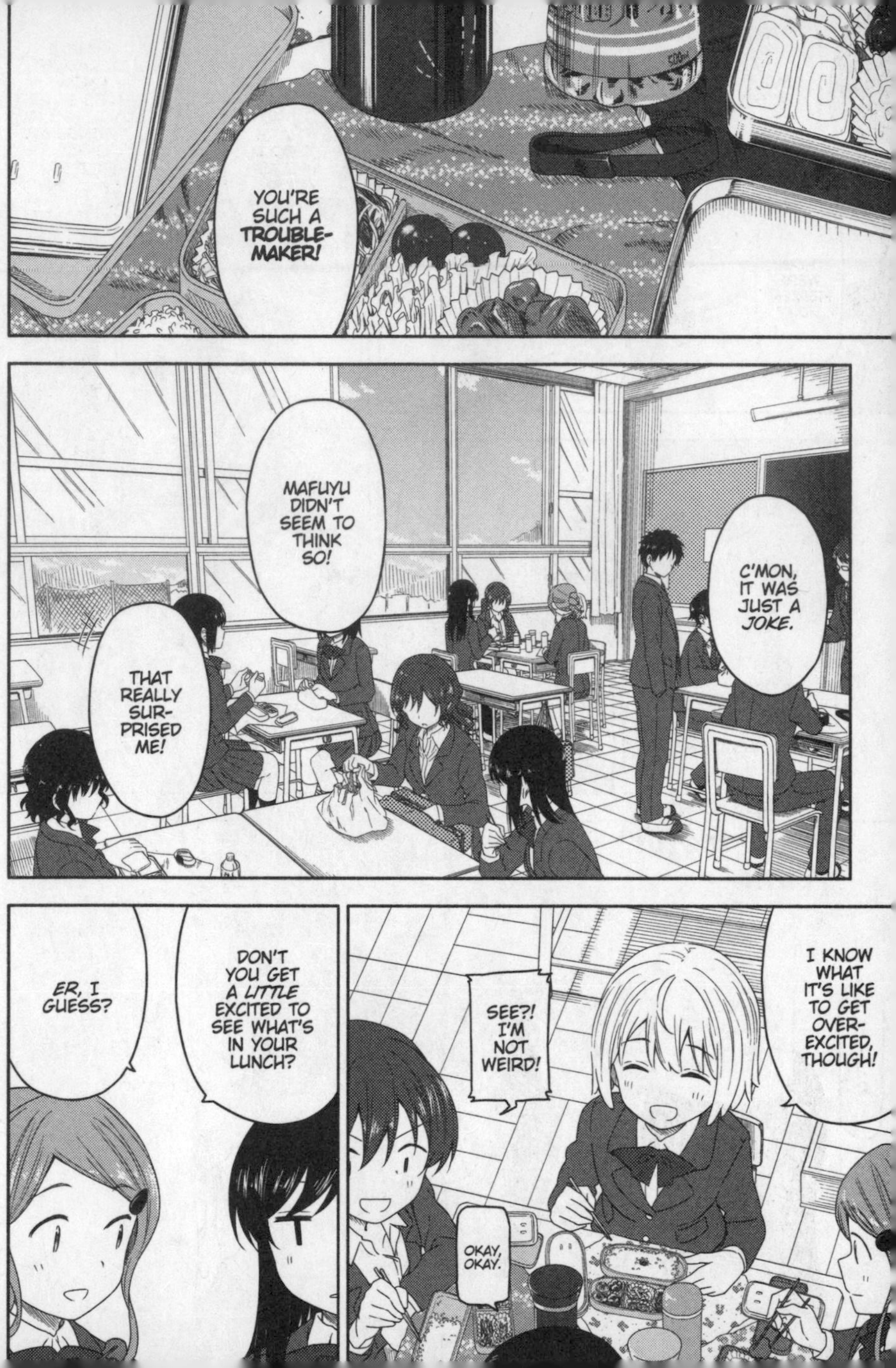
YOU'RE SUCH A TROUBLE-MAKER!
C'MON, IT WAS JUST A *JOKE.*
MAFUYU DIDN'T SEEM TO THINK SO!
THAT REALLY SUR-PRISED ME!
I KNOW WHAT IT'S LIKE TO GET OVER-EXCITED, THOUGH!
SEE?! I'M NOT WEIRD!
OKAY, OKAY.
DON'T YOU GET A *LITTLE* EXCITED TO SEE WHAT'S IN YOUR LUNCH?
ER, I GUESS?

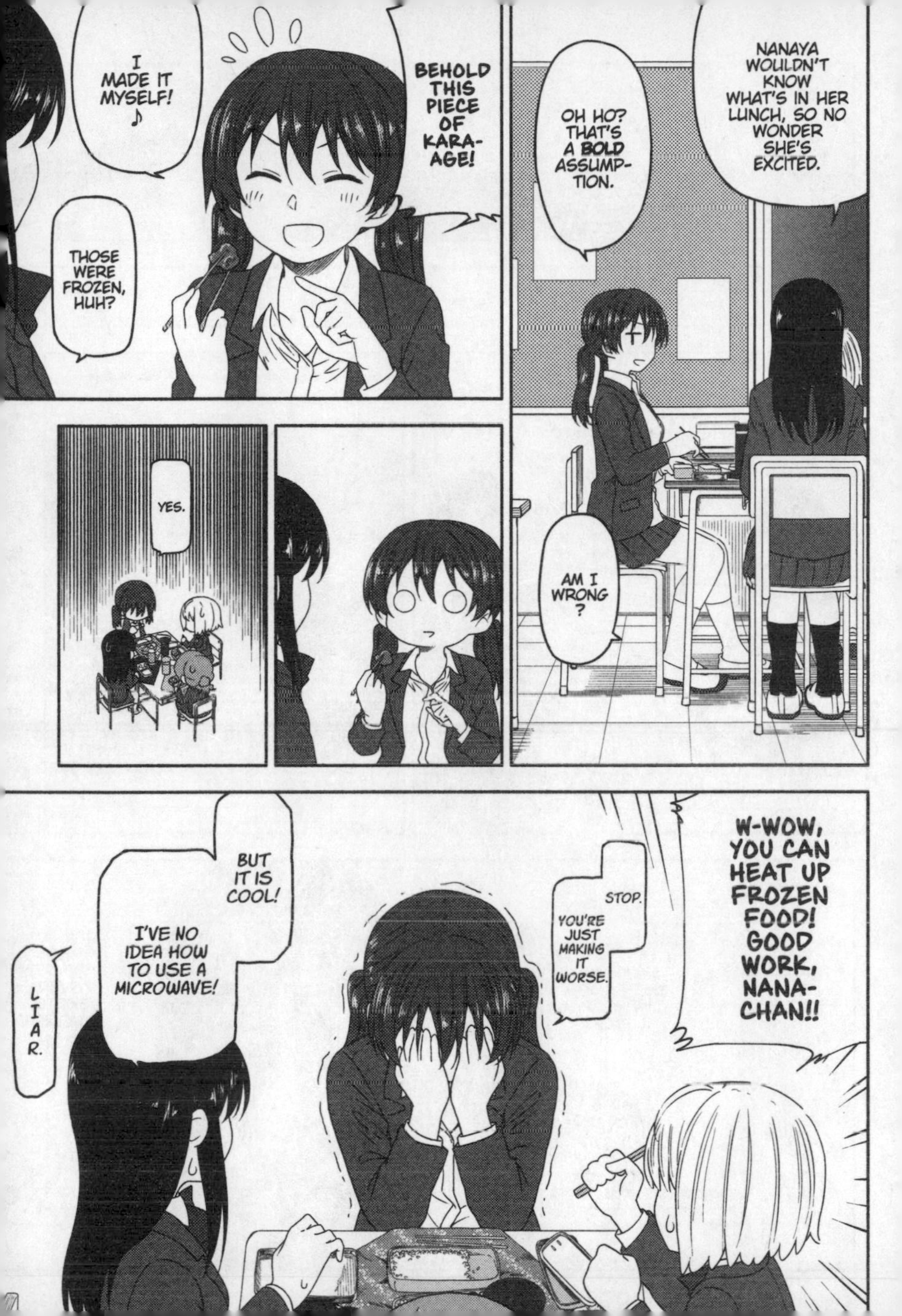
NANAYA WOULDN'T KNOW WHAT'S IN HER LUNCH, SO NO WONDER SHE'S EXCITED.
OH HO? THAT'S A BOLD ASSUMPTION.
AM I WRONG?
BEHOLD THIS PIECE OF KARA-AGE!
I MADE IT MYSELF! ♪
THOSE WERE FROZEN, HUH?
YES.
W-WOW, YOU CAN HEAT UP FROZEN FOOD! GOOD WORK, NANA-CHAN!!
STOP.
YOU'RE JUST MAKING IT WORSE.
BUT IT IS COOL!
I'VE NO IDEA HOW TO USE A MICROWAVE!
LIAR.

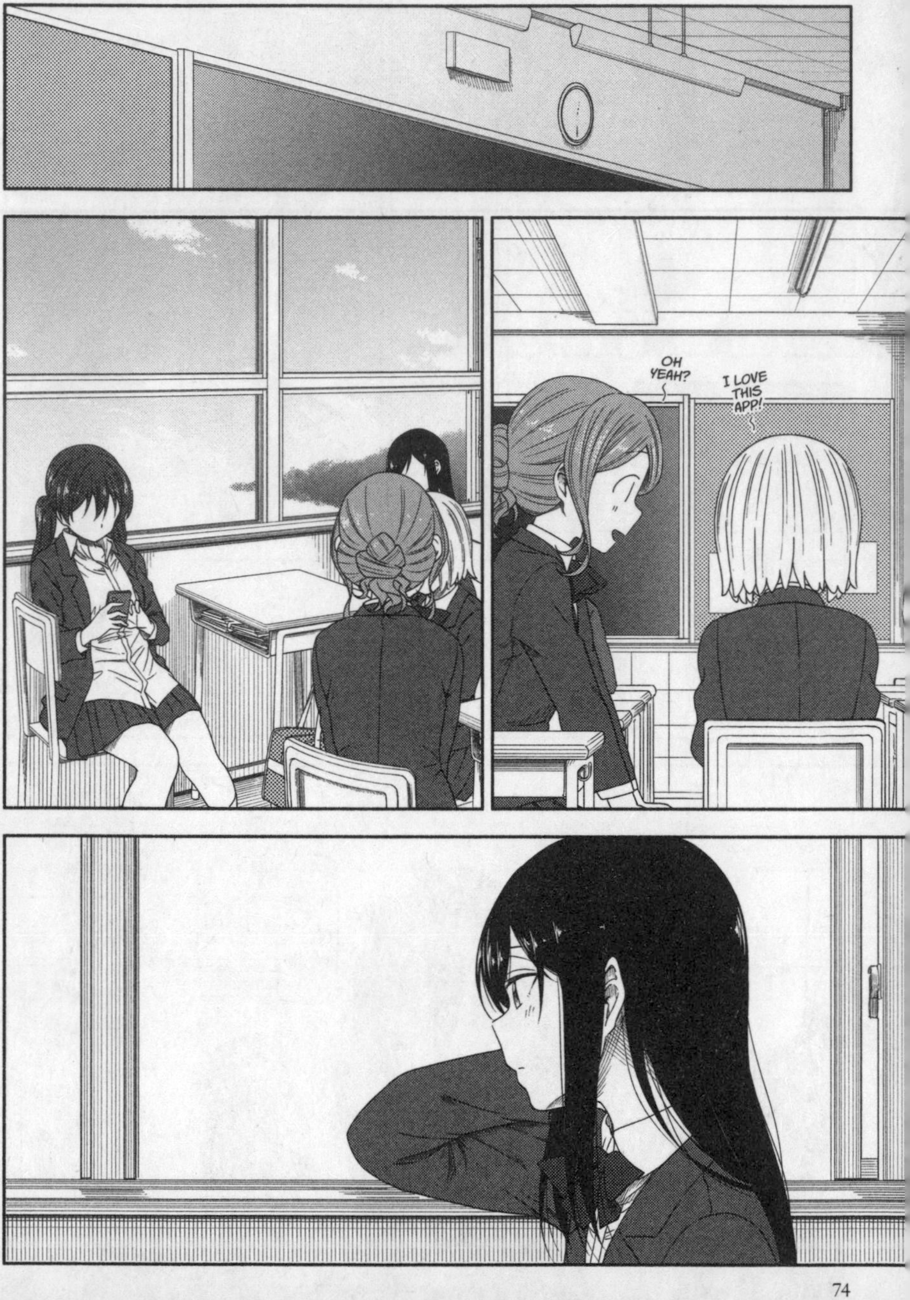
I LOVE THIS APP!
OH YEAH?

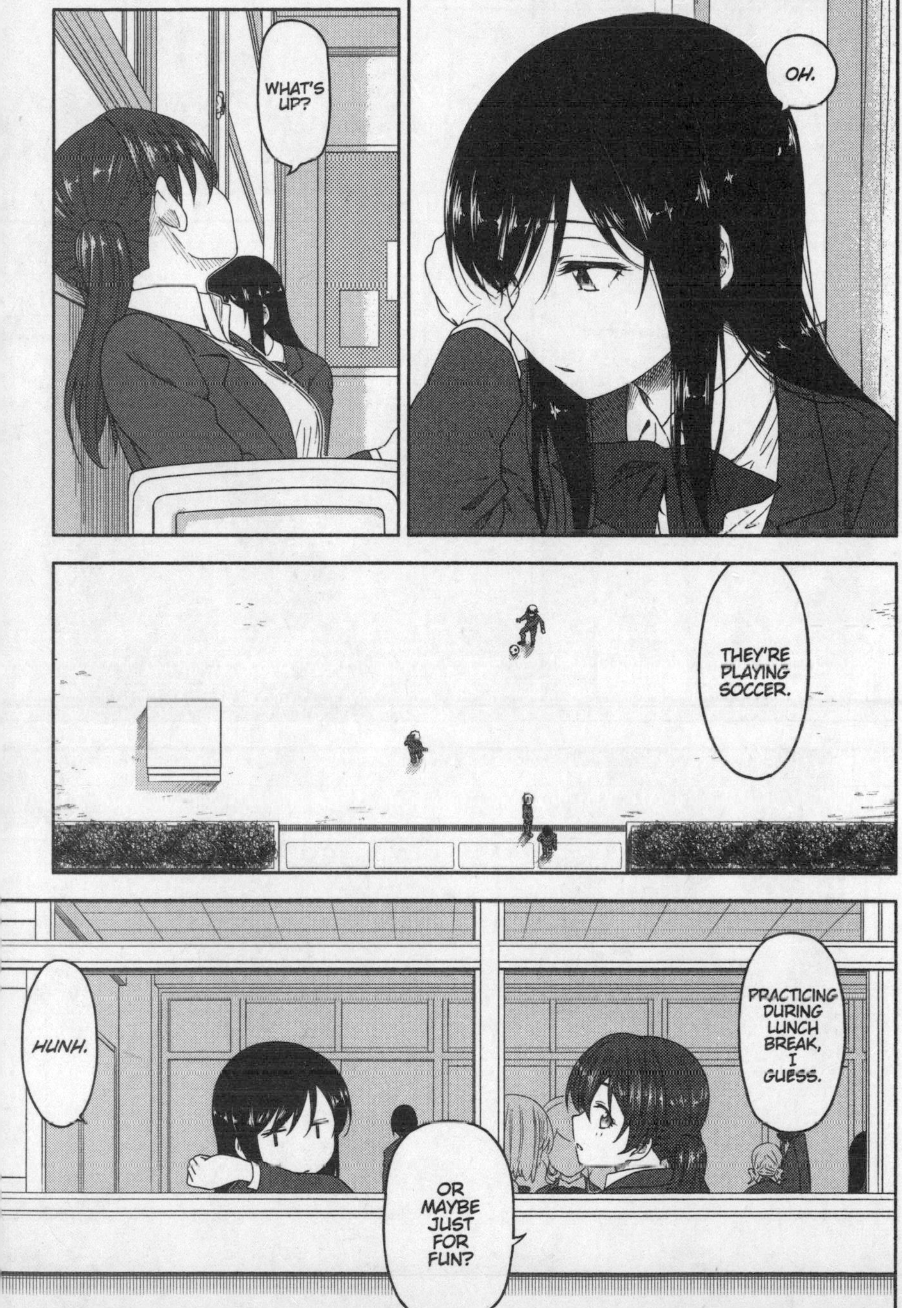
OH.
WHAT'S UP?
THEY'RE PLAYING SOCCER.
PRACTICING DURING LUNCH BREAK, I GUESS.
OR MAYBE JUST FOR FUN?
HUNH.

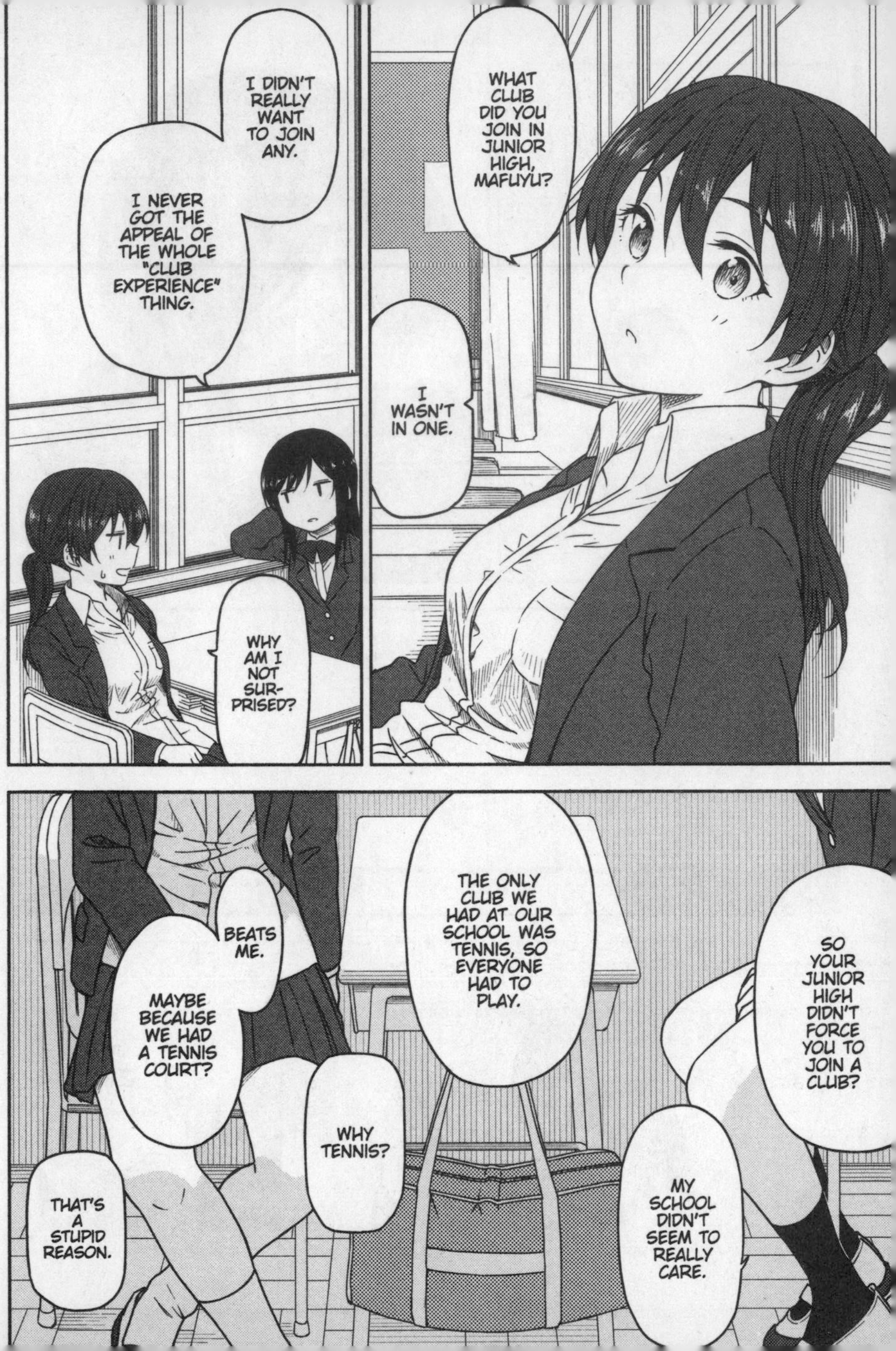
WHAT CLUB DID YOU JOIN IN JUNIOR HIGH, MAFUYU?
I WASN'T IN ONE.
I DIDN'T REALLY WANT TO JOIN ANY.
I NEVER GOT THE APPEAL OF THE WHOLE "CLUB EXPERIENCE" THING.
WHY AM I NOT SUR-PRISED?
SO YOUR JUNIOR HIGH DIDN'T FORCE YOU TO JOIN A CLUB?
MY SCHOOL DIDN'T SEEM TO REALLY CARE.
THE ONLY CLUB WE HAD AT OUR SCHOOL WAS TENNIS, SO EVERYONE HAD TO PLAY.
WHY TENNIS?
BEATS ME.
MAYBE BECAUSE WE HAD A TENNIS COURT?
THAT'S A STUPID REASON.

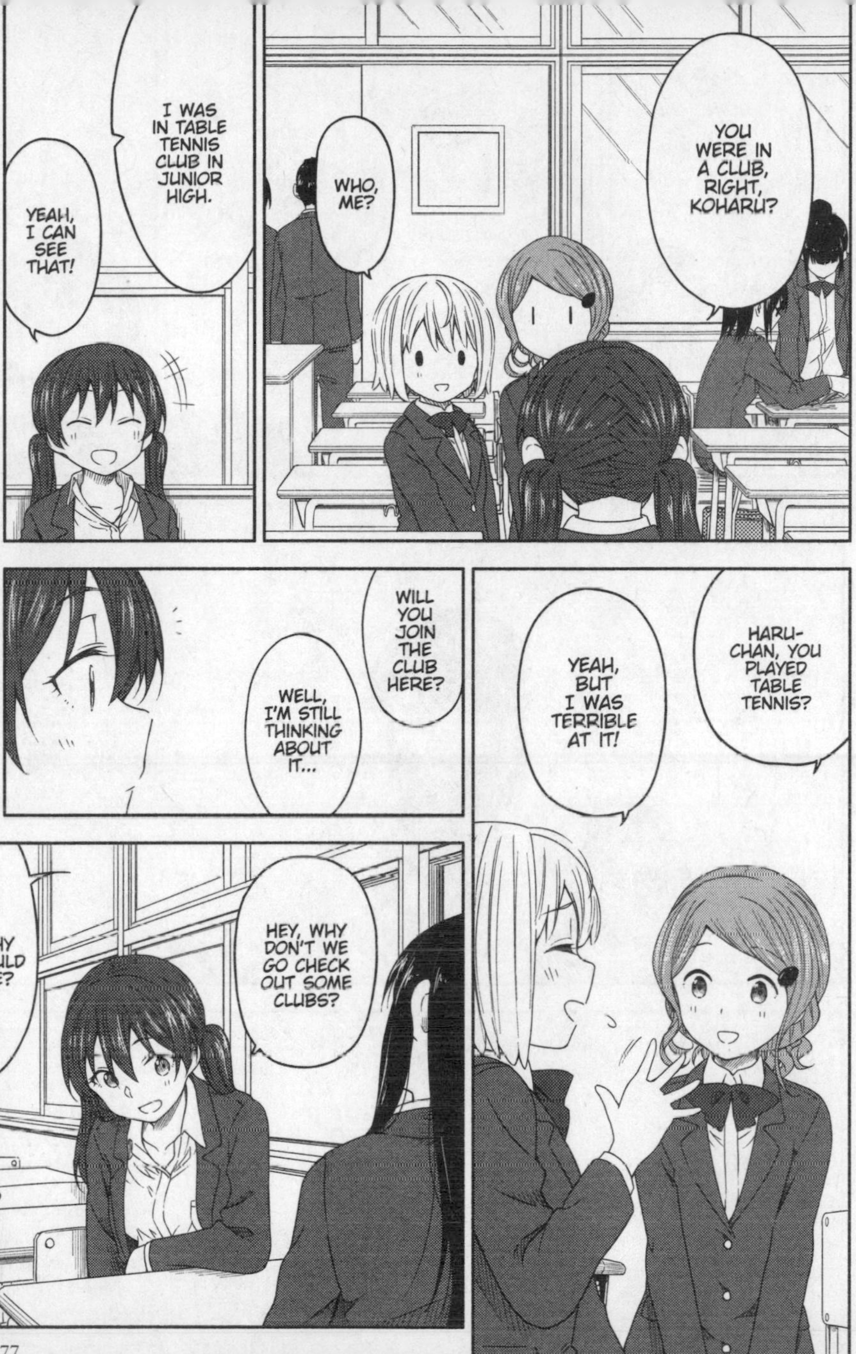
YOU WERE IN A CLUB, RIGHT, KOHARU?
WHO, ME?
I WAS IN TABLE TENNIS CLUB IN JUNIOR HIGH.
YEAH, I CAN SEE THAT!
HARU-CHAN, YOU PLAYED TABLE TENNIS?
YEAH, BUT I WAS TERRIBLE AT IT!
WILL YOU JOIN THE CLUB HERE?
WELL, I'M STILL THINKING ABOUT IT...
HEY, WHY DON'T WE GO CHECK OUT SOME CLUBS?
WHY WOULD WE?

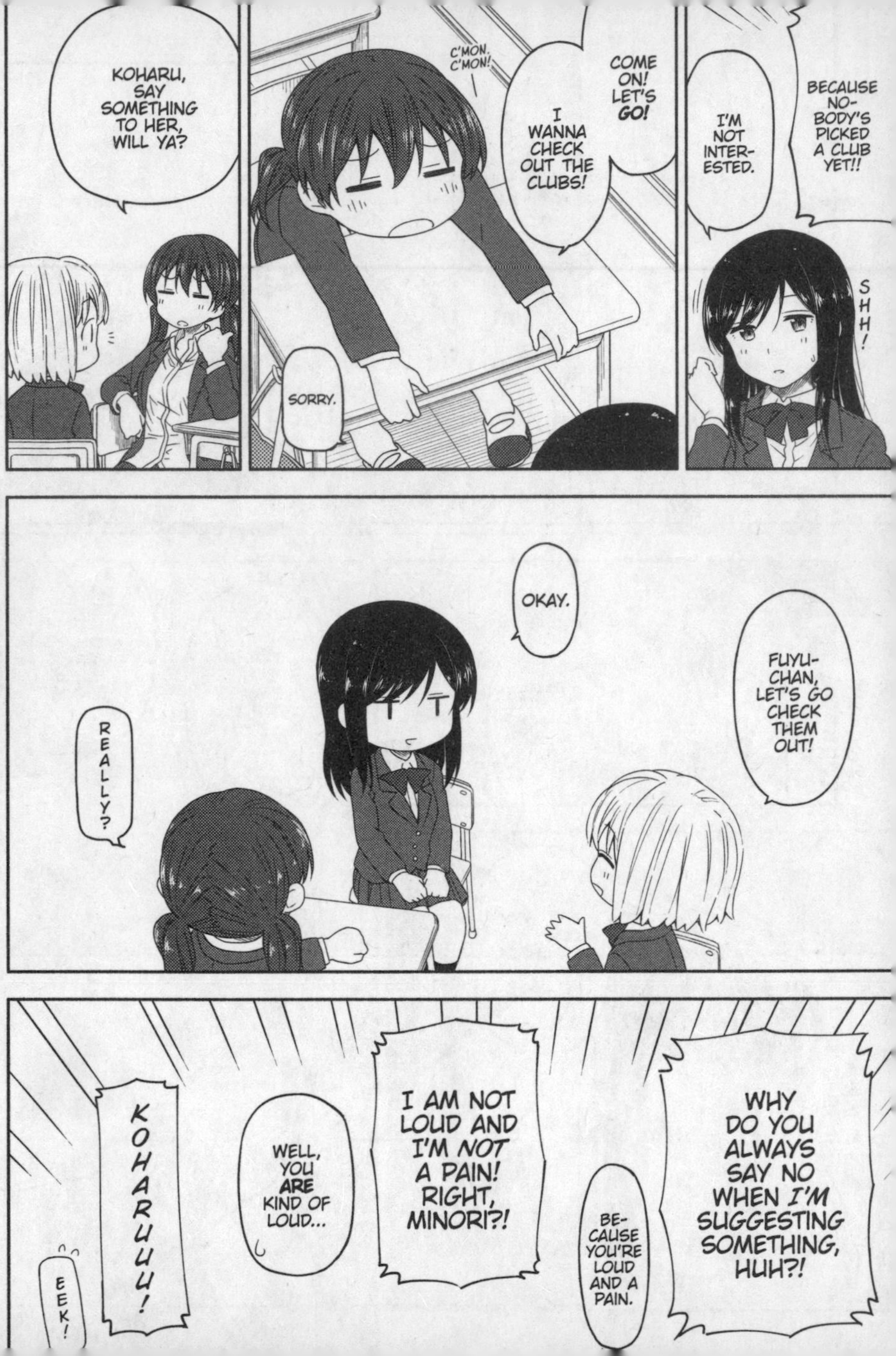
BECAUSE NO-BODY'S PICKED A CLUB YET!!
I'M NOT INTER-ESTED.
SHH!
COME ON! LET'S GO!
I WANNA CHECK OUT THE CLUBS!
C'MON. C'MON!
SORRY.
KOHARU, SAY SOMETHING TO HER, WILL YA?
FUYU-CHAN, LET'S GO CHECK THEM OUT!
OKAY.
REALLY?
WHY DO YOU ALWAYS SAY NO WHEN I'M SUGGESTING SOMETHING, HUH?!
BE-CAUSE YOU'RE LOUD AND A PAIN.
I AM NOT LOUD AND I'M NOT A PAIN! RIGHT, MINORI?!
WELL, YOU ARE KIND OF LOUD...
KOHARUUU!
EEK!

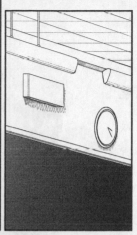

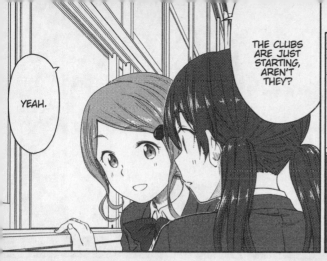

THE CLUBS ARE JUST STARTING, AREN'T THEY?
YEAH.
I CAN'T BELIEVE SHE'S STILL ASLEEP...
FUYU-CHAN!
SHE'S BEEN OUT COLD SINCE SIXTH PERIOD.
YAAAAWN!

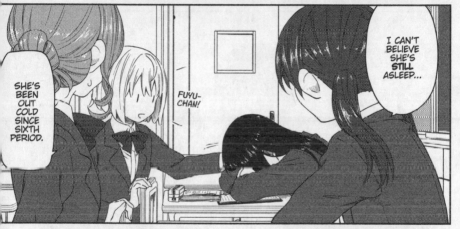

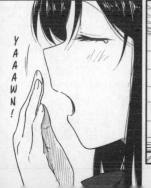

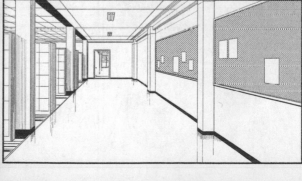

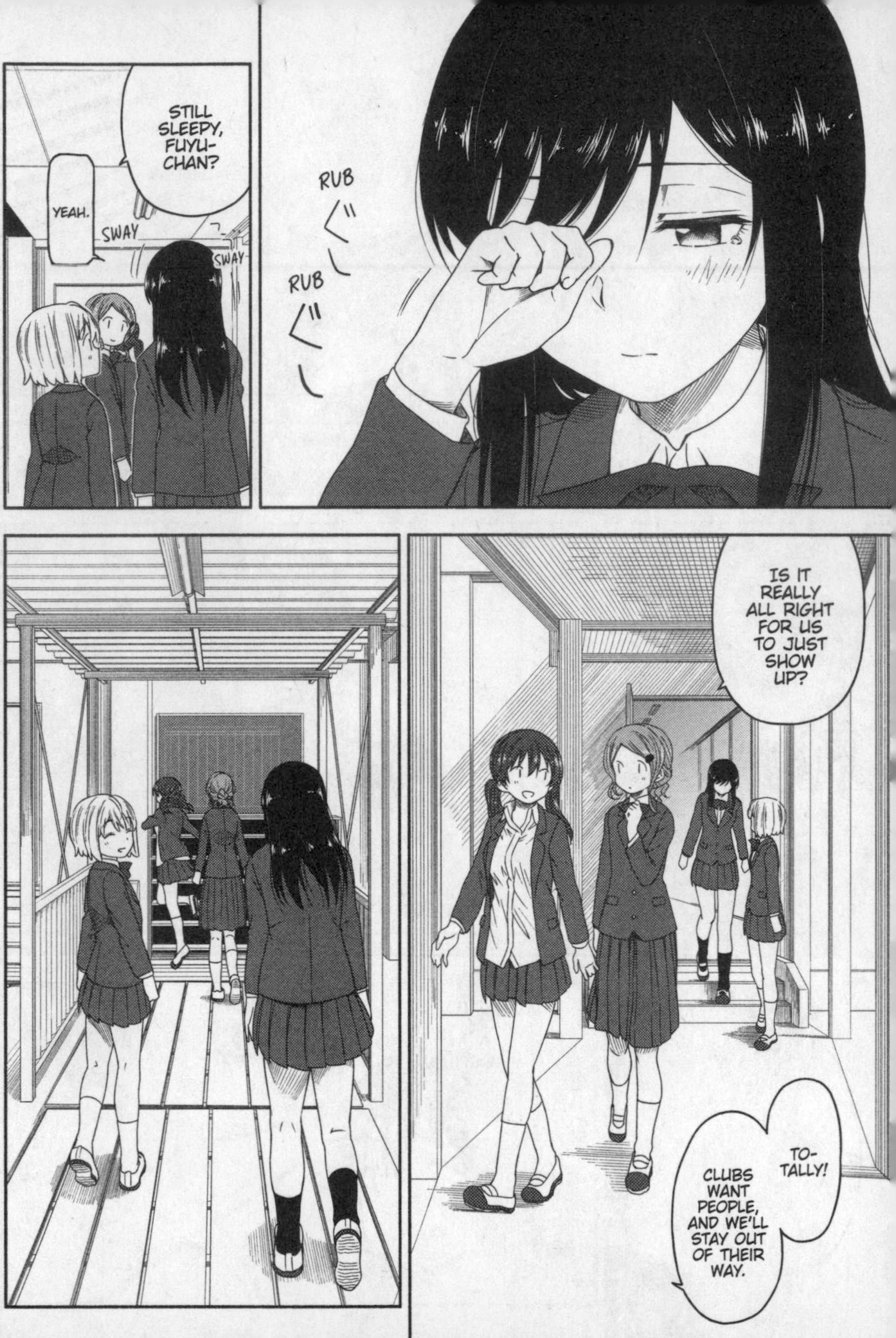
RUB
RUB
STILL SLEEPY, FUYU-CHAN?
YEAH.
SWAY
SWAY
IS IT REALLY ALL RIGHT FOR US TO JUST SHOW UP?
TO-TALLY!
CLUBS WANT PEOPLE, AND WE'LL STAY OUT OF THEIR WAY.

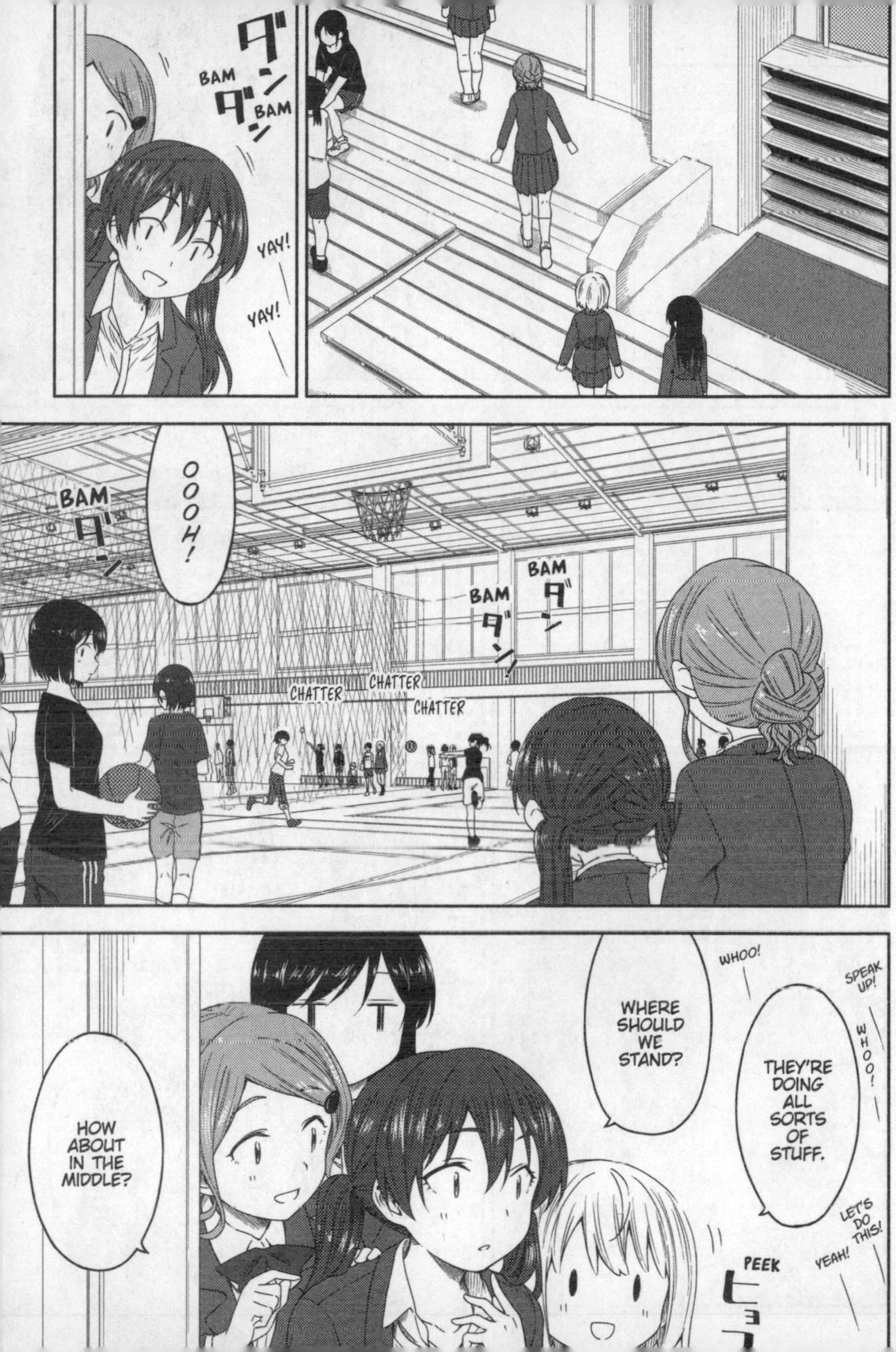
BAM
BAM
YAY!
YAY!
OOOH!
BAM
BAM
BAM
CHATTER
CHATTER
CHATTER
SPEAK UP!
WHOO!
THEY'RE DOING ALL SORTS OF STUFF.
WHOO!
WHERE SHOULD WE STAND?
HOW ABOUT IN THE MIDDLE?
LET'S DO THIS!
YEAH!
PEEK

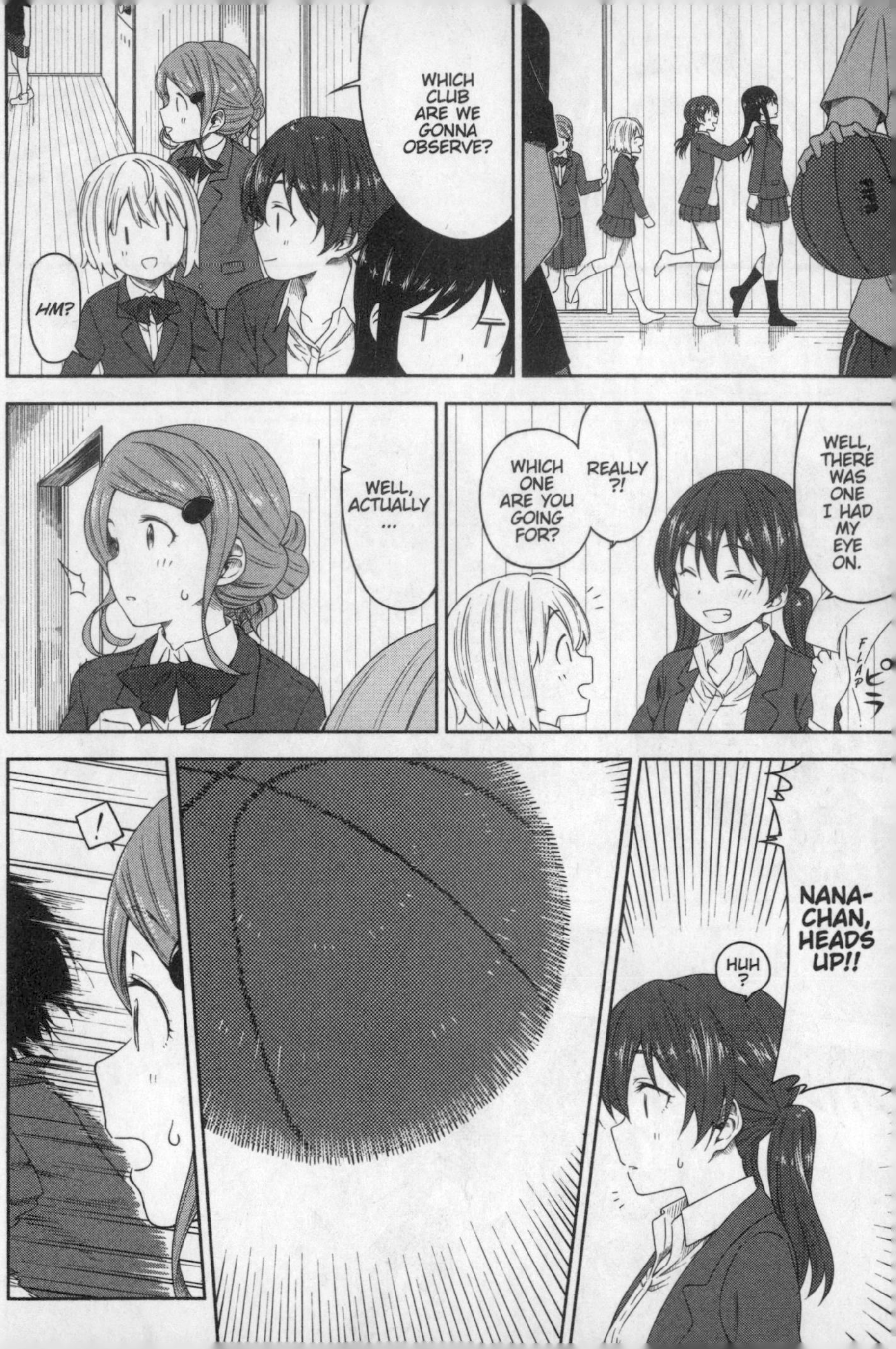
WHICH CLUB ARE WE GONNA OBSERVE?
HM?
WELL, THERE WAS ONE I HAD MY EYE ON.
FLAP
REALLY?!
WHICH ONE ARE YOU GOING FOR?
WELL, ACTUALLY...
NANA-CHAN, HEADS UP!!
HUH?
!

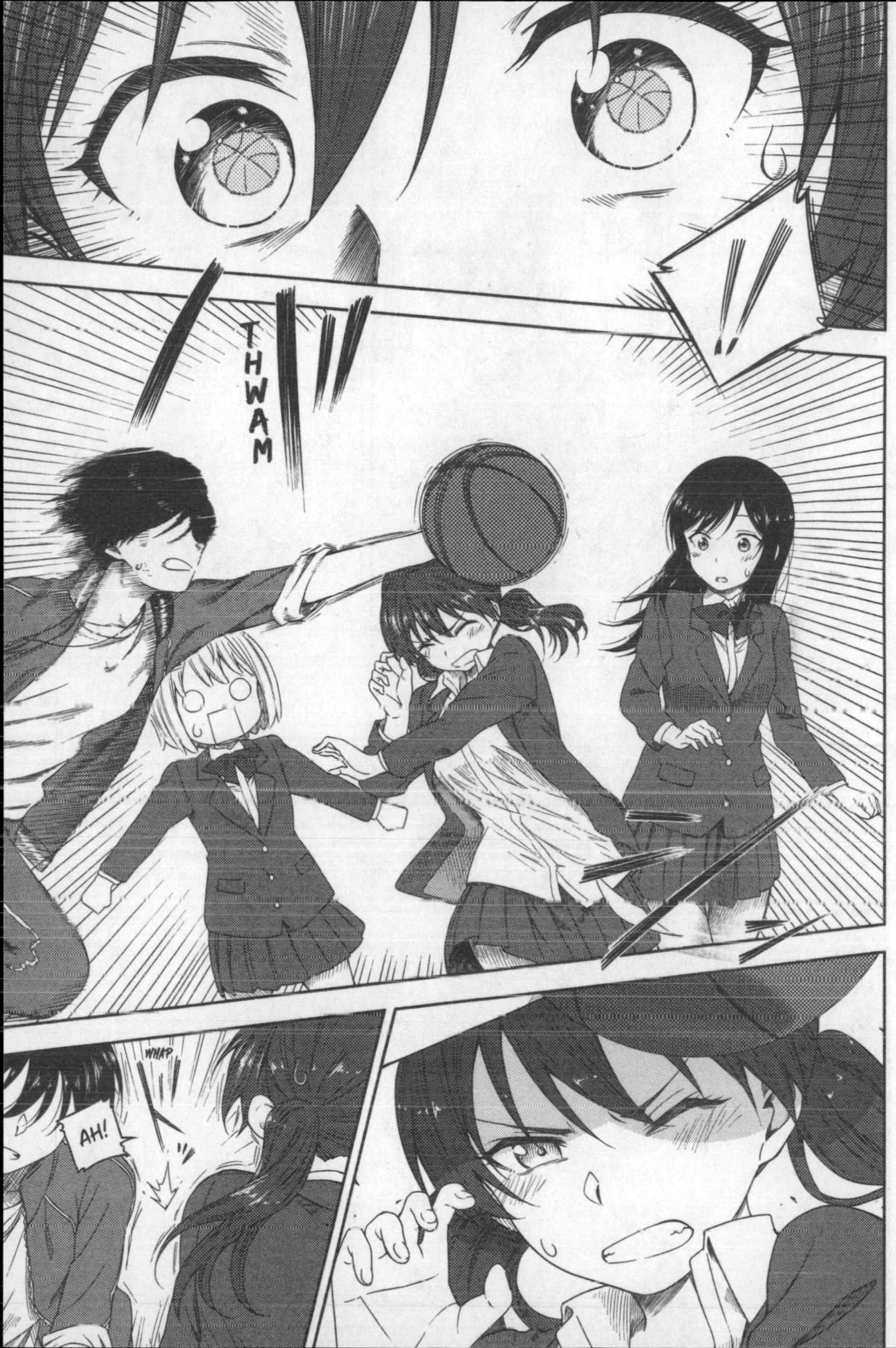
THWAM
WHAP
AH!

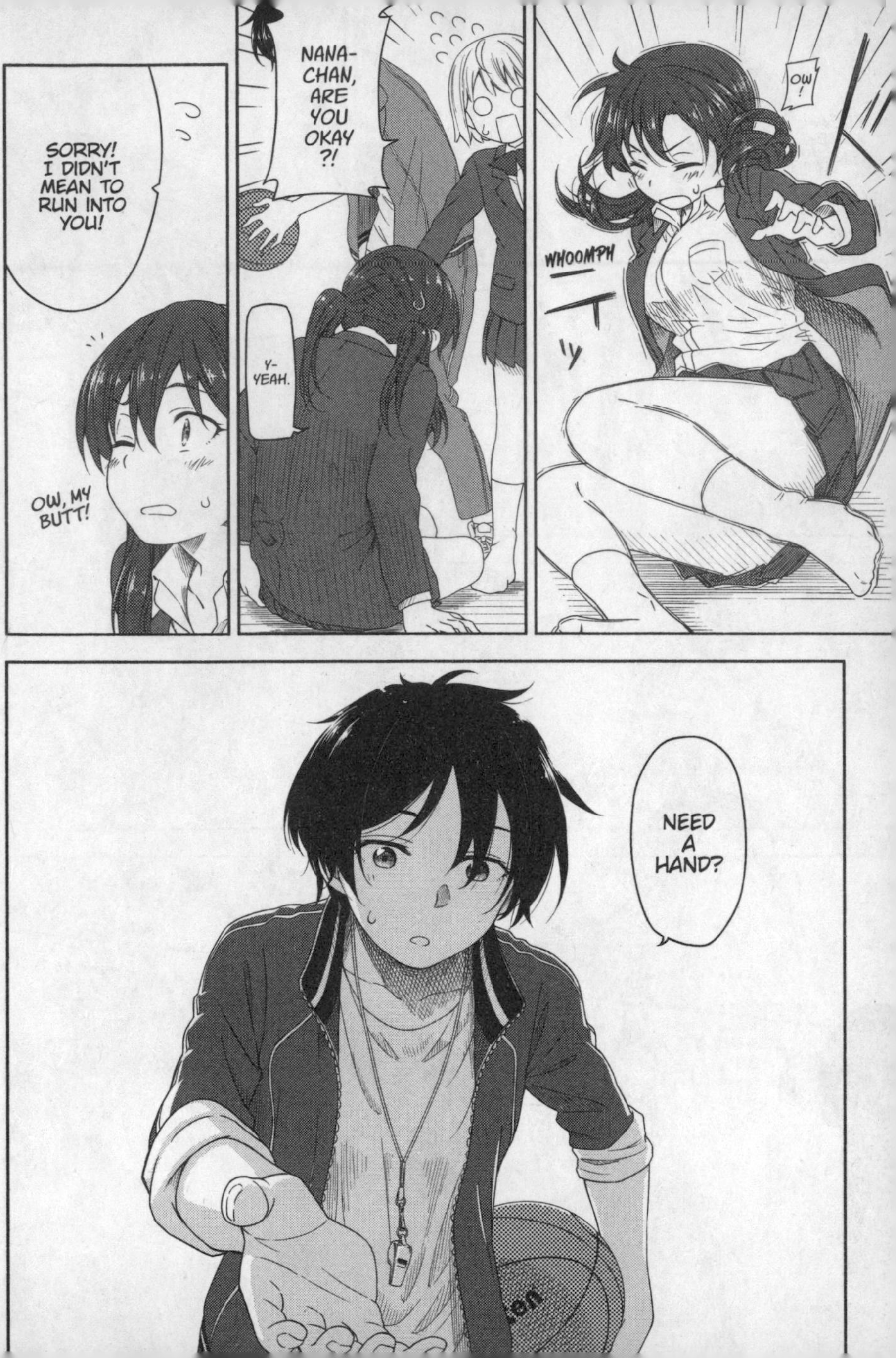
OW!
WHOOMPH
NANA-CHAN, ARE YOU OKAY?!
Y-YEAH.
SORRY! I DIDN'T MEAN TO RUN INTO YOU!
OW, MY BUTT!
NEED A HAND?

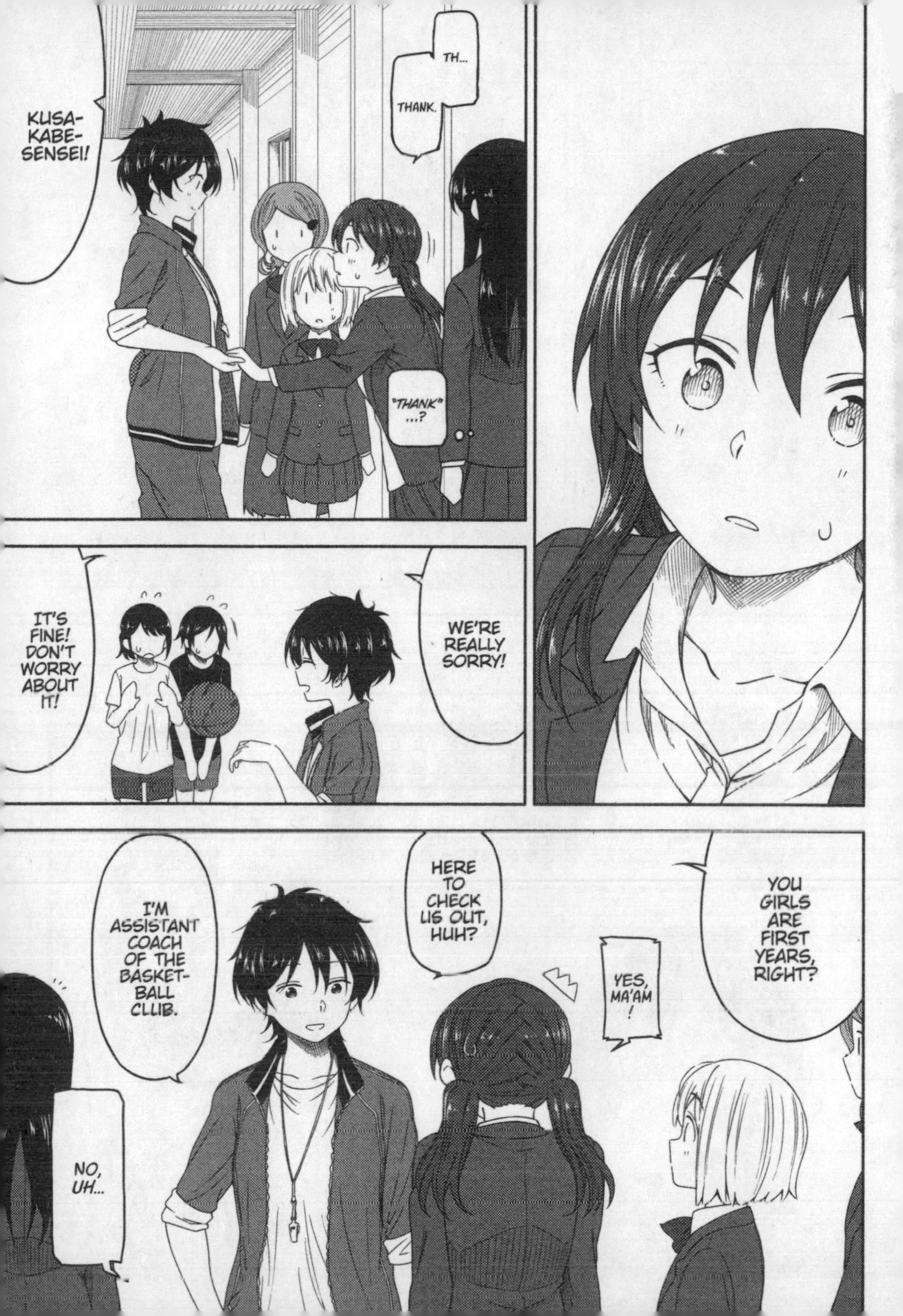
TH...
THANK.
KUSA-KABE-SENSEI!
"THANK"...?
WE'RE REALLY SORRY!
IT'S FINE! DON'T WORRY ABOUT IT!
YOU GIRLS ARE FIRST YEARS, RIGHT?
YES, MA'AM!
HERE TO CHECK US OUT, HUH?
I'M ASSISTANT COACH OF THE BASKET-BALL CLUB.
NO, UH...

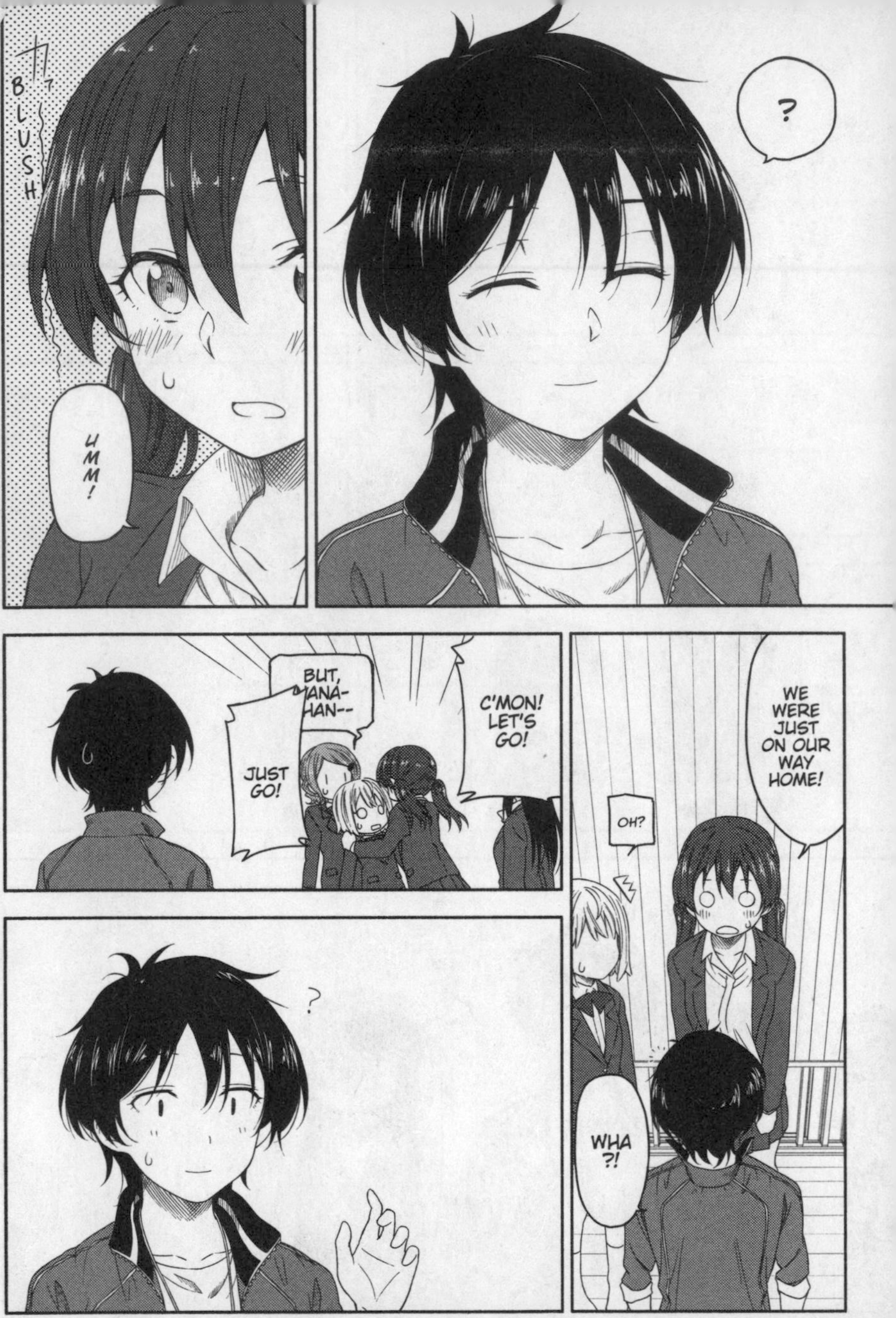
?
BLUSH
UMM!
WE WERE JUST ON OUR WAY HOME!
OH?
WHA ?!
C'MON! LET'S GO!
BUT, HANA-HAN--
JUST GO!
?

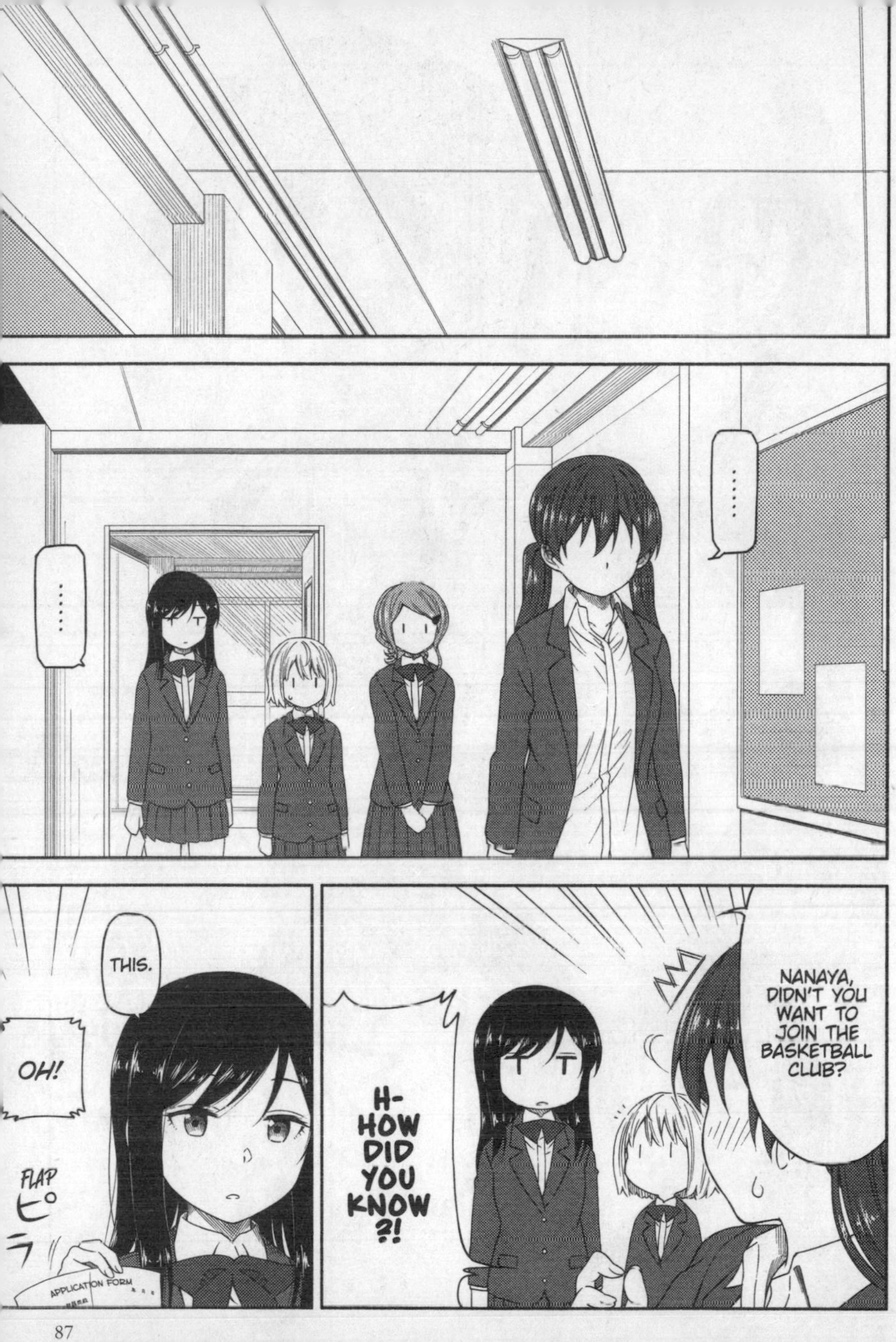
......
......
NANAYA, DIDN'T YOU WANT TO JOIN THE BASKETBALL CLUB?
H-HOW DID YOU KNOW?!
THIS.
OH!
FLAP
ピラ
APPLICATION FORM

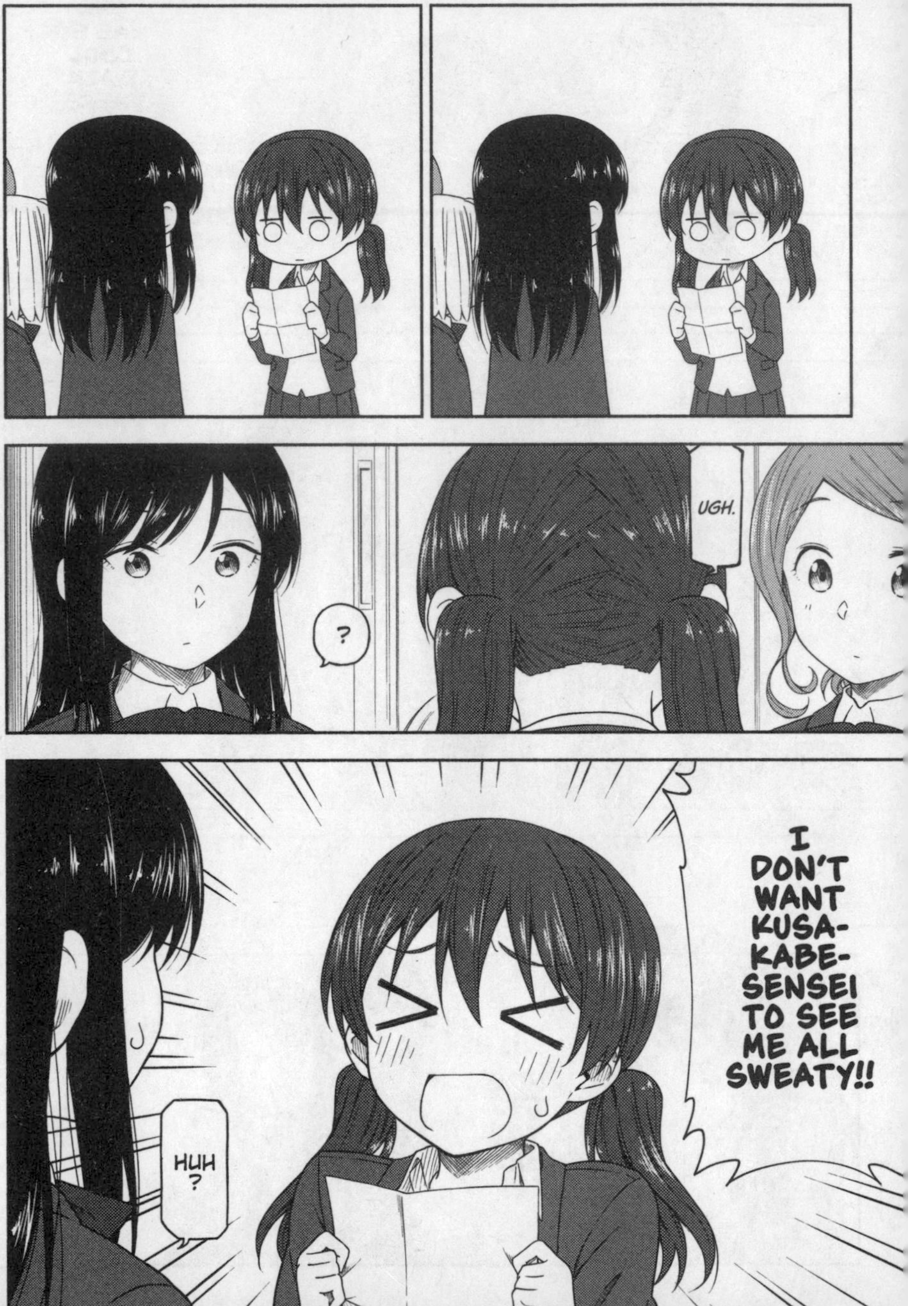
UGH.
?
I DON'T WANT KUSAKABE-SENSEI TO SEE ME ALL SWEATY!!
HUH?

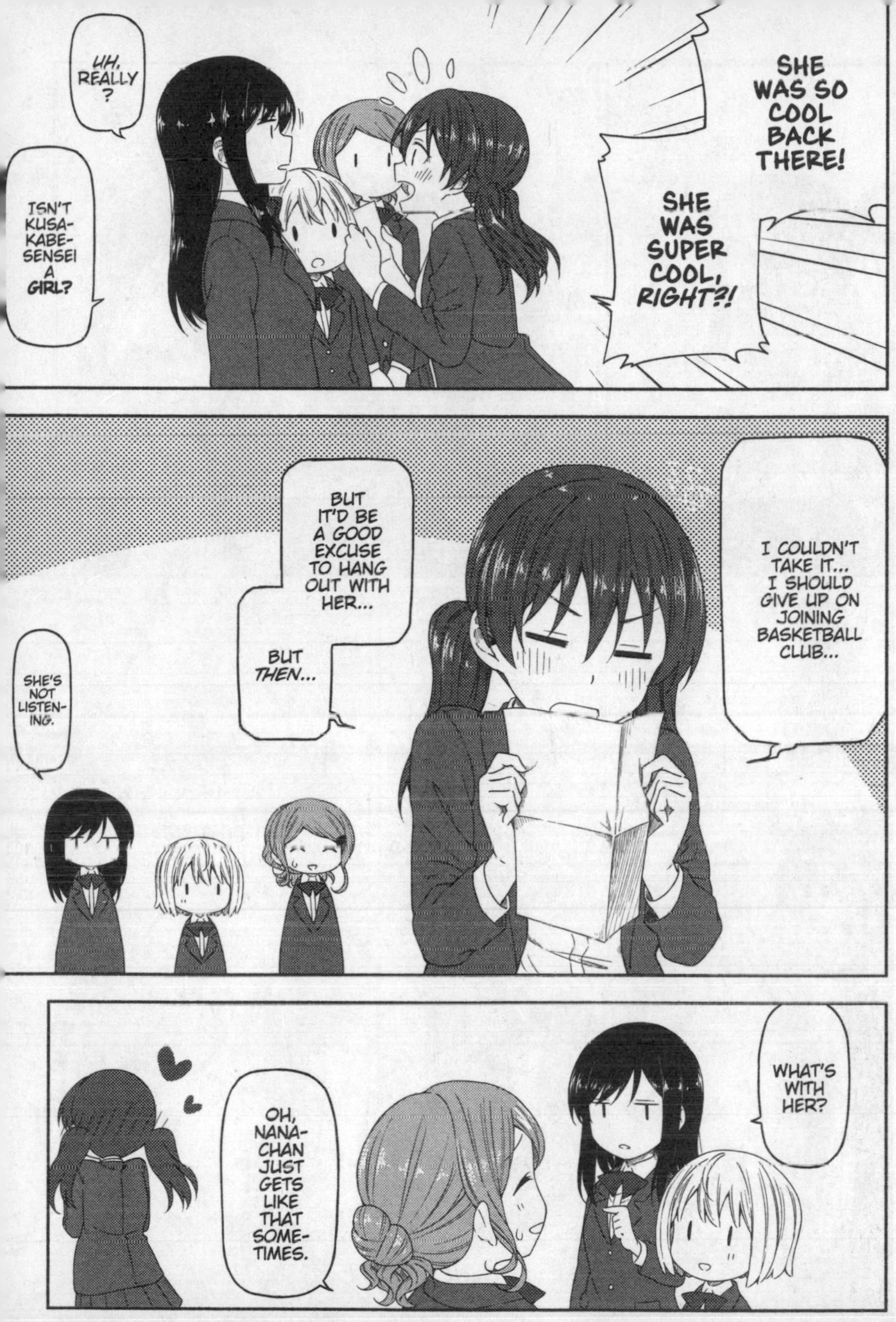
SHE WAS SO COOL BACK THERE!
SHE WAS SUPER COOL, RIGHT?!
UH, REALLY?
ISN'T KUSA-KABE-SENSEI A GIRL?
I COULDN'T TAKE IT... I SHOULD GIVE UP ON JOINING BASKETBALL CLUB...
BUT IT'D BE A GOOD EXCUSE TO HANG OUT WITH HER...
BUT *THEN*...
SHE'S NOT LISTEN-ING.
WHAT'S WITH HER?
OH, NANA-CHAN JUST GETS LIKE THAT SOME-TIMES.

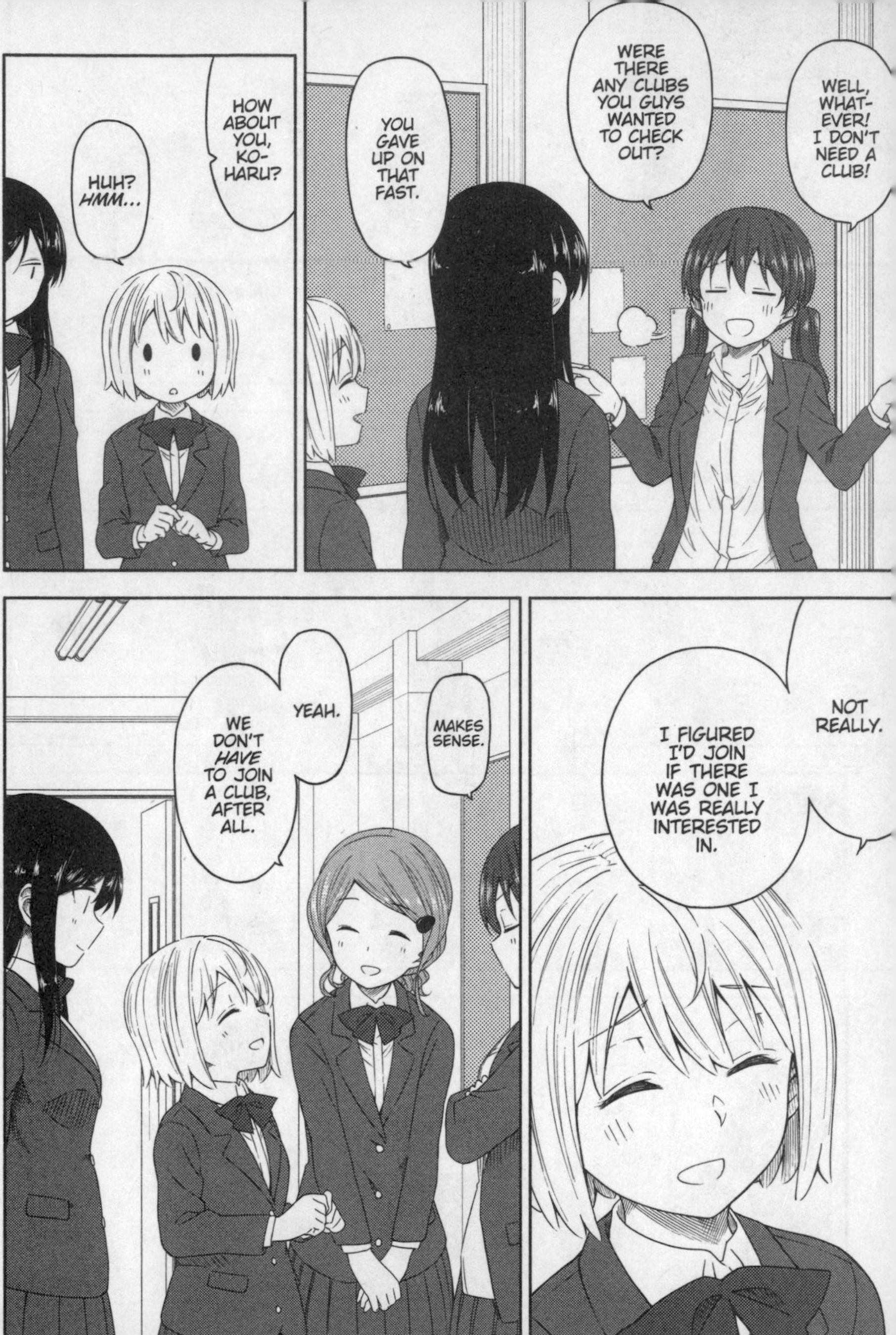
WELL, WHAT-EVER! I DON'T NEED A CLUB!
WERE THERE ANY CLUBS YOU GUYS WANTED TO CHECK OUT?
YOU GAVE UP ON THAT FAST.
HOW ABOUT YOU, KO-HARU?
HUH? *HMM...*
NOT REALLY.
I FIGURED I'D JOIN IF THERE WAS ONE I WAS REALLY INTERESTED IN.
MAKES SENSE.
YEAH.
WE DON'T *HAVE* TO JOIN A CLUB, AFTER ALL.

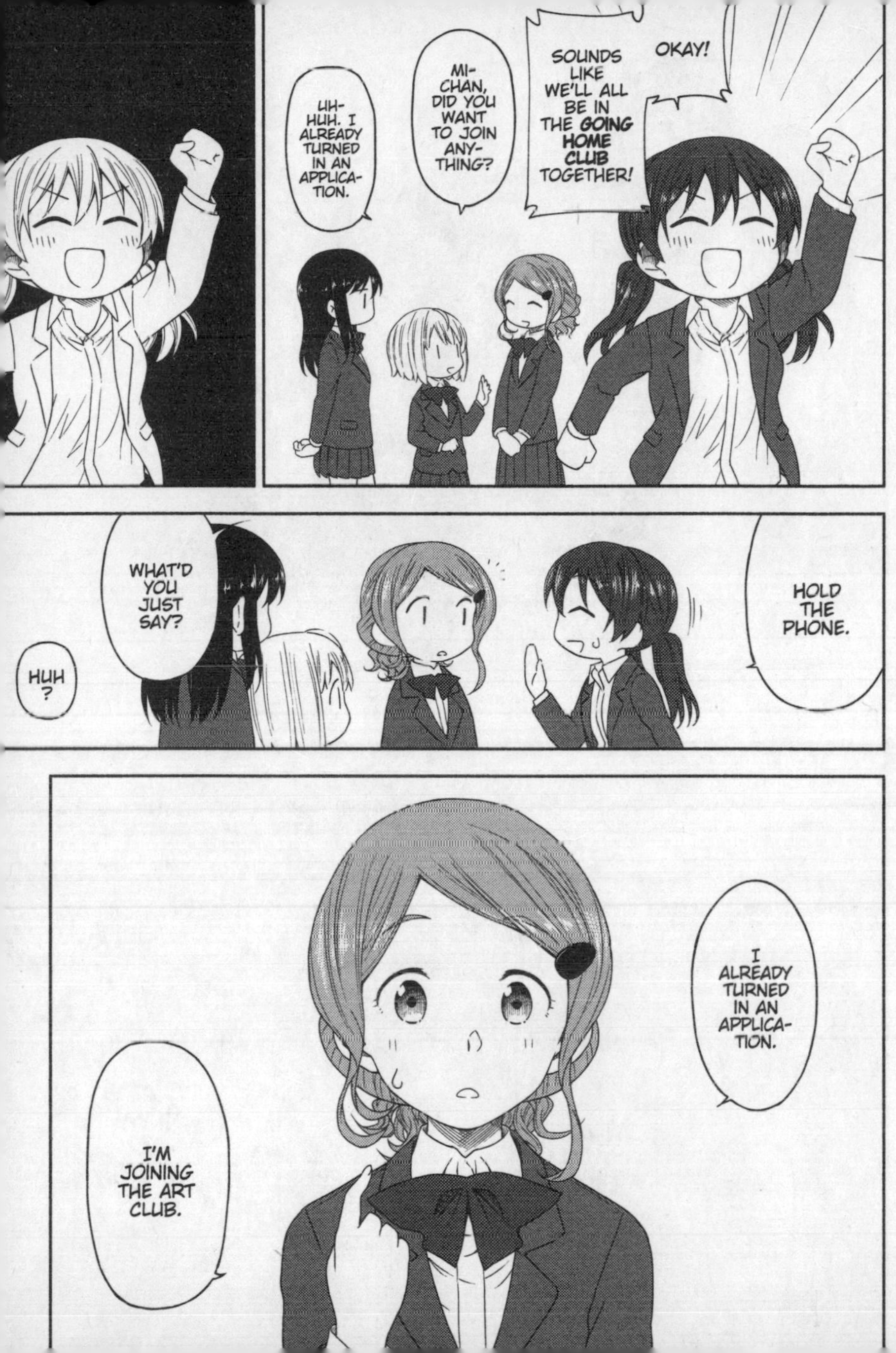
OKAY!
SOUNDS LIKE WE'LL ALL BE IN THE **GOING HOME CLUB** TOGETHER!
MI-CHAN, DID YOU WANT TO JOIN ANY-THING?
UH-HUH. I ALREADY TURNED IN AN APPLICA-TION.
HOLD THE PHONE.
WHAT'D YOU JUST SAY?
HUH?
I ALREADY TURNED IN AN APPLICA-TION.
I'M JOINING THE ART CLUB.

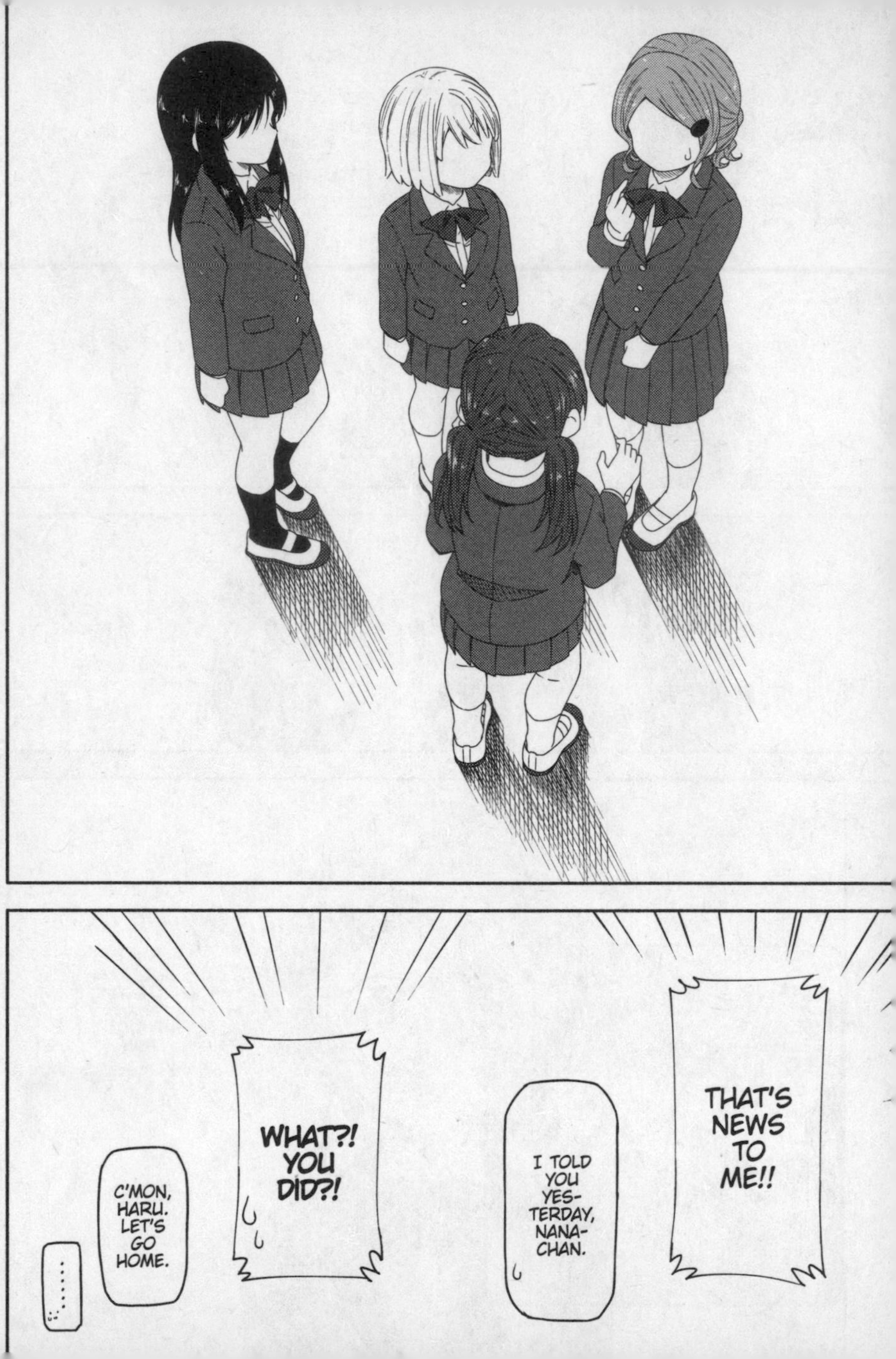
THAT'S NEWS TO ME!!
I TOLD YOU YES-TERDAY, NANA-CHAN.
WHAT?! YOU DID?!
C'MON, HARU. LET'S GO HOME.
......

Our Wonderful Days

story & art by Kei Hamuro

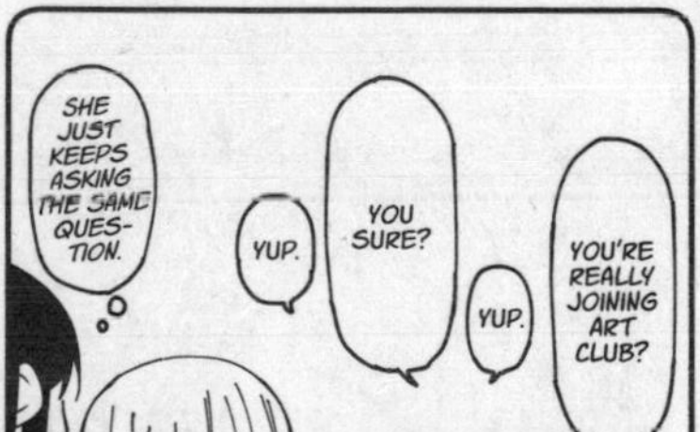

YOU'RE REALLY JOINING ART CLUB?
YUP.
YOU SURE?
YUP.
SHE JUST KEEPS ASKING THE SAME QUES-TION.

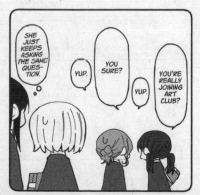

Our Wonderful Days

Tsurezure Biyori

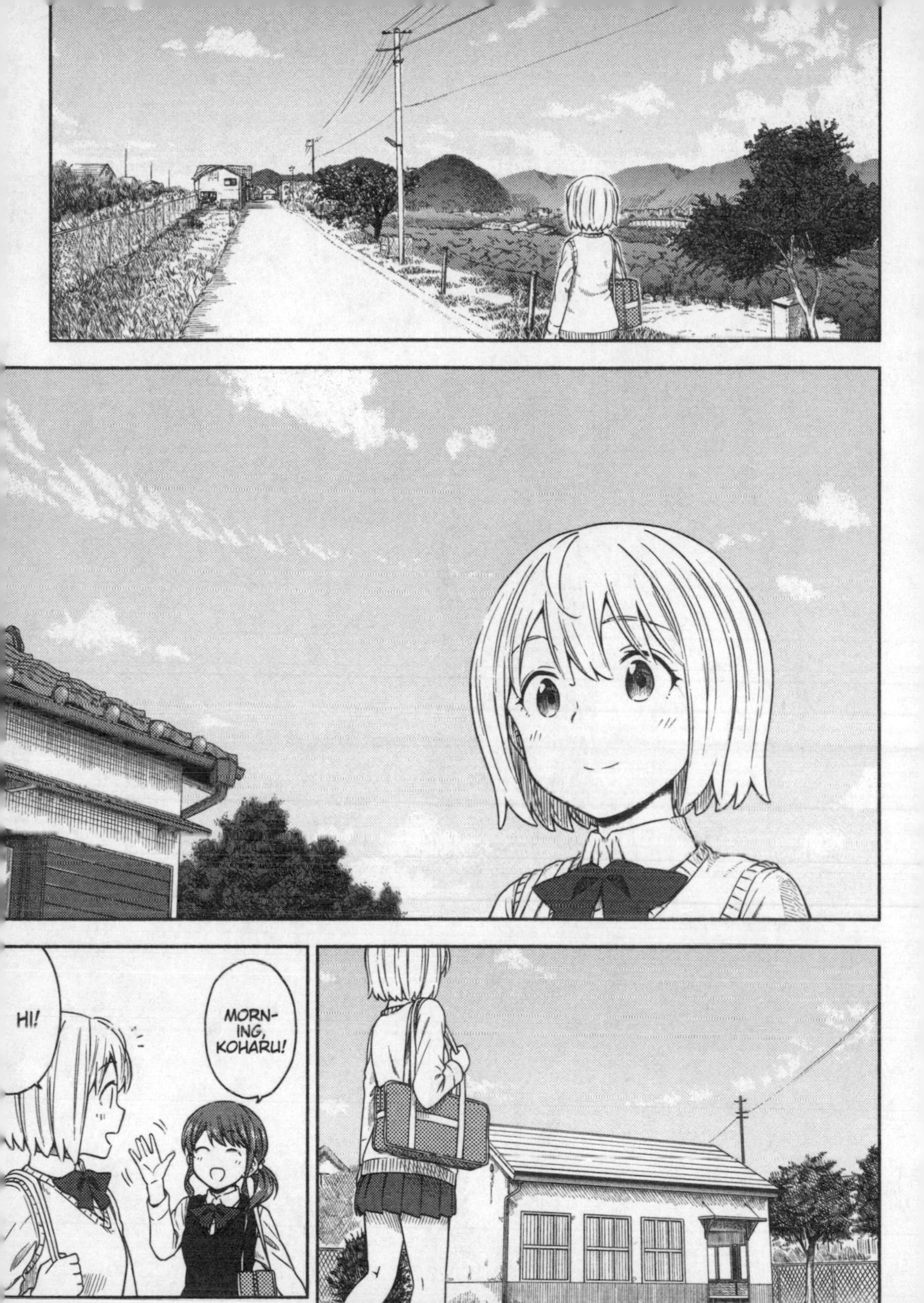
MORN-
ING,
KOHARU!
HI!

Chapter 4
The Smell of Art Supplies and Alcohol

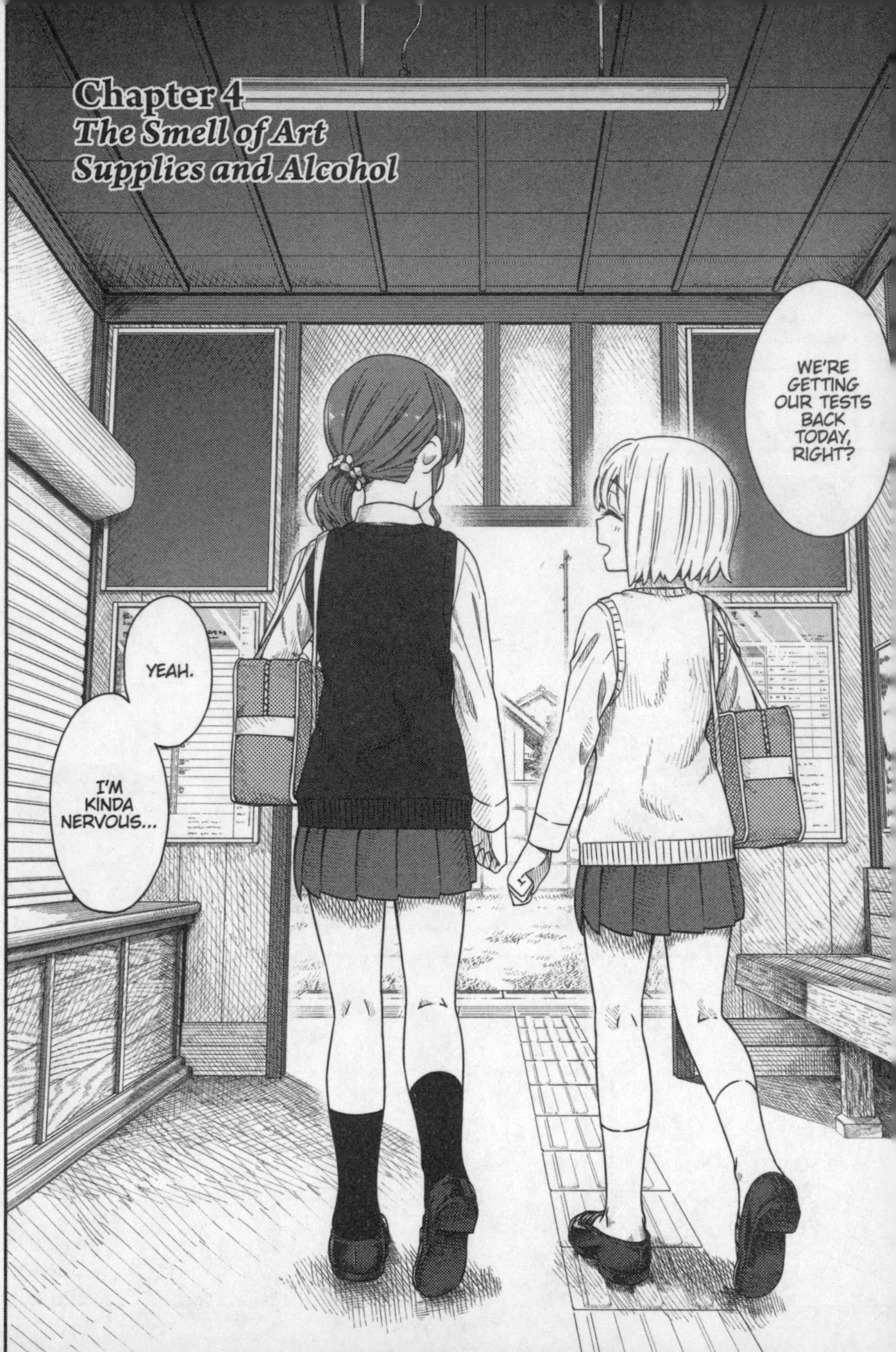
WE'RE GETTING OUR TESTS BACK TODAY, RIGHT?
YEAH.
I'M KINDA NERVOUS...

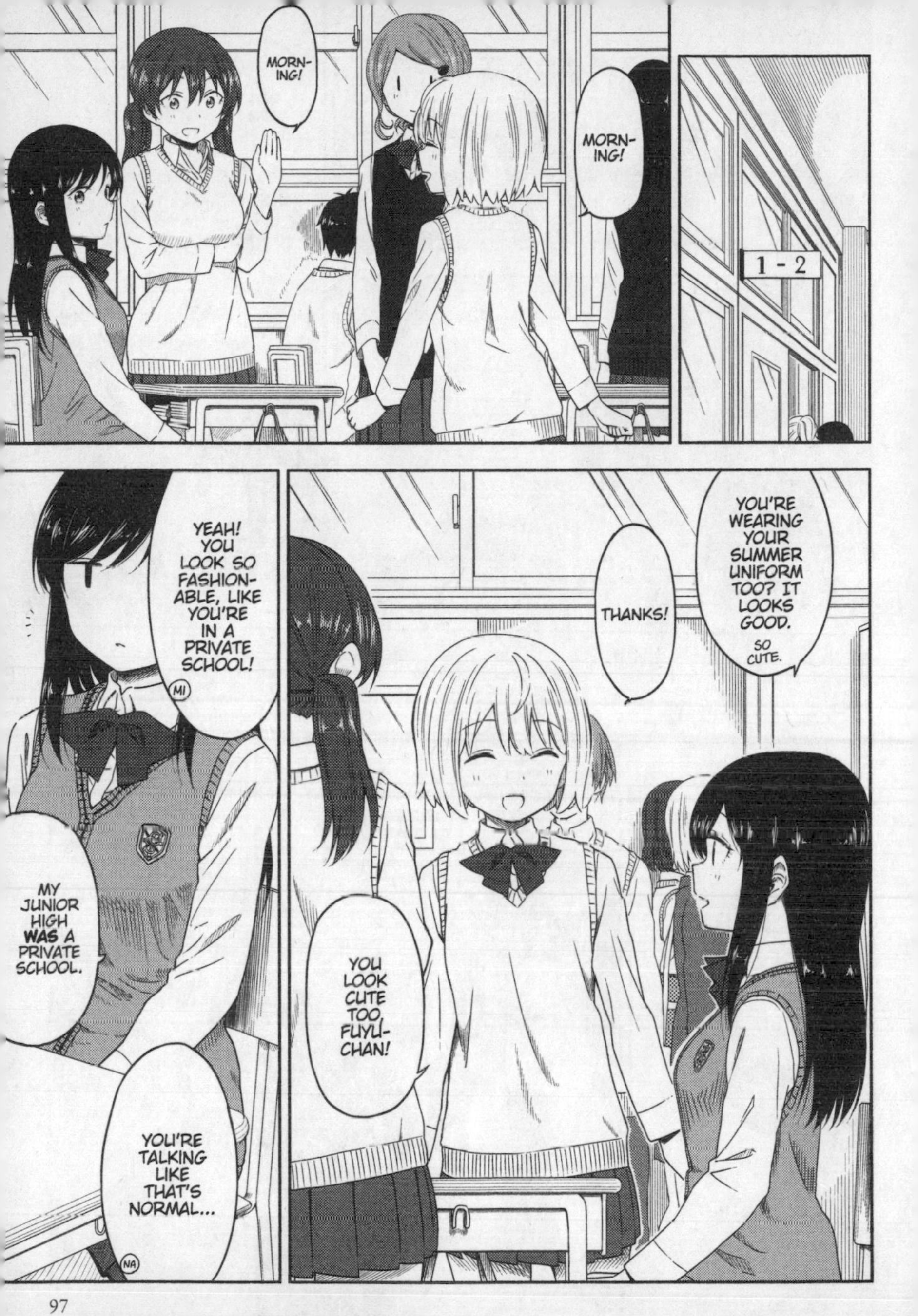
1 - 2
MORN-ING!
MORN-ING!
YOU'RE WEARING YOUR SUMMER UNIFORM TOO? IT LOOKS GOOD.
SO CUTE.
THANKS!
YOU LOOK CUTE TOO, FUYU-CHAN!
YEAH! YOU LOOK SO FASHION-ABLE, LIKE YOU'RE IN A PRIVATE SCHOOL!
MI
MY JUNIOR HIGH **WAS** A PRIVATE SCHOOL.
YOU'RE TALKING LIKE THAT'S NORMAL...
NA

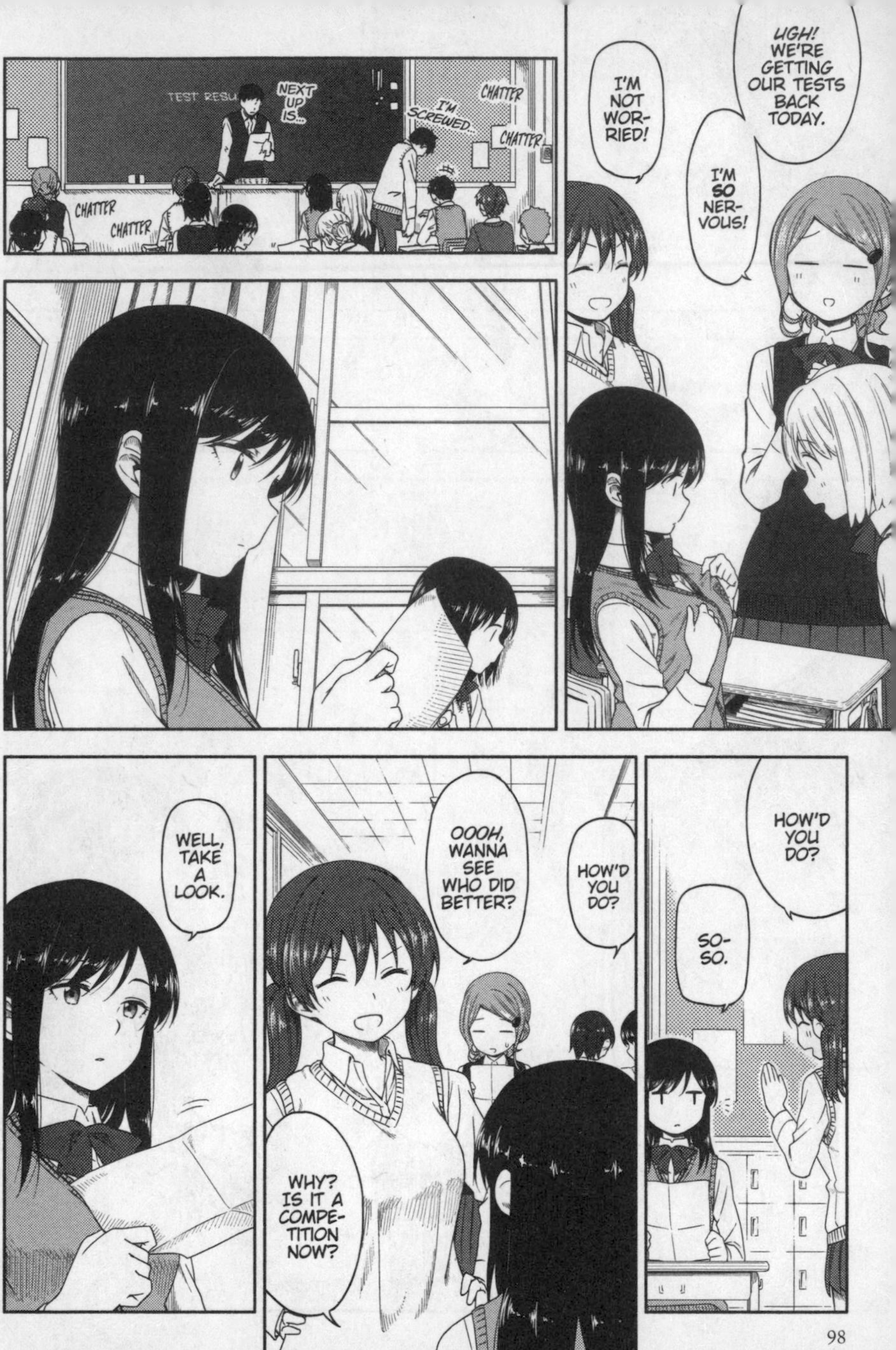
UGH! WE'RE GETTING OUR TESTS BACK TODAY.
I'M NOT WORRIED!
I'M SO NERVOUS!
TEST RESU
NEXT UP IS...
CHATTER
I'M SCREWED...
CHATTER
CHATTER
CHATTER
HOW'D YOU DO?
SO-SO.
HOW'D YOU DO?
OOOH, WANNA SEE WHO DID BETTER?
WHY? IS IT A COMPETITION NOW?
WELL, TAKE A LOOK.

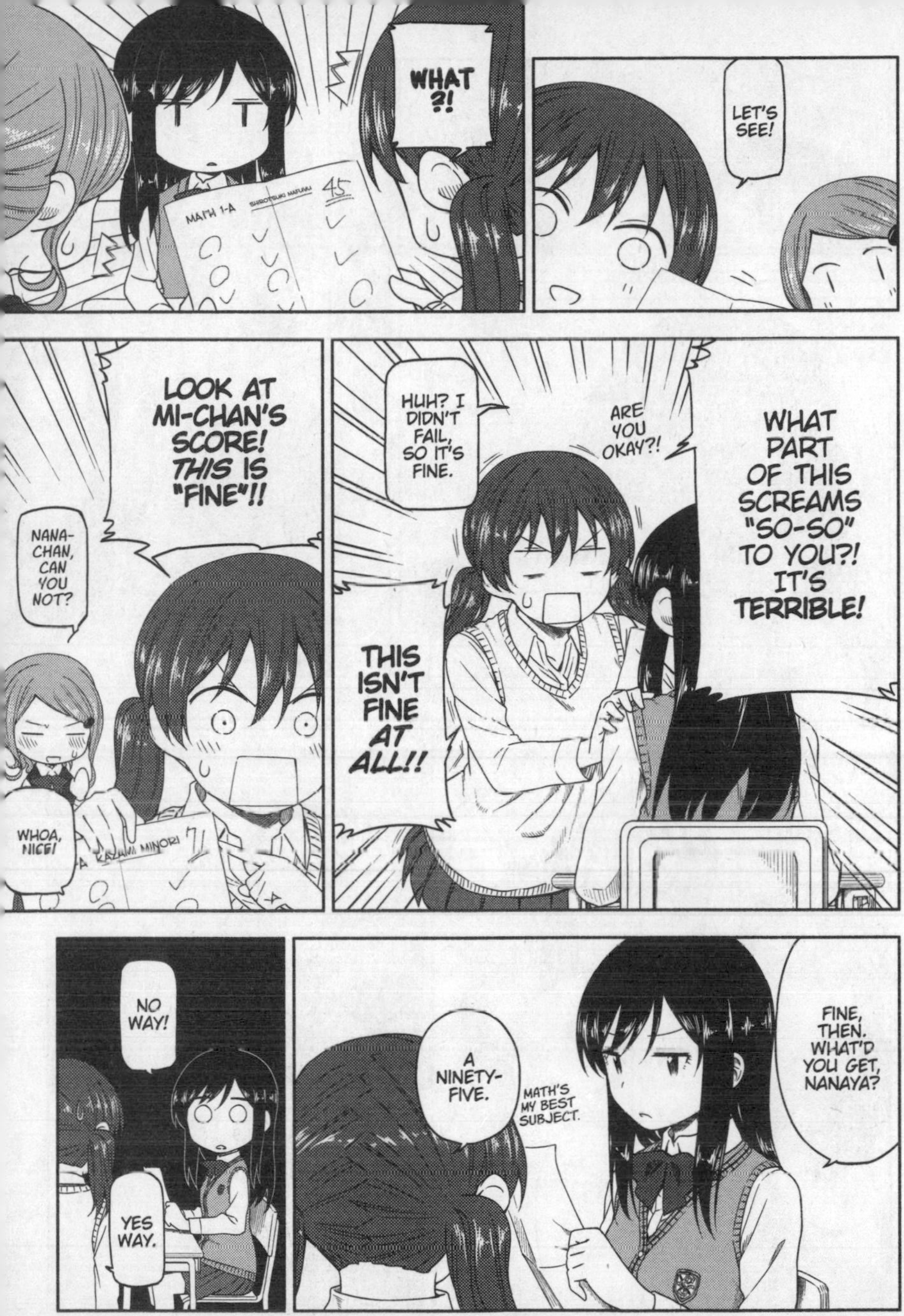
LET'S SEE!
WHAT ?!
MATH 1-A
45
ARE YOU OKAY?!
HUH? I DIDN'T FAIL, SO IT'S FINE.
WHAT PART OF THIS SCREAMS "SO-SO" TO YOU?! IT'S TERRIBLE!
THIS ISN'T FINE AT ALL!!
LOOK AT MI-CHAN'S SCORE! THIS IS "FINE"!!
NANA-CHAN, CAN YOU NOT?
WHOA, NICE!
KAZAMI MINORI
71
FINE, THEN. WHAT'D YOU GET, NANAYA?
A NINETY-FIVE.
MATH'S MY BEST SUBJECT.
NO WAY!
YES WAY.

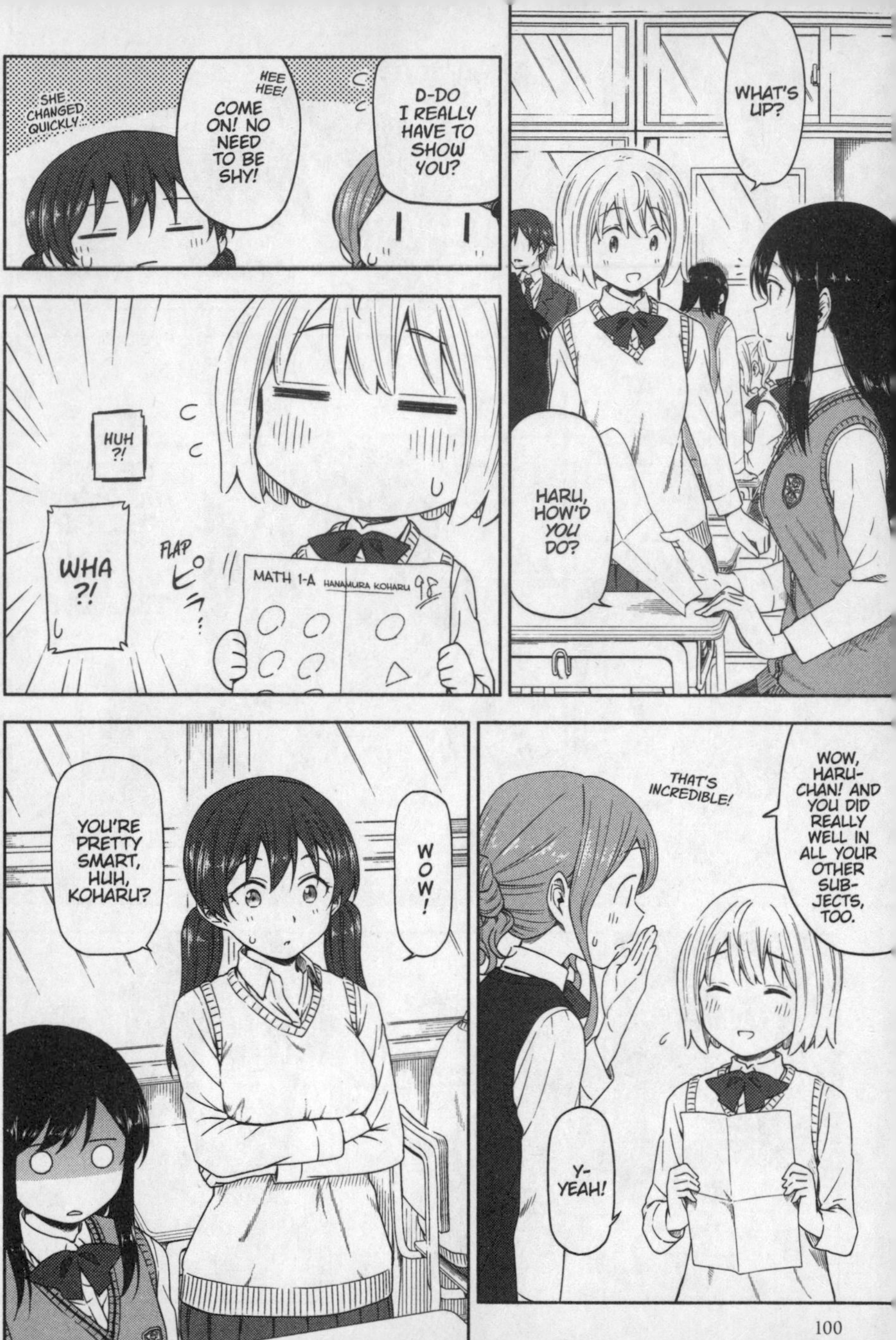
WHAT'S UP?
HARU, HOW'D YOU DO?
D-DO I REALLY HAVE TO SHOW YOU?
HEE HEE!
COME ON! NO NEED TO BE SHY!
SHE CHANGED QUICKLY...
HUH ?!
FLAP
WHA ?!
MATH 1-A HANAMURA KOHARU 98
WOW, HARU-CHAN! AND YOU DID REALLY WELL IN ALL YOUR OTHER SUBJECTS, TOO.
THAT'S INCREDIBLE!
Y-YEAH!
WOW!
YOU'RE PRETTY SMART, HUH, KOHARU?

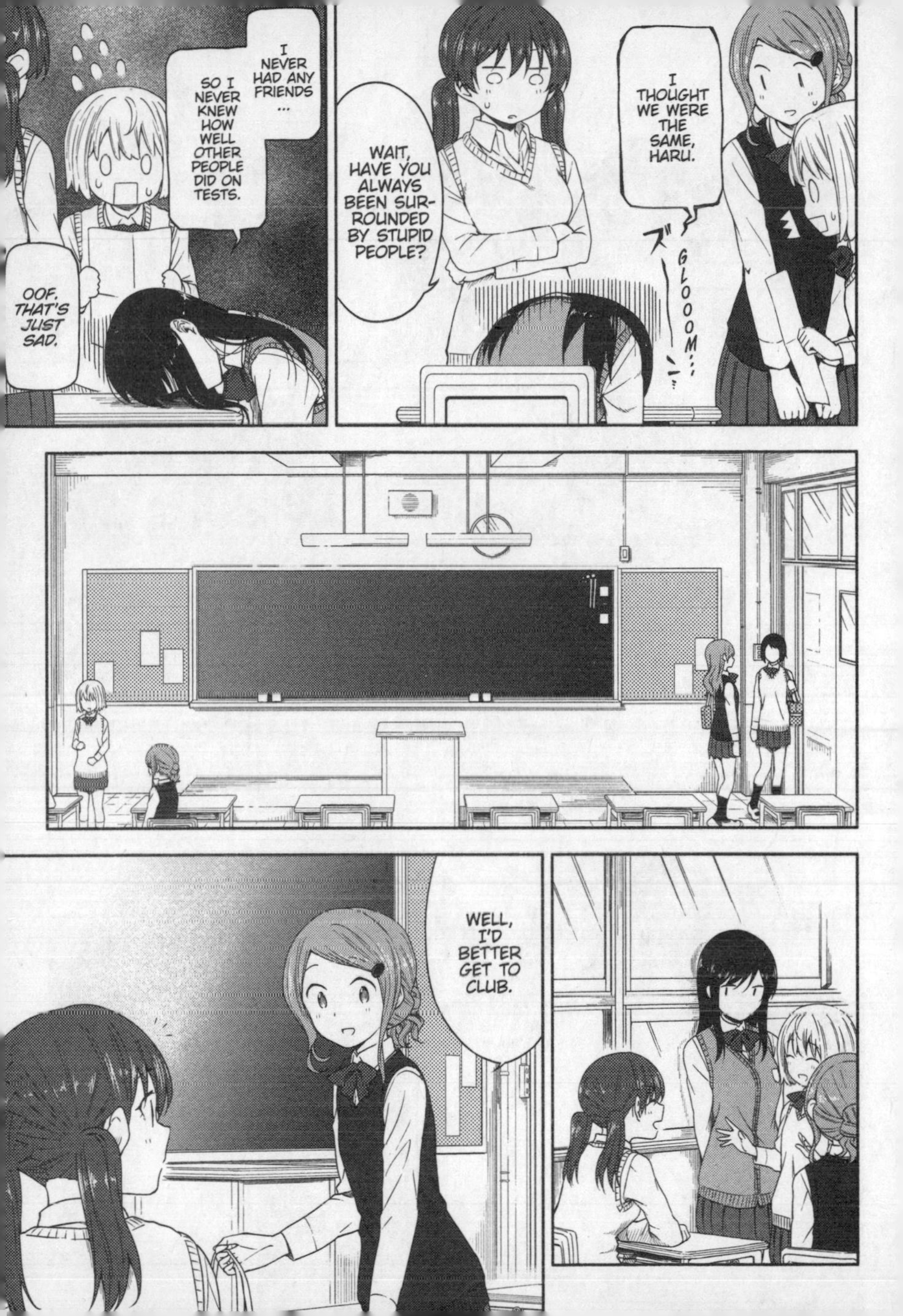
I THOUGHT WE WERE THE SAME, HARU.
WAIT, HAVE YOU ALWAYS BEEN SURROUNDED BY STUPID PEOPLE?
ズ
GLOOOM...
I NEVER HAD ANY FRIENDS ...
SO I NEVER KNEW HOW WELL OTHER PEOPLE DID ON TESTS.
OOF. THAT'S JUST SAD.
WELL, I'D BETTER GET TO CLUB.

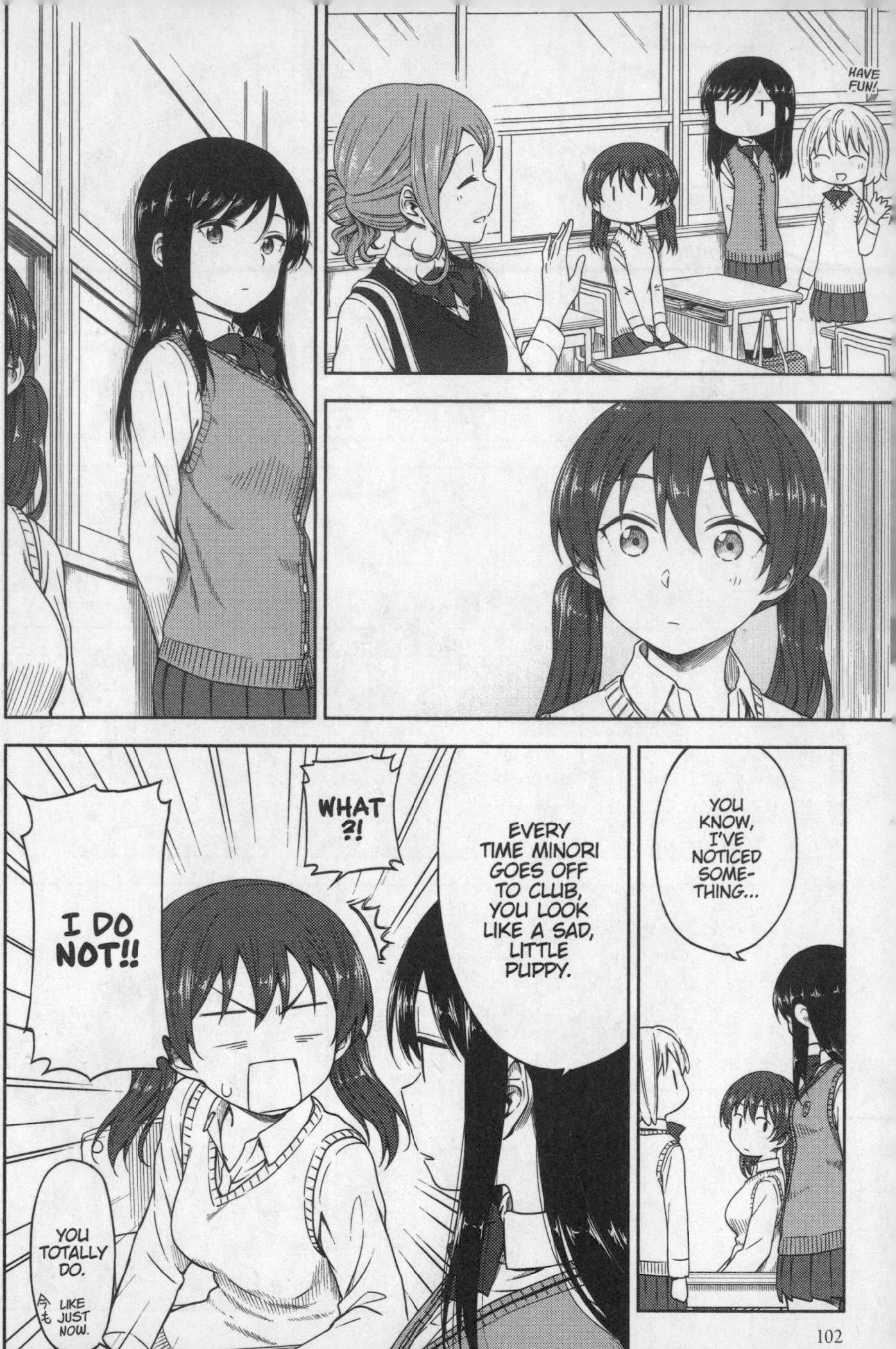
HAVE FUN!
YOU KNOW, I'VE NOTICED SOME-THING...
EVERY TIME MINORI GOES OFF TO CLUB, YOU LOOK LIKE A SAD, LITTLE PUPPY.
WHAT?!
I DO NOT!!
YOU TOTALLY DO.
今も LIKE JUST NOW.

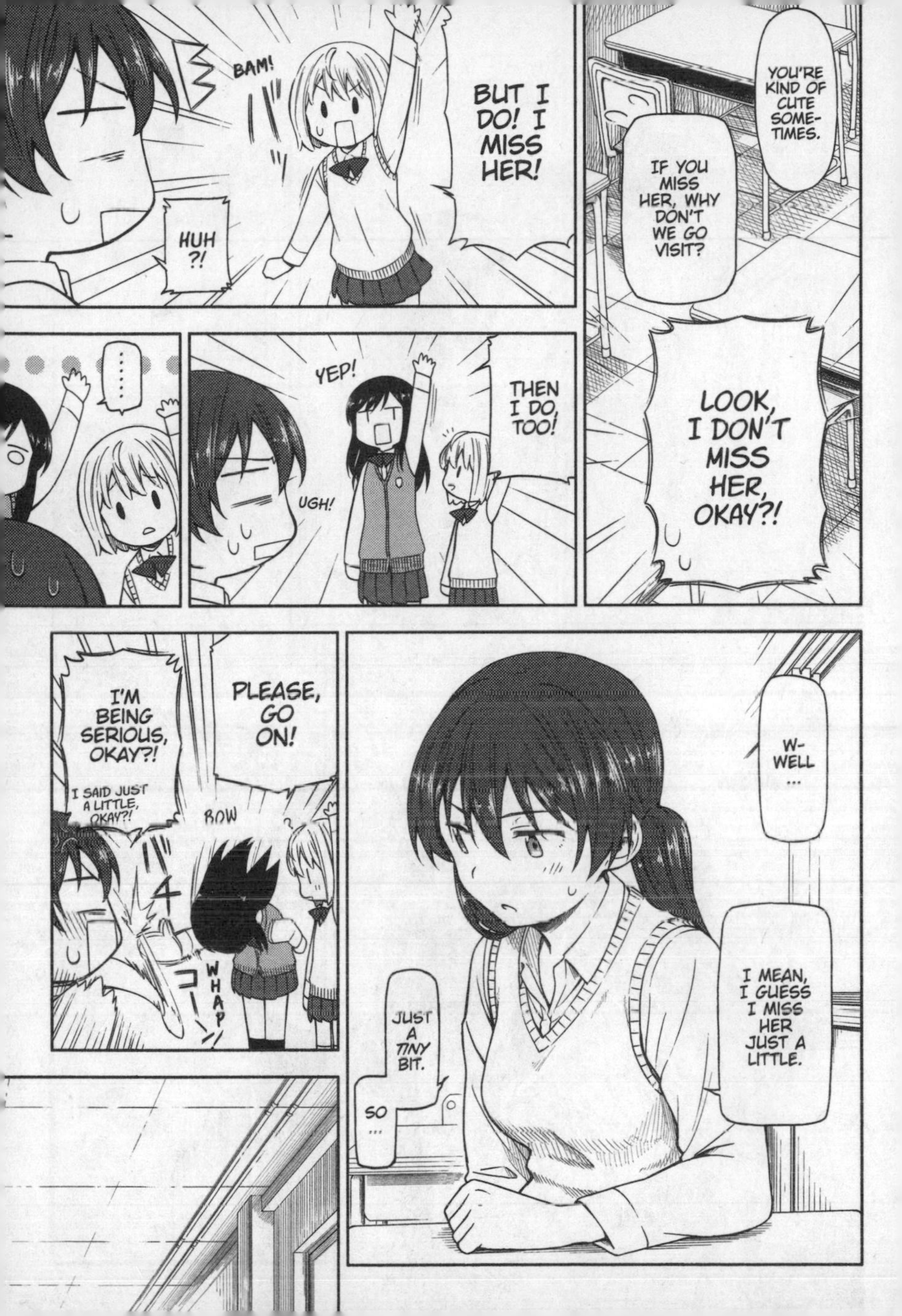
YOU'RE KIND OF CUTE SOME-TIMES.
IF YOU MISS HER, WHY DON'T WE GO VISIT?
LOOK, I DON'T MISS HER, OKAY?!
BUT I DO! I MISS HER!
BAM!
HUH ?!
THEN I DO, TOO!
YEP!
UGH!
......
W-WELL ...
I MEAN, I GUESS I MISS HER JUST A LITTLE.
JUST A TINY BIT.
SO ...
PLEASE, GO ON!
I'M BEING SERIOUS, OKAY?!
I SAID JUST A LITTLE, OKAY?!
BOW
WHAP

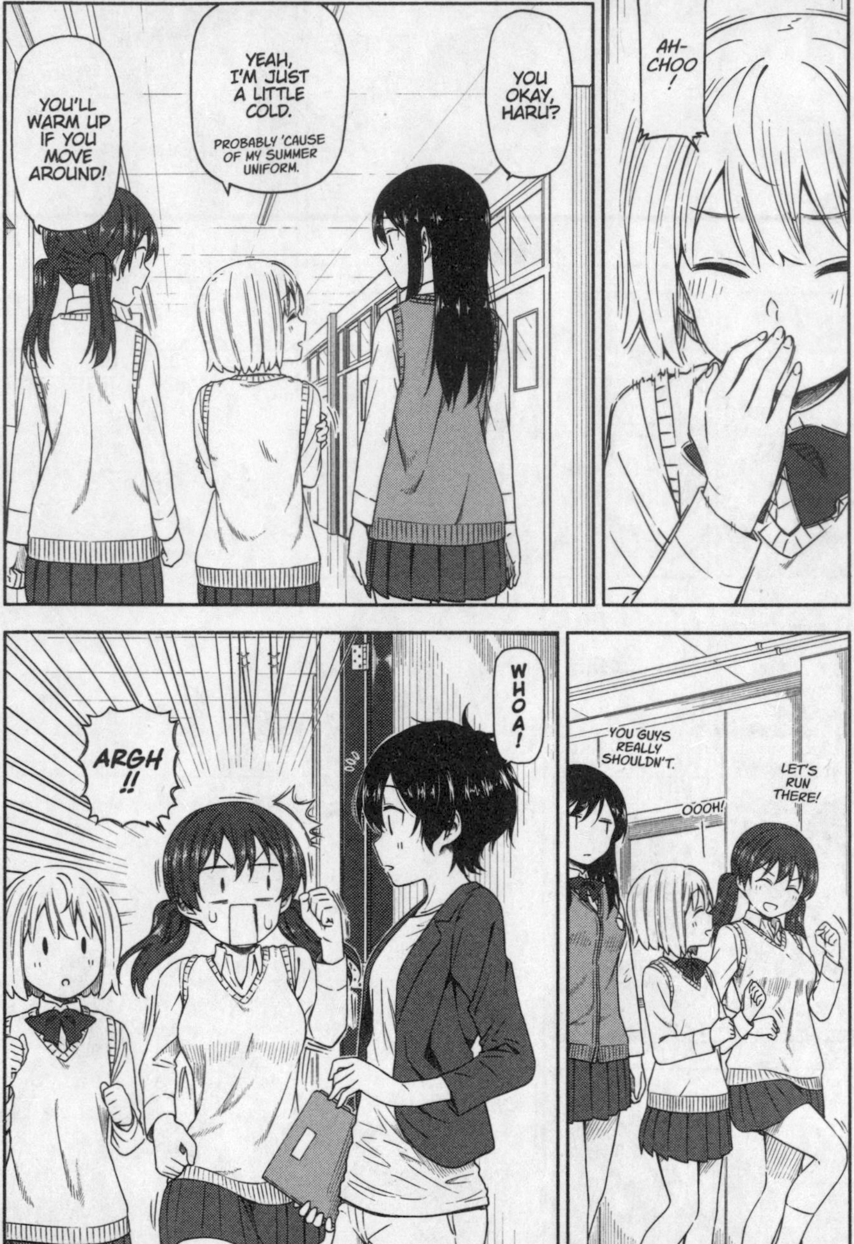
AH-CHOO!
YOU OKAY, HARU?
YEAH, I'M JUST A LITTLE COLD.
PROBABLY 'CAUSE OF MY SUMMER UNIFORM.
YOU'LL WARM UP IF YOU MOVE AROUND!
LET'S RUN THERE!
OOOH!
YOU GUYS REALLY SHOULDN'T.
WHOA!
ARGH!!

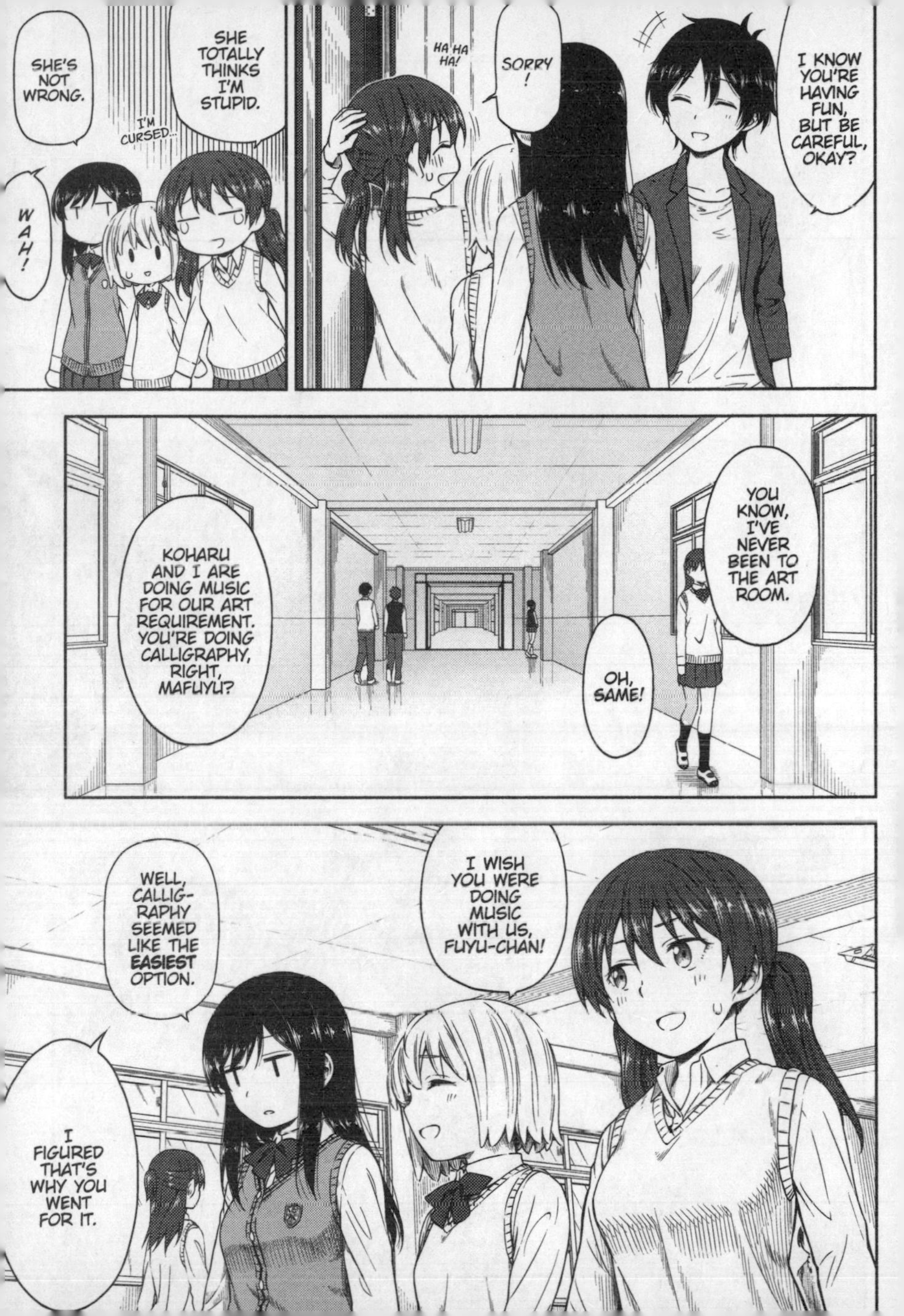
I KNOW YOU'RE HAVING FUN, BUT BE CAREFUL, OKAY?
SORRY!
HA HA HA!
SHE TOTALLY THINKS I'M STUPID.
SHE'S NOT WRONG.
I'M CURSED...
WAH!
YOU KNOW, I'VE NEVER BEEN TO THE ART ROOM.
OH, SAME!
KOHARU AND I ARE DOING MUSIC FOR OUR ART REQUIREMENT. YOU'RE DOING CALLIGRAPHY, RIGHT, MAFUYU?
I WISH YOU WERE DOING MUSIC WITH US, FUYU-CHAN!
WELL, CALLIGRAPHY SEEMED LIKE THE EASIEST OPTION.
I FIGURED THAT'S WHY YOU WENT FOR IT.

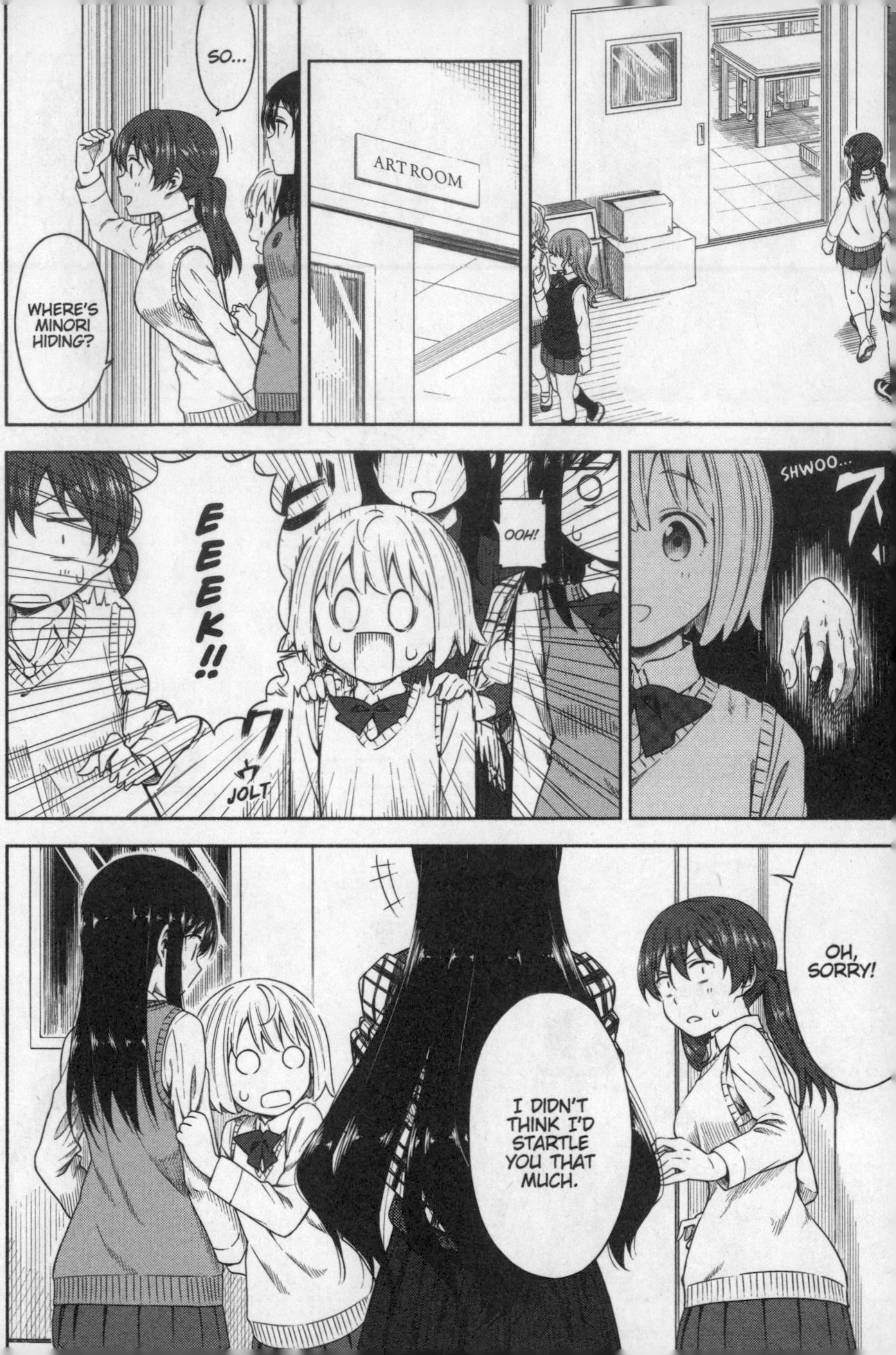
ART ROOM
SO...
WHERE'S MINORI HIDING?
SHWOO...
OOH!
EEEEK!!
JOLT
OH, SORRY!
I DIDN'T THINK I'D STARTLE YOU THAT MUCH.

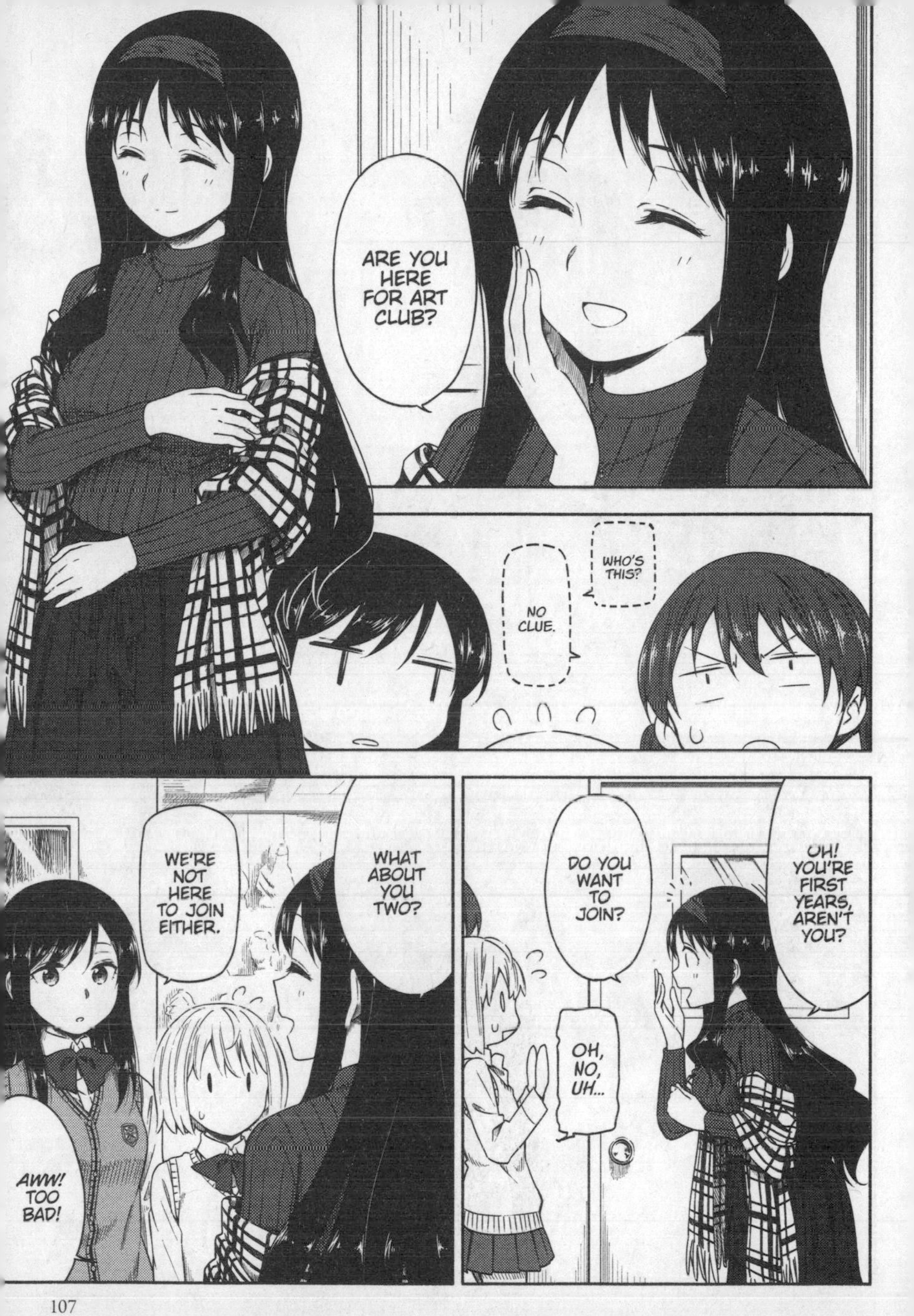

ARE YOU HERE FOR ART CLUB?
WHO'S THIS?
NO CLUE.
OH! YOU'RE FIRST YEARS, AREN'T YOU?
DO YOU WANT TO JOIN?
OH, NO, UH...
WHAT ABOUT YOU TWO?
WE'RE NOT HERE TO JOIN EITHER.
AWW! TOO BAD!

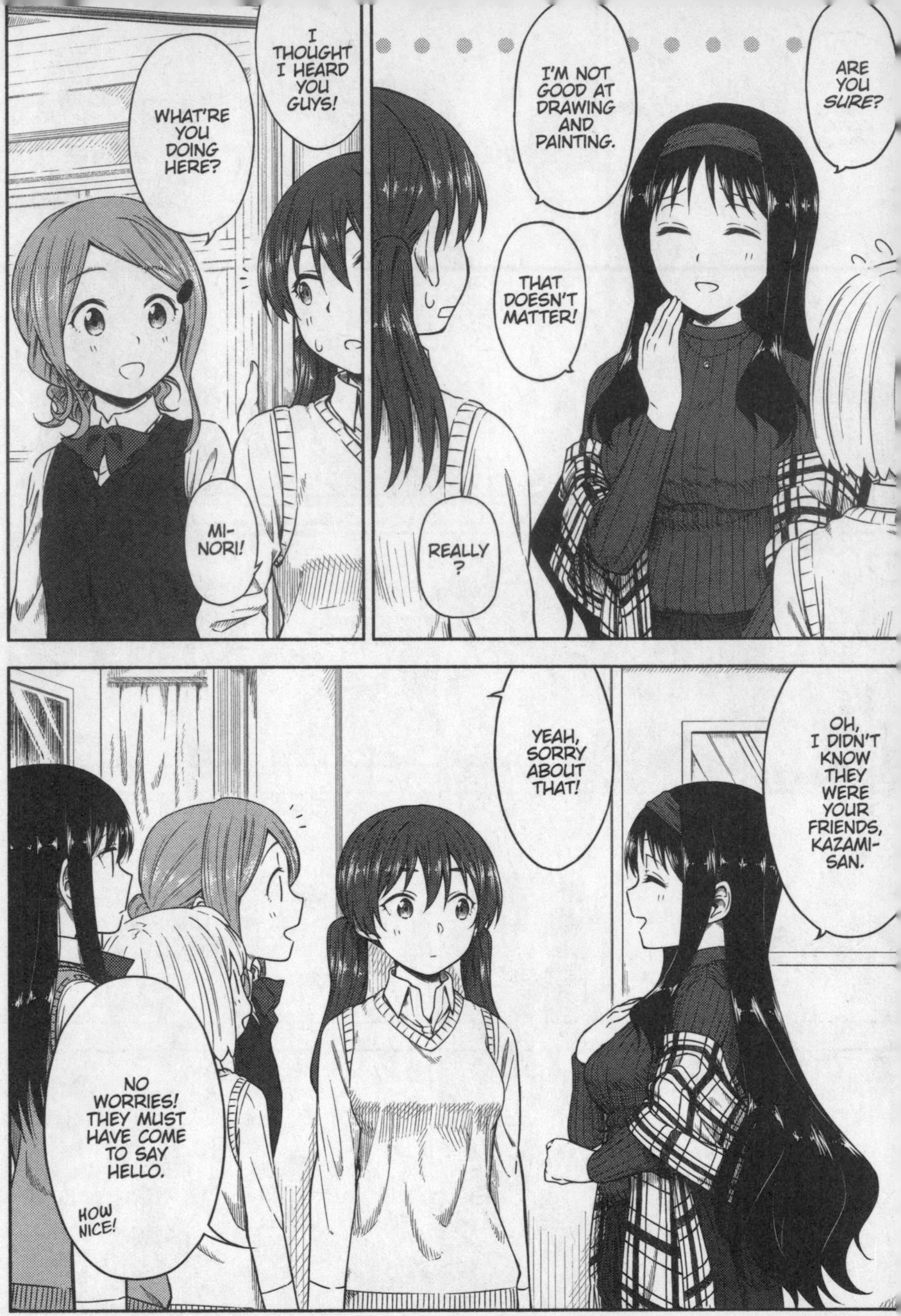
ARE YOU SURE?
I'M NOT GOOD AT DRAWING AND PAINTING.
THAT DOESN'T MATTER!
REALLY?
I THOUGHT I HEARD YOU GUYS!
WHAT'RE YOU DOING HERE?
MI-NORI!
OH, I DIDN'T KNOW THEY WERE YOUR FRIENDS, KAZAMI-SAN.
YEAH, SORRY ABOUT THAT!
NO WORRIES! THEY MUST HAVE COME TO SAY HELLO.
HOW NICE!

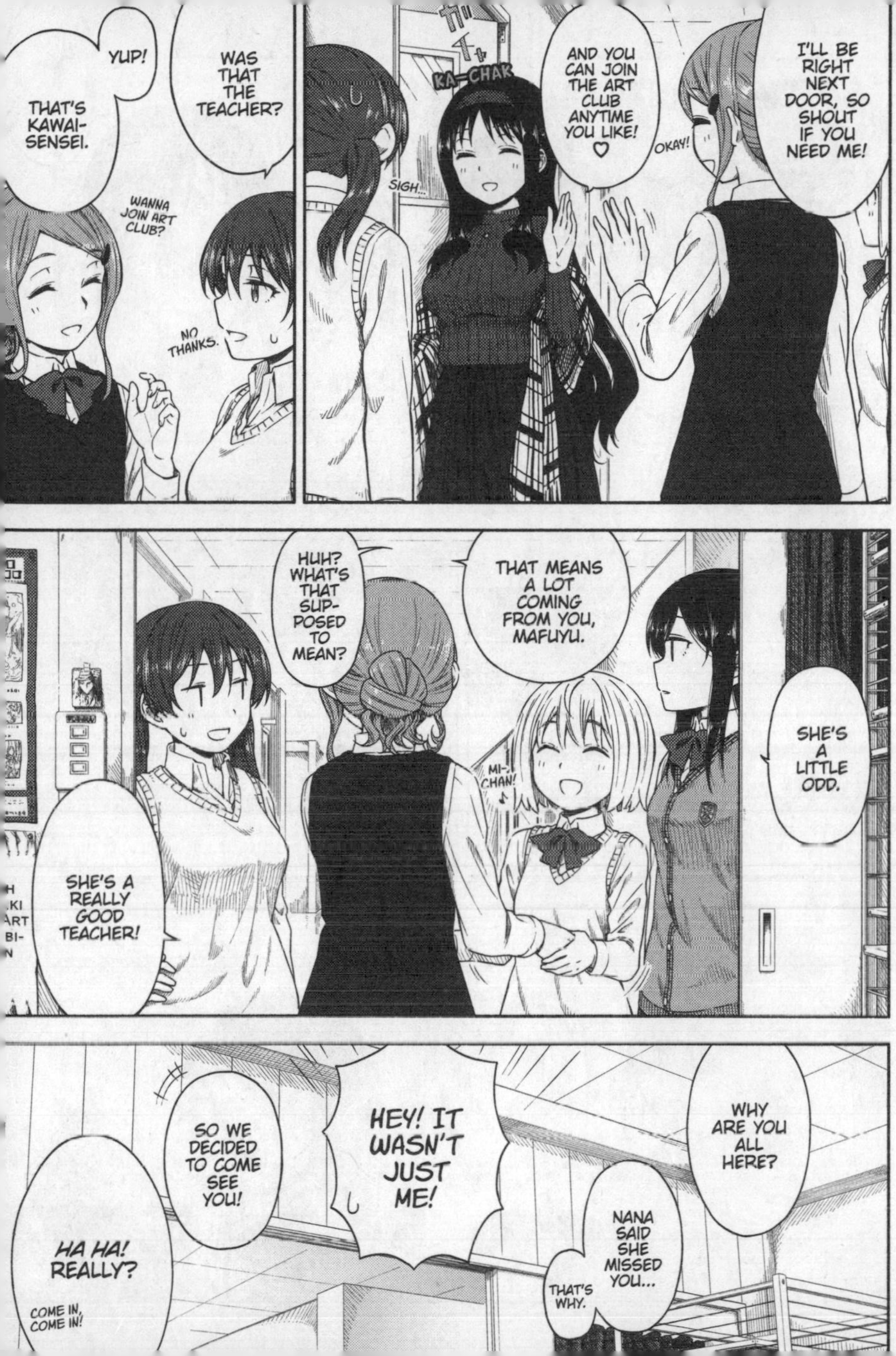
KA-CHAK
I'LL BE RIGHT NEXT DOOR, SO SHOUT IF YOU NEED ME!
OKAY!
AND YOU CAN JOIN THE ART CLUB ANYTIME YOU LIKE! ♡
SIGH...
WAS THAT THE TEACHER?
YUP!
THAT'S KAWAI-SENSEI.
WANNA JOIN ART CLUB?
NO THANKS.
SHE'S A LITTLE ODD.
THAT MEANS A LOT COMING FROM YOU, MAFUYU.
HUH? WHAT'S THAT SUPPOSED TO MEAN?
MI-CHAN! ♪
SHE'S A REALLY GOOD TEACHER!
WHY ARE YOU ALL HERE?
NANA SAID SHE MISSED YOU...
THAT'S WHY.
HEY! IT WASN'T JUST ME!
SO WE DECIDED TO COME SEE YOU!
HA HA! REALLY?
COME IN, COME IN!

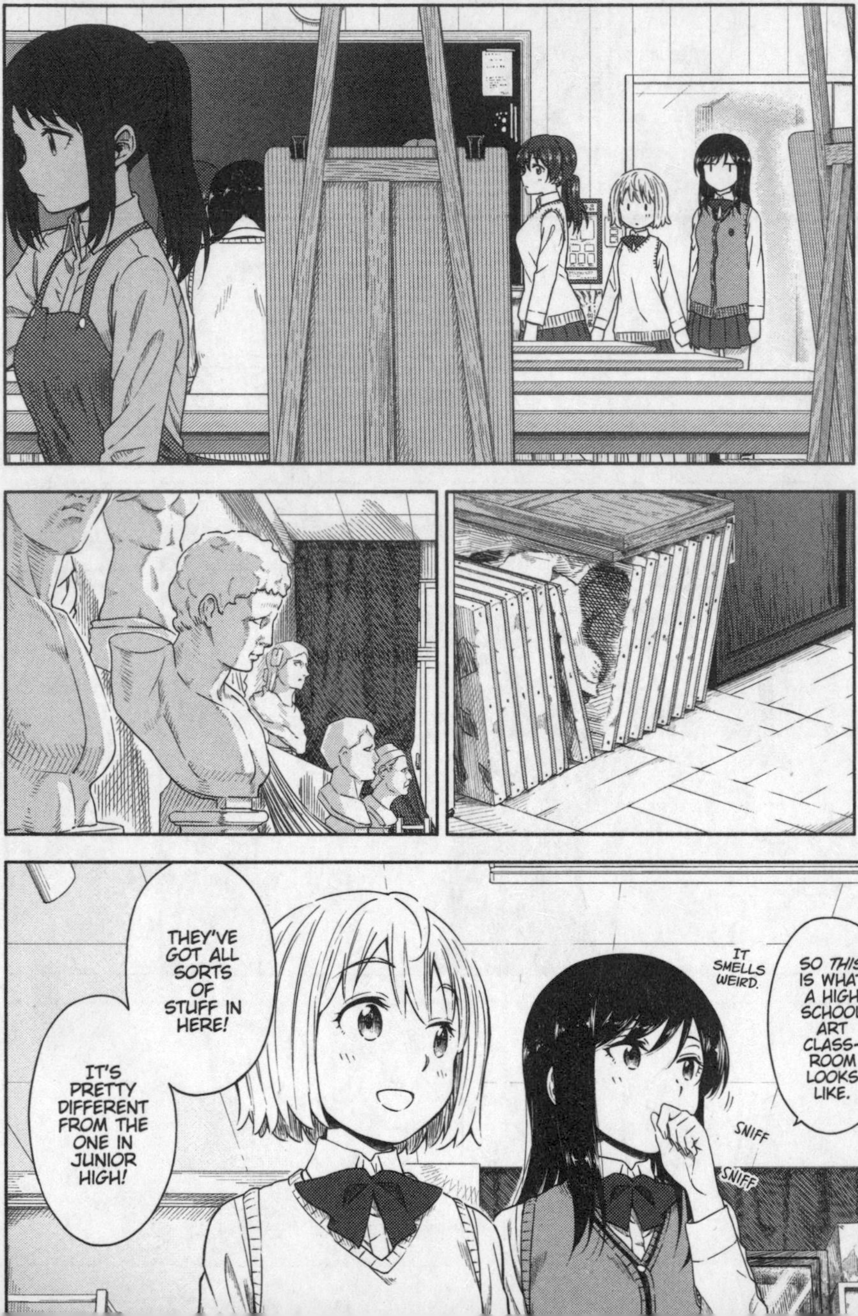
SO THIS IS WHAT A HIGH SCHOOL ART CLASSROOM LOOKS LIKE.
IT SMELLS WEIRD.
SNIFF
SNIFF
THEY'VE GOT ALL SORTS OF STUFF IN HERE!
IT'S PRETTY DIFFERENT FROM THE ONE IN JUNIOR HIGH!

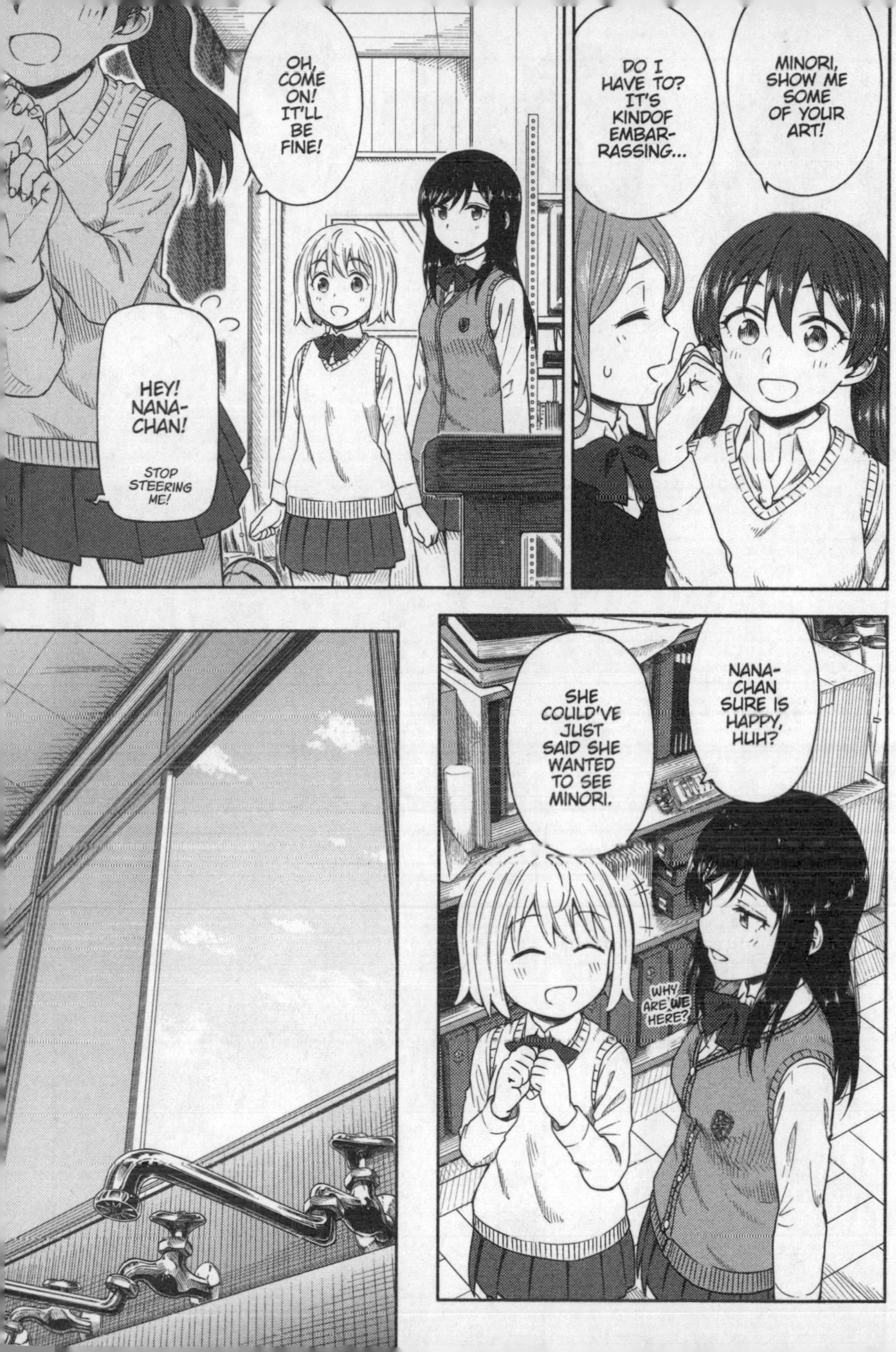
MINORI, SHOW ME SOME OF YOUR ART!
DO I HAVE TO? IT'S KINDOF EMBAR-RASSING...
OH, COME ON! IT'LL BE FINE!
HEY! NANA-CHAN!
STOP STEERING ME!
NANA-CHAN SURE IS HAPPY, HUH?
SHE COULD'VE JUST SAID SHE WANTED TO SEE MINORI.
WHY ARE WE HERE?

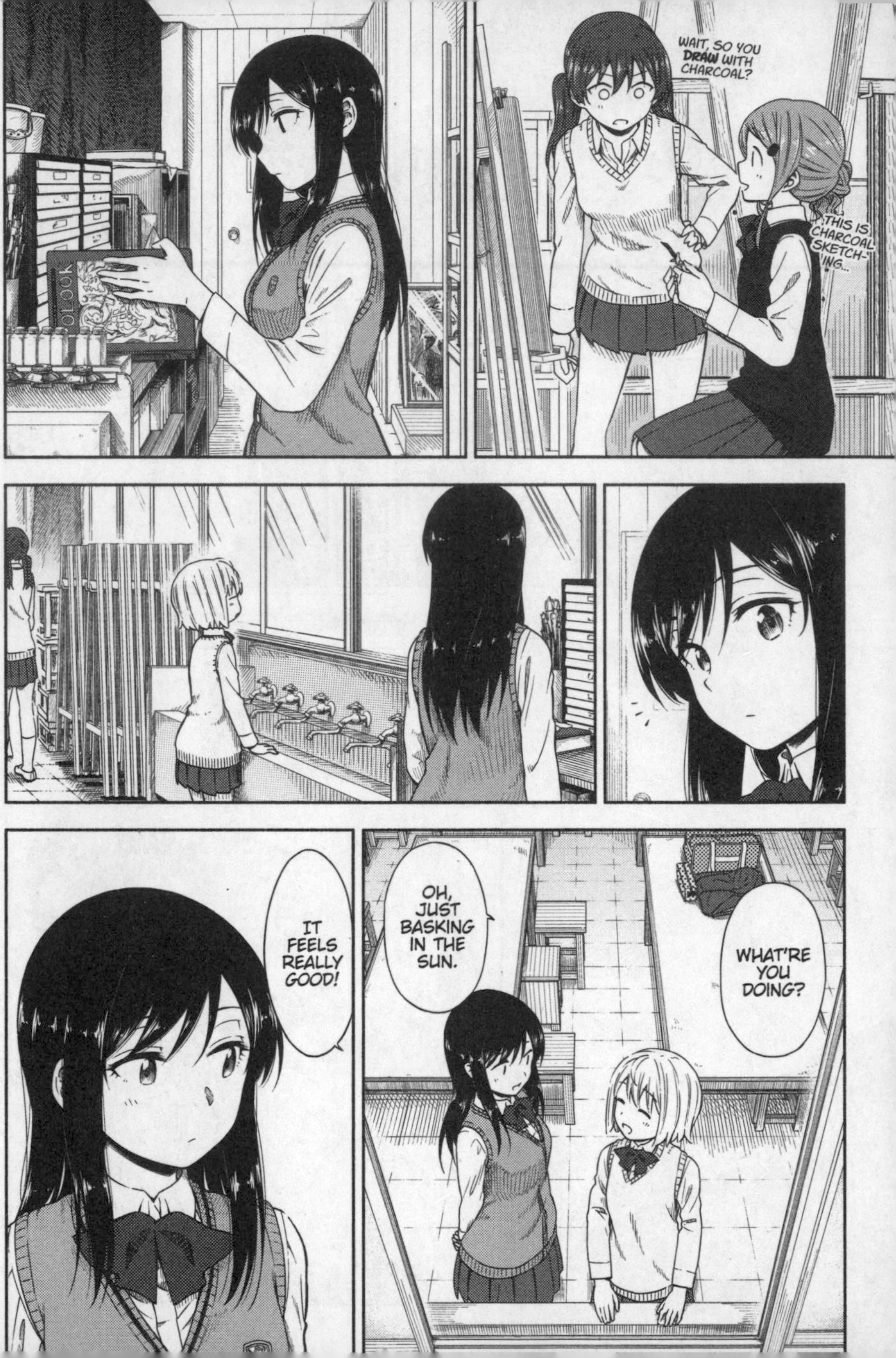
WAIT, SO YOU DRAW WITH CHARCOAL?
THIS IS CHARCOAL SKETCHING...
WHAT'RE YOU DOING?
OH, JUST BASKING IN THE SUN.
IT FEELS REALLY GOOD!

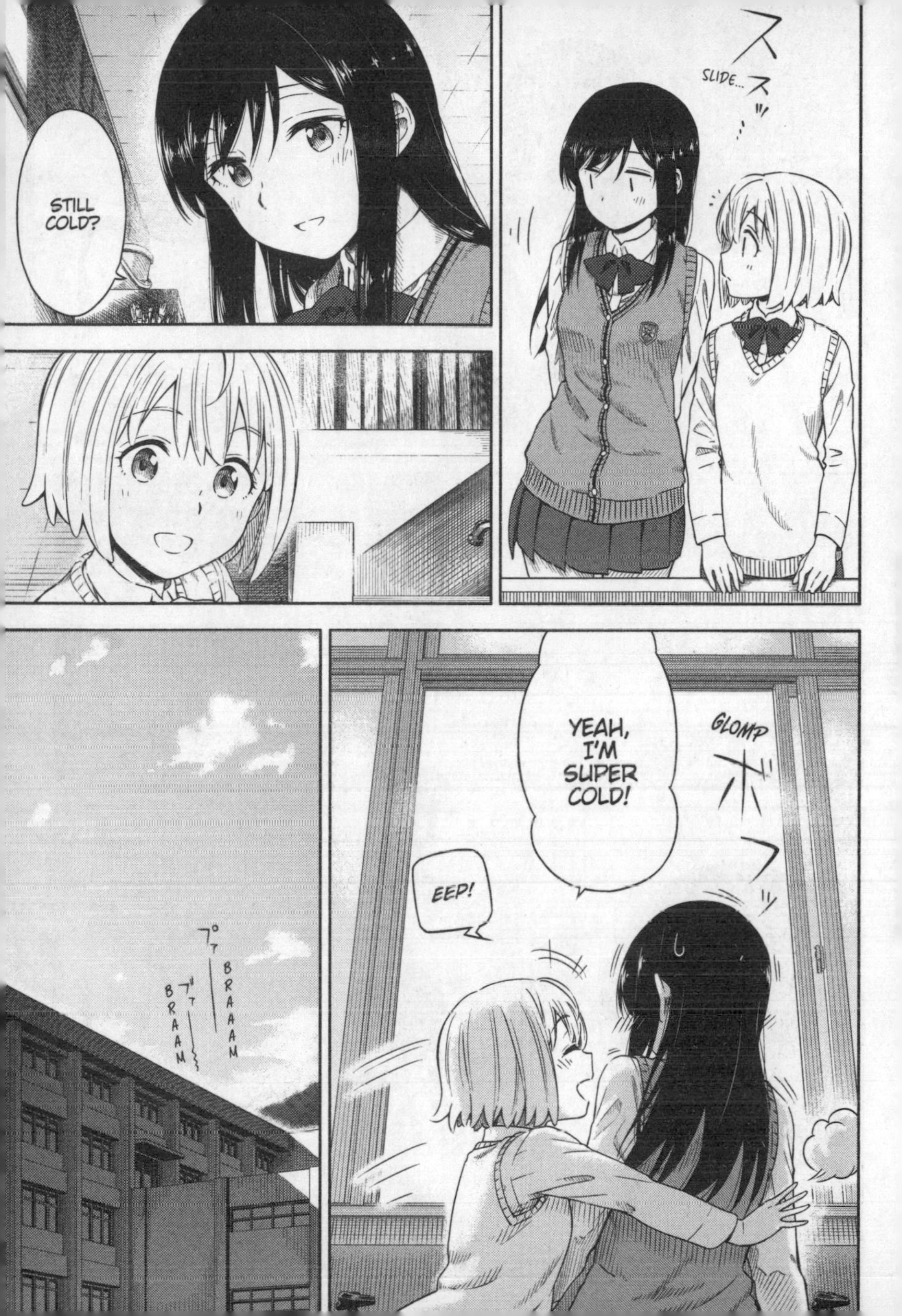
SLIDE...
STILL COLD?
GLOMP
YEAH, I'M SUPER COLD!
EEP!
BRAAAM
BRAAM

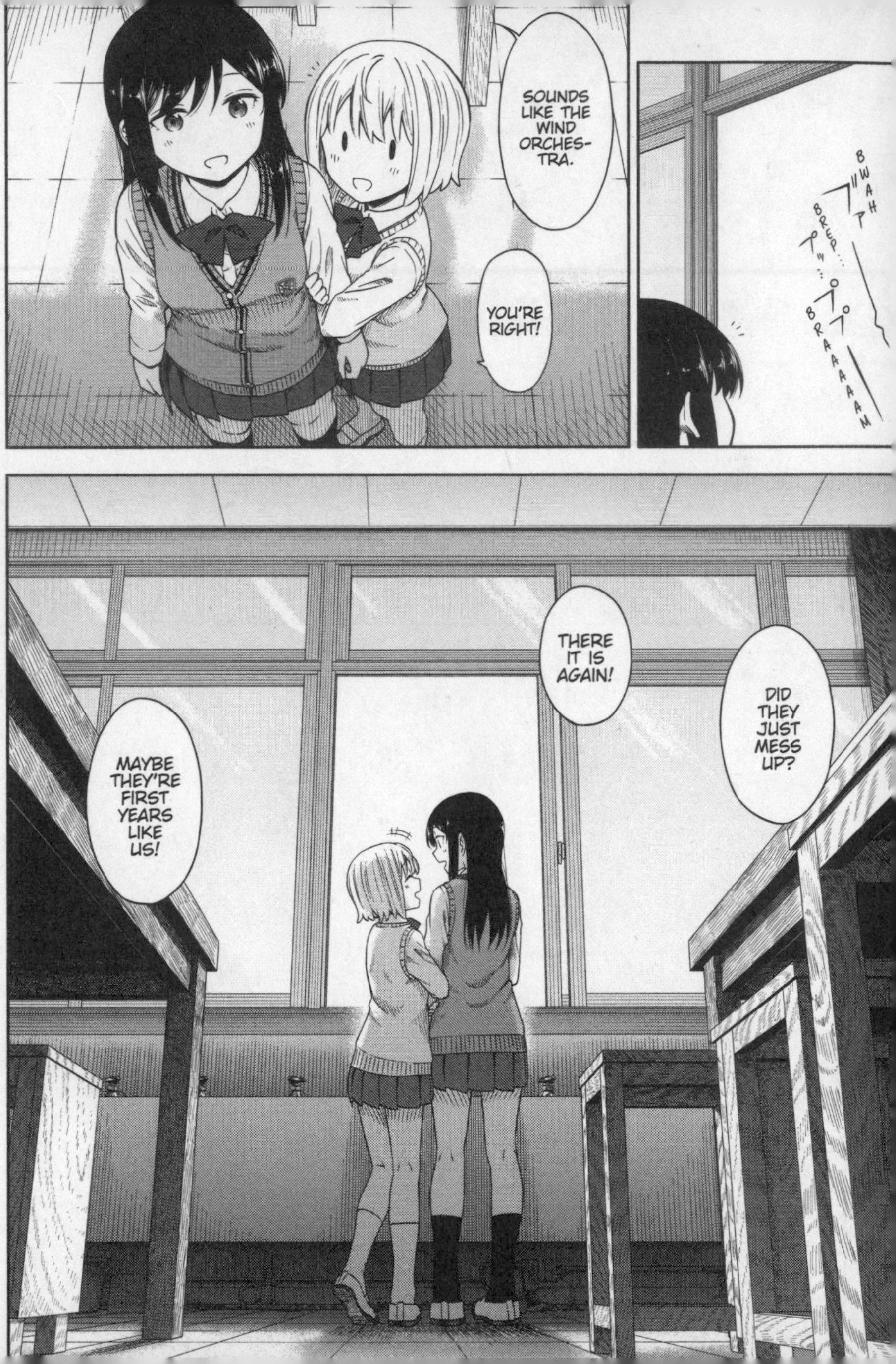
BWAH
BREP...
BRAAAAAAAM
SOUNDS LIKE THE WIND ORCHES-TRA.
YOU'RE RIGHT!
DID THEY JUST MESS UP?
THERE IT IS AGAIN!
MAYBE THEY'RE FIRST YEARS LIKE US!

Our Wonderful Days

story & art by Kei Hamuro

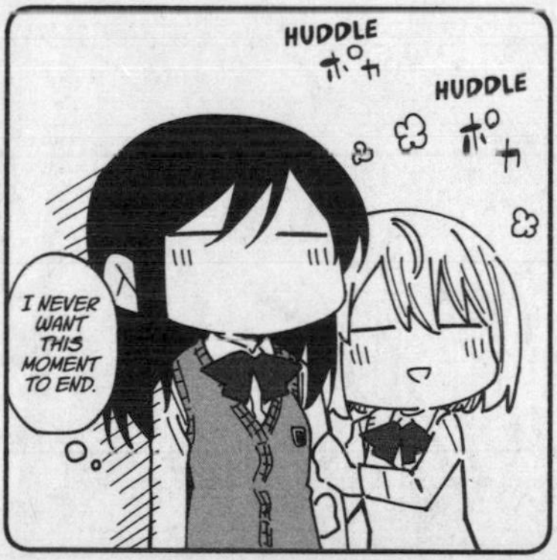
HUDDLE
ポカ
HUDDLE
ポカ
I NEVER WANT THIS MOMENT TO END.

Our Wonderful Days
Tsurezure Biyori

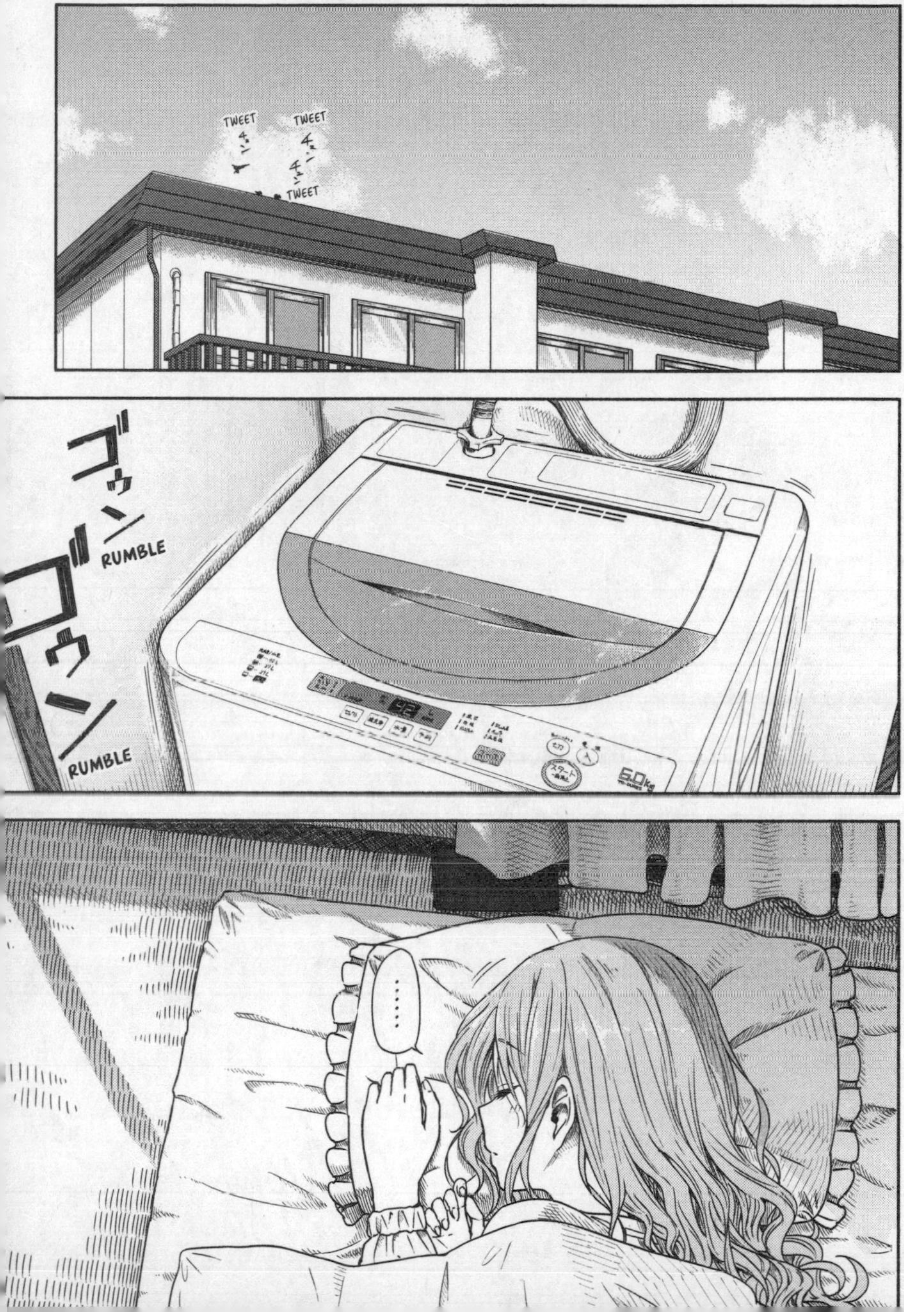
TWEET
チュン
TWEET
チュン
チュン
TWEET
ゴウン
RUMBLE
ゴウン
RUMBLE
6.0kg
……

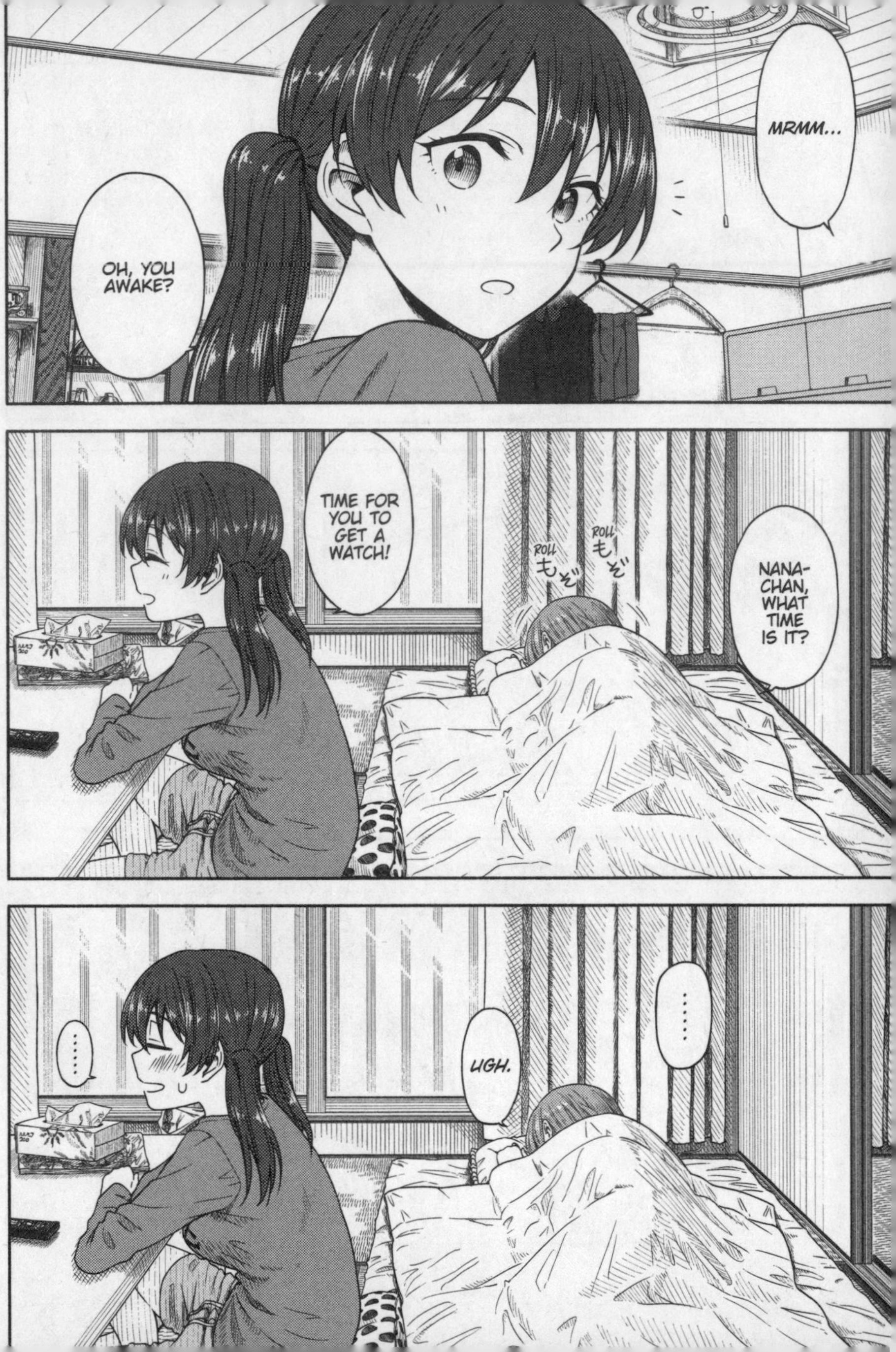
MRMM...
OH, YOU AWAKE?
NANA-CHAN, WHAT TIME IS IT?
ROLL もぞ
ROLL もぞ
TIME FOR YOU TO GET A WATCH!
......
UGH.
......

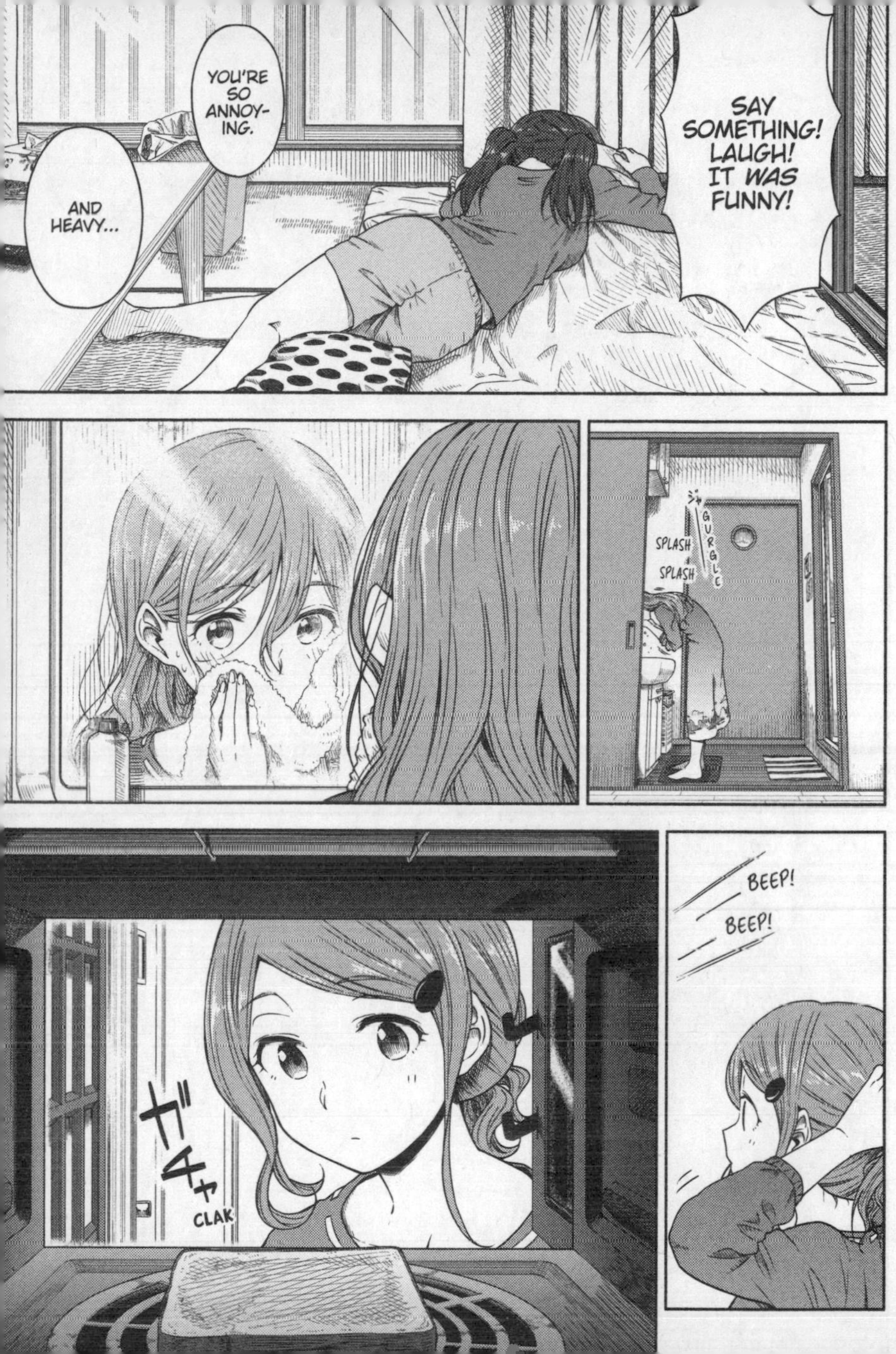
SAY SOMETHING! LAUGH! IT WAS FUNNY!
YOU'RE SO ANNOY-ING.
AND HEAVY...
ジャ
GURGLE
SPLASH
SPLASH
BEEP!
BEEP!
ガチャ
CLAK

Chapter 5
Omurice

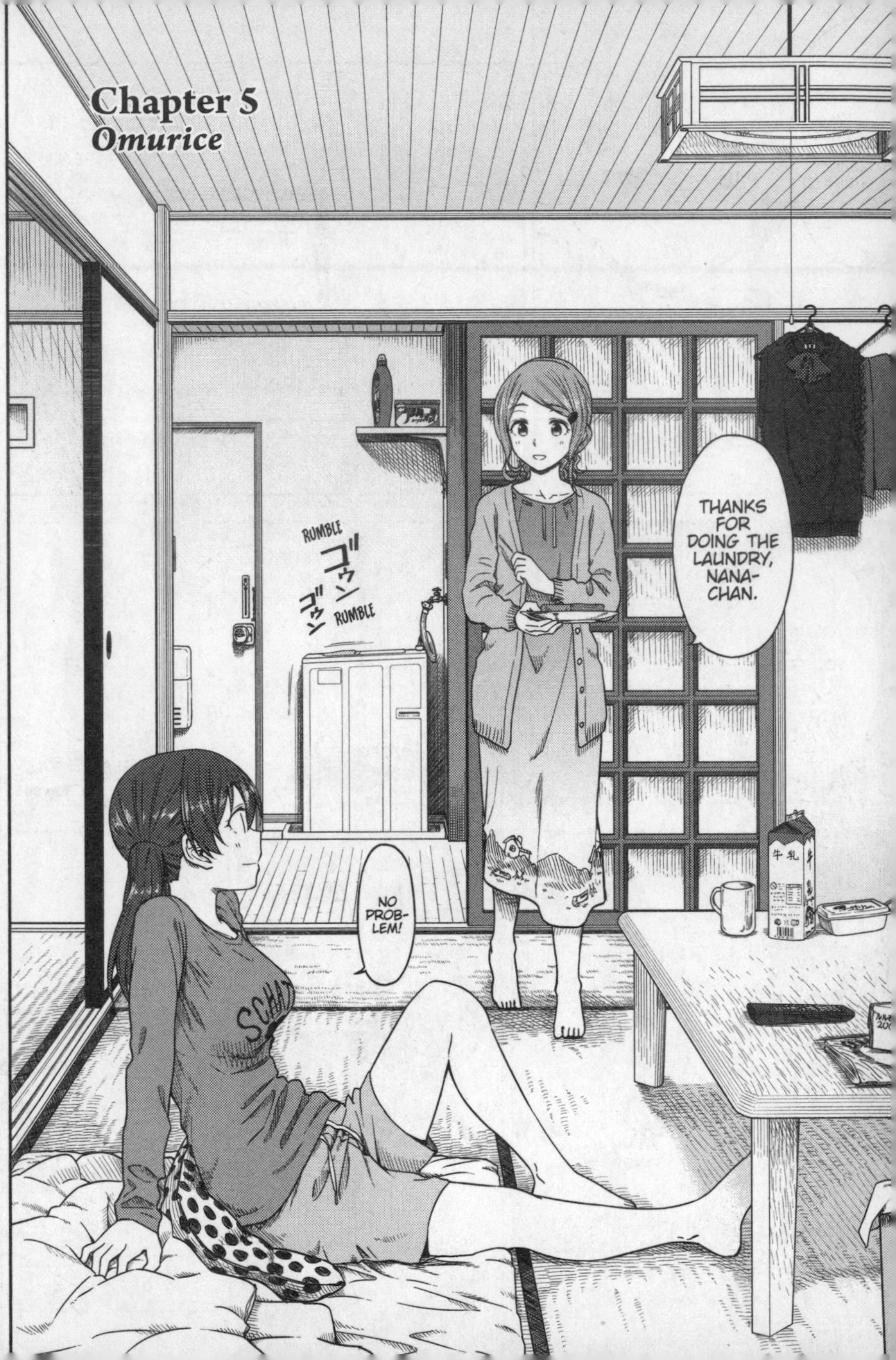
THANKS FOR DOING THE LAUNDRY, NANA-CHAN.
RUMBLE ゴウン
ゴウン RUMBLE
NO PROBLEM!

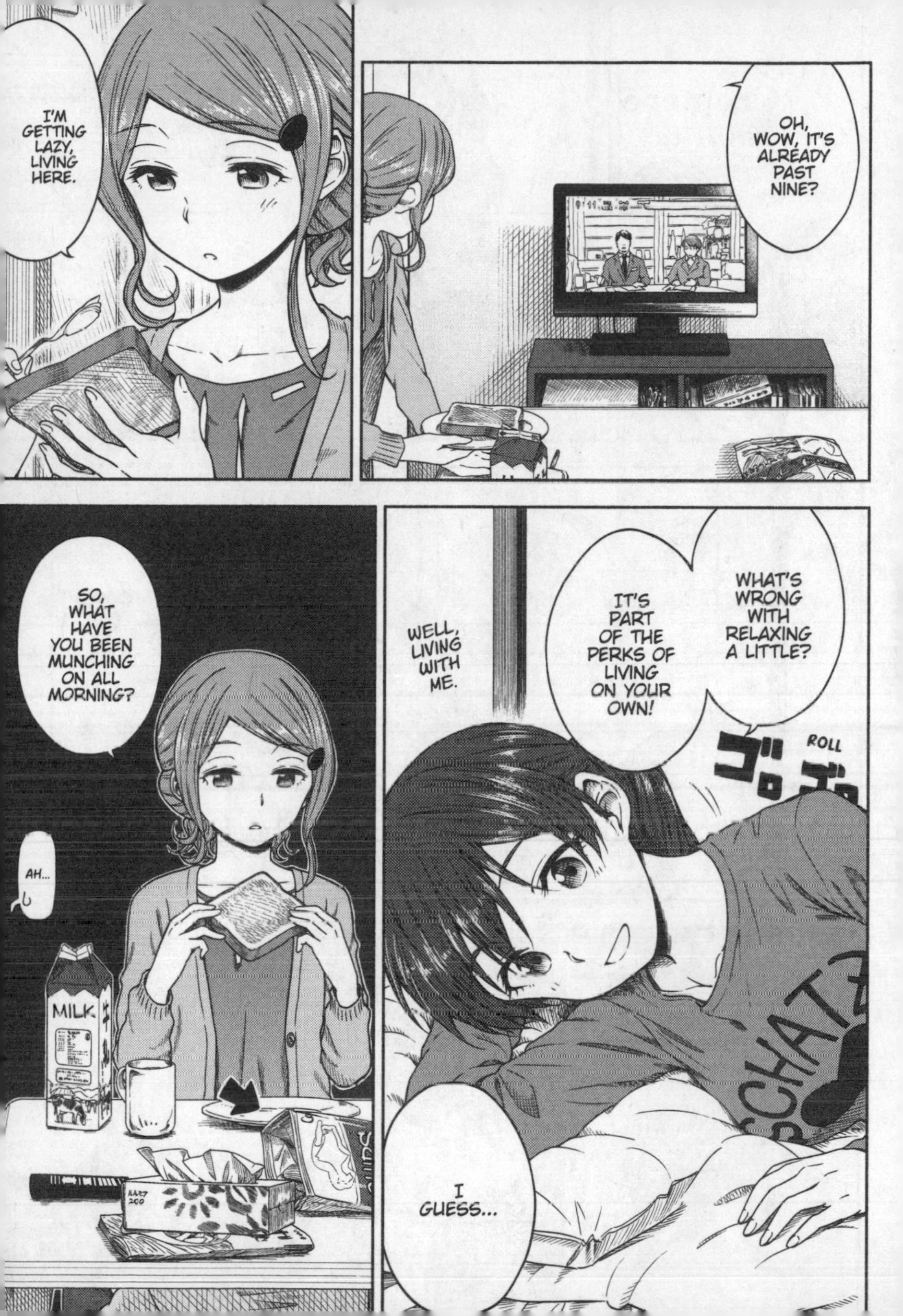
OH, WOW, IT'S ALREADY PAST NINE?
I'M GETTING LAZY, LIVING HERE.
WHAT'S WRONG WITH RELAXING A LITTLE?
IT'S PART OF THE PERKS OF LIVING ON YOUR OWN!
ROLL
WELL, LIVING WITH ME.
I GUESS...
SO, WHAT HAVE YOU BEEN MUNCHING ON ALL MORNING?
AH...
...
MILK

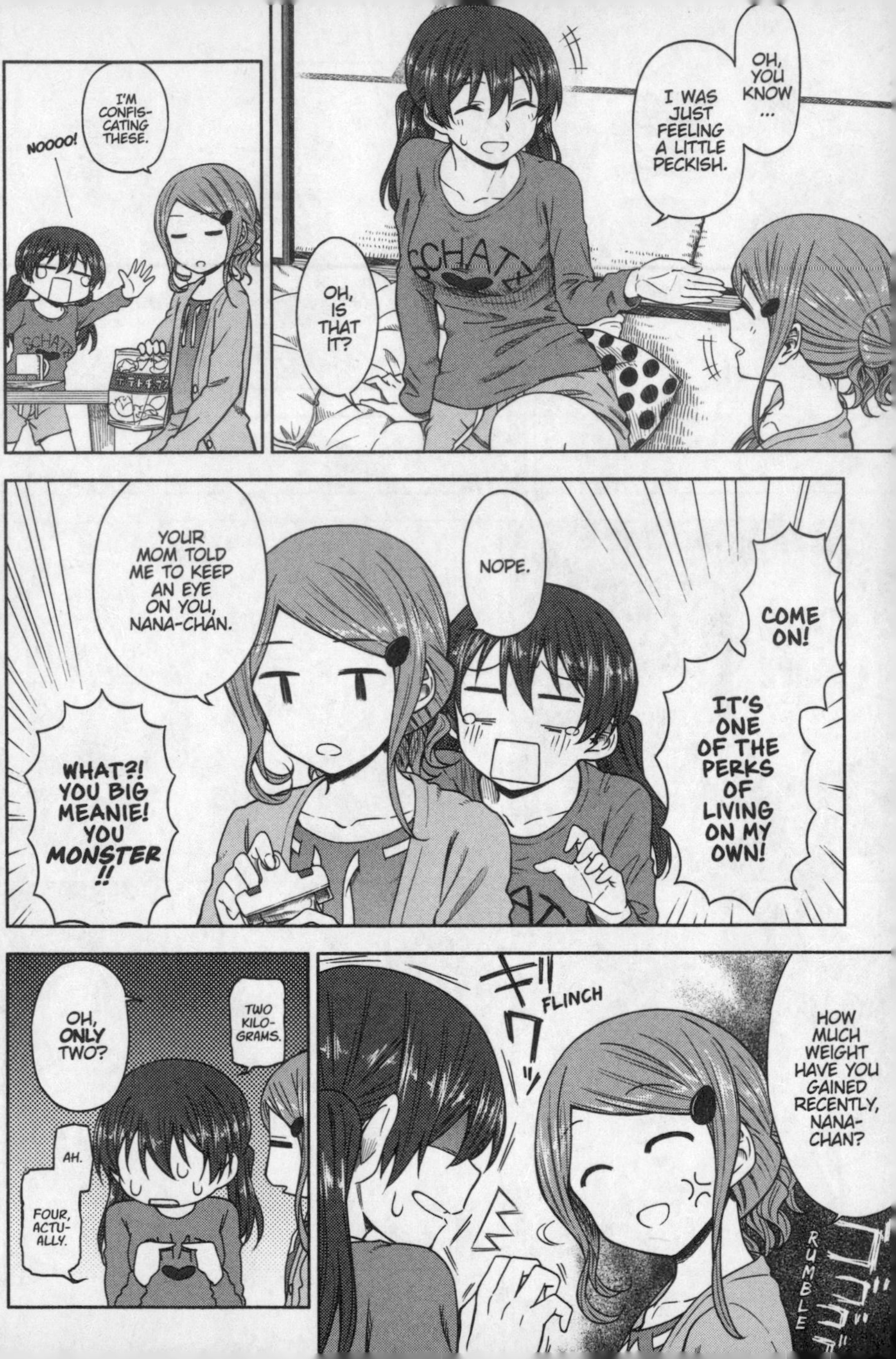
OH, YOU KNOW ... I WAS JUST FEELING A LITTLE PECKISH.
OH, IS THAT IT?
I'M CONFISCATING THESE.
NOOOO!
COME ON! IT'S ONE OF THE PERKS OF LIVING ON MY OWN!
NOPE.
YOUR MOM TOLD ME TO KEEP AN EYE ON YOU, NANA-CHAN.
WHAT?! YOU BIG MEANIE! YOU MONSTER!!
HOW MUCH WEIGHT HAVE YOU GAINED RECENTLY, NANA-CHAN?
RUMBLE
FLINCH
TWO KILOGRAMS.
OH, ONLY TWO?
AH.
FOUR, ACTUALLY.

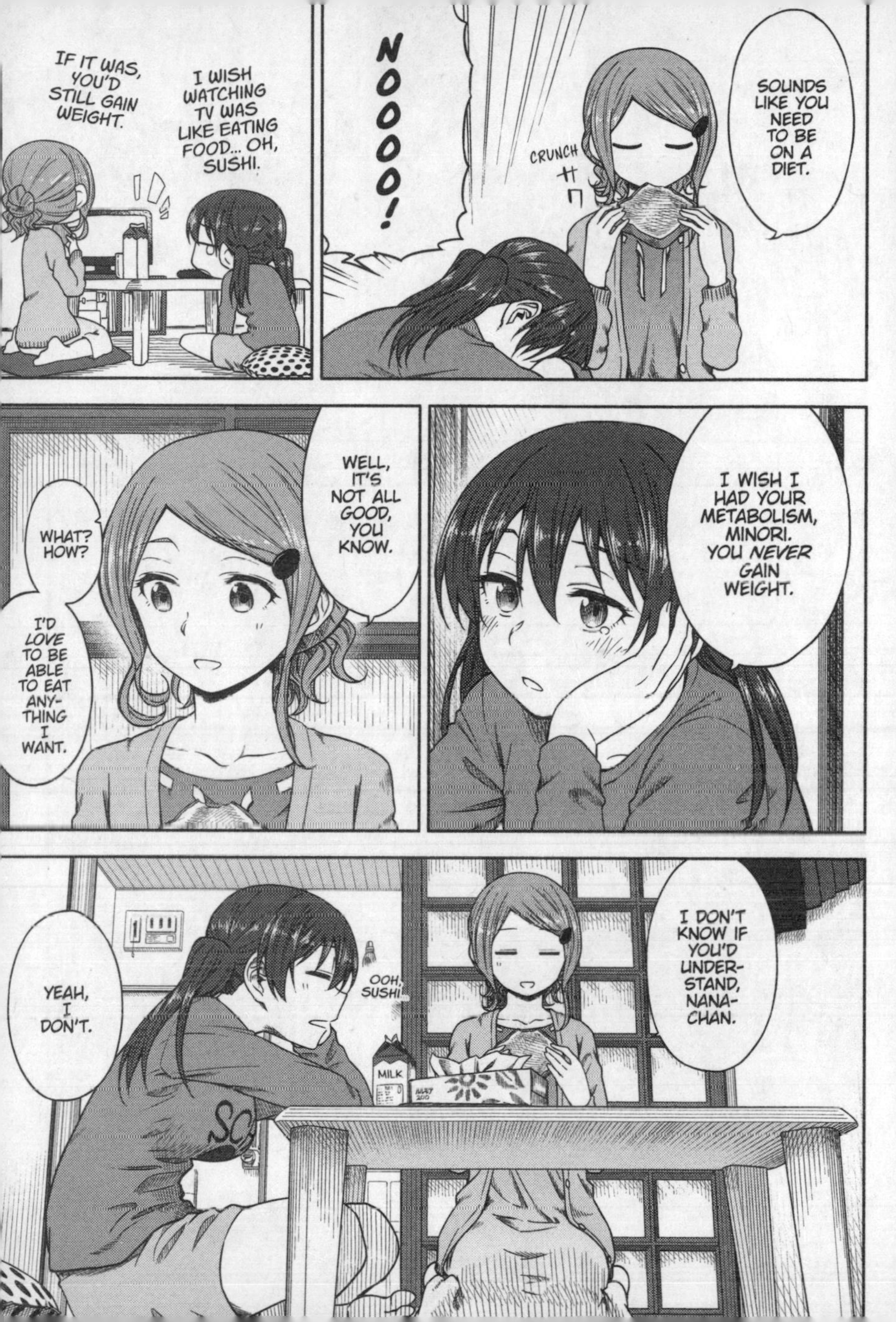
SOUNDS LIKE YOU NEED TO BE ON A DIET.
CRUNCH
サク
NOOOOO!
I WISH WATCHING TV WAS LIKE EATING FOOD... OH, SUSHI.
IF IT WAS, YOU'D STILL GAIN WEIGHT.
I WISH I HAD YOUR METABOLISM, MINORI. YOU *NEVER* GAIN WEIGHT.
WELL, IT'S NOT ALL GOOD, YOU KNOW.
WHAT? HOW?
I'D *LOVE* TO BE ABLE TO EAT ANYTHING I WANT.
I DON'T KNOW IF YOU'D UNDERSTAND, NANA-CHAN.
OOH, SUSHI!...
YEAH, I DON'T.

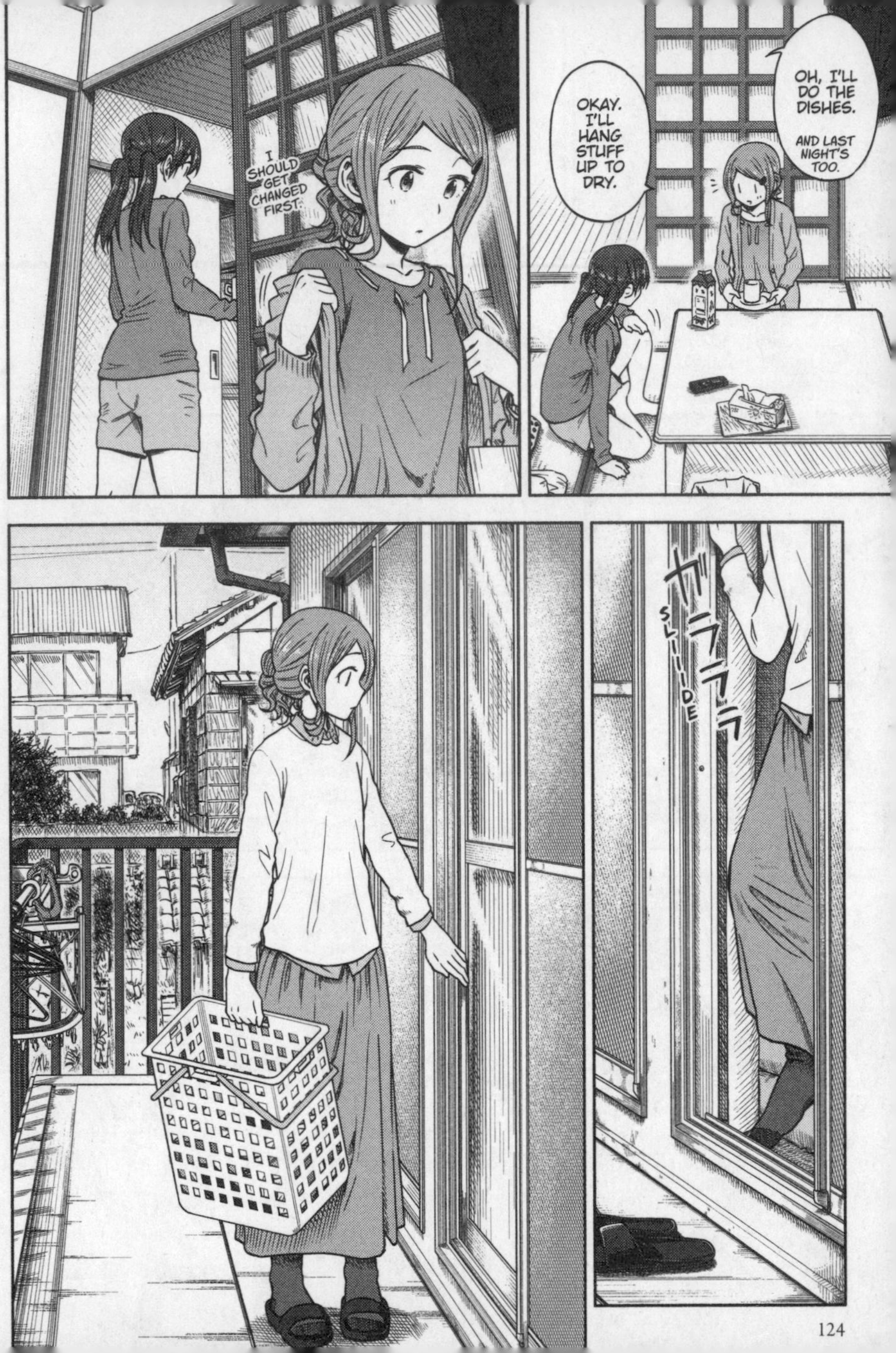
OH, I'LL DO THE DISHES.
AND LAST NIGHT'S TOO.
OKAY. I'LL HANG STUFF UP TO DRY.
I SHOULD GET CHANGED FIRST.
SLIIIDE

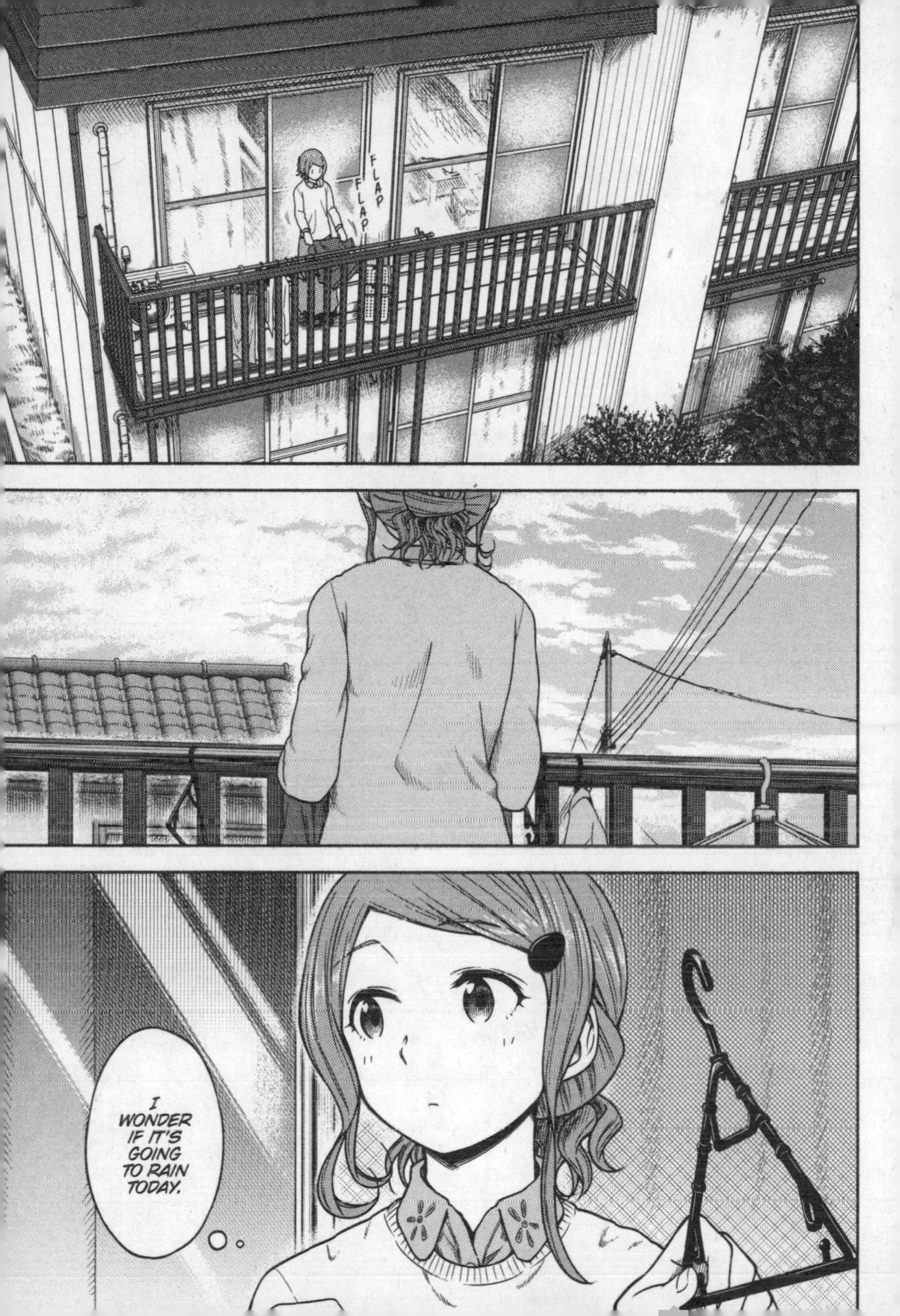
FLAP FLAP
I WONDER IF IT'S GOING TO RAIN TODAY.

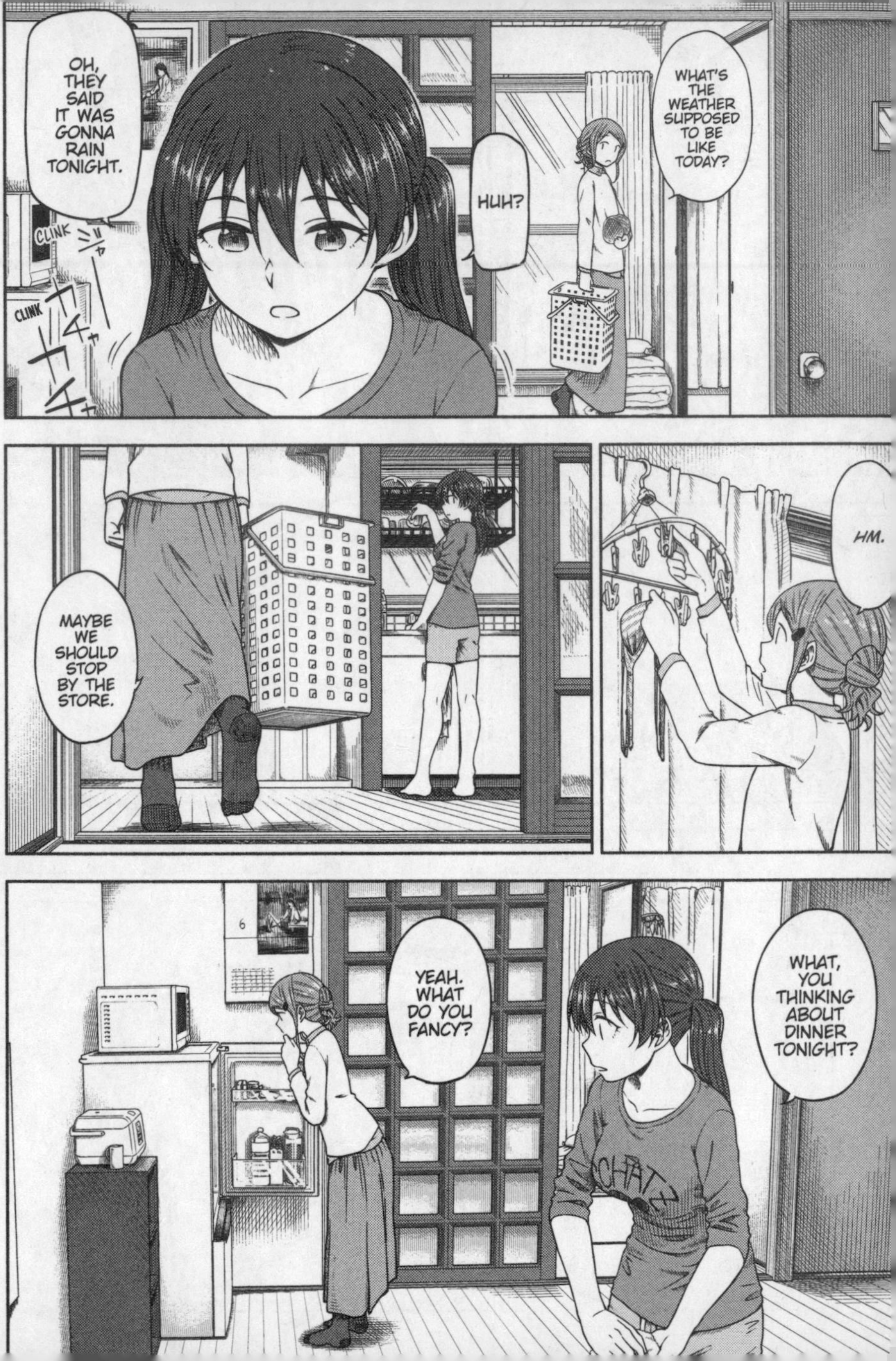
WHAT'S THE WEATHER SUPPOSED TO BE LIKE TODAY?
HUH?
OH, THEY SAID IT WAS GONNA RAIN TONIGHT.
CLINK
CLINK
HM.
MAYBE WE SHOULD STOP BY THE STORE.
WHAT, YOU THINKING ABOUT DINNER TONIGHT?
YEAH. WHAT DO YOU FANCY?

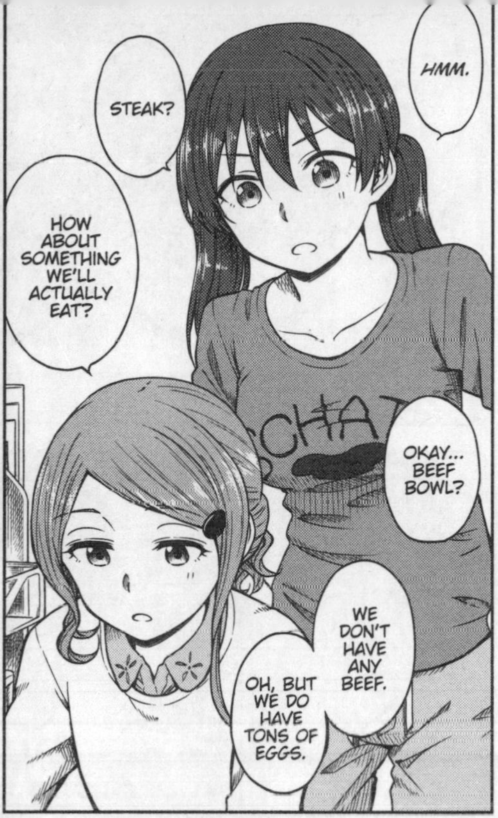
HMM.
STEAK?
HOW ABOUT SOMETHING WE'LL ACTUALLY EAT?
OKAY... BEEF BOWL?
WE DON'T HAVE ANY BEEF.
OH, BUT WE DO HAVE TONS OF EGGS.

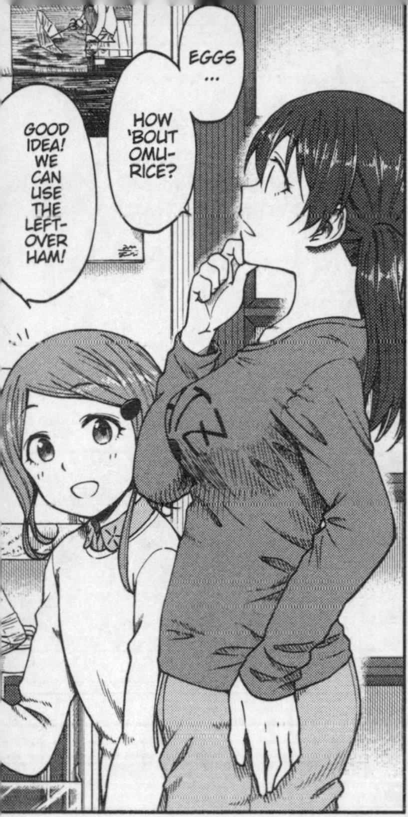
EGGS...
HOW 'BOUT OMU-RICE?
GOOD IDEA! WE CAN USE THE LEFT-OVER HAM!

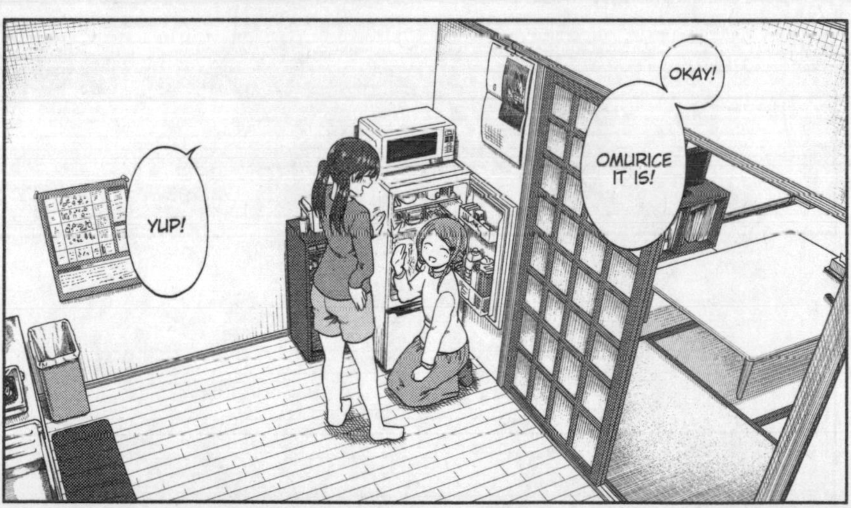
OKAY!
OMURICE IT IS!
YUP!

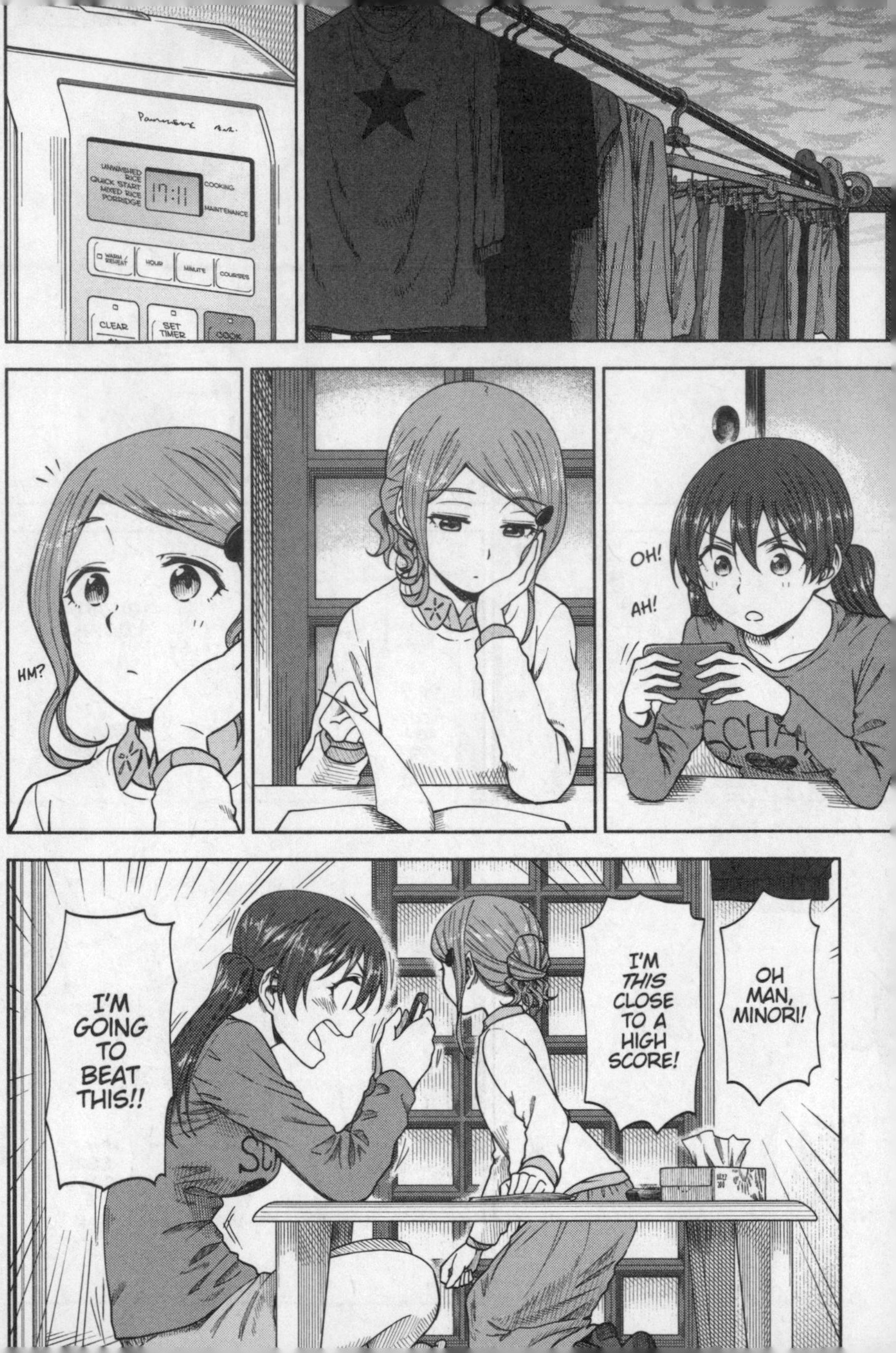
UNWASHED RICE
QUICK START
MIXED RICE
PORRIDGE
17:11
COOKING
MAINTENANCE
WARM/REHEAT
HOUR
MINUTE
COURSES
CLEAR
SET TIMER
COOK
OH!
AH!
HM?
OH MAN, MINORI!
I'M THIS CLOSE TO A HIGH SCORE!
I'M GOING TO BEAT THIS!!

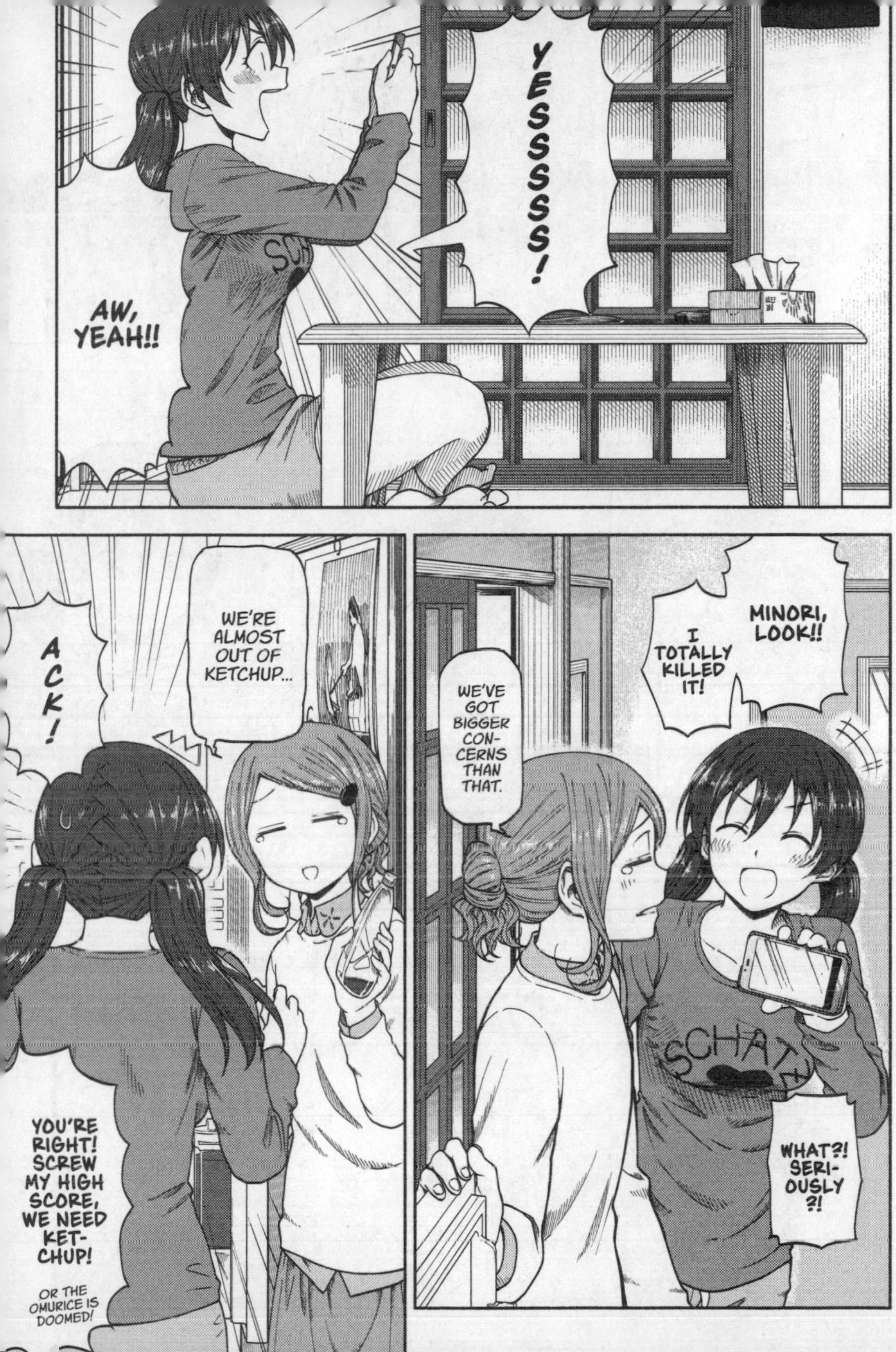
YESSSSSS!
AW, YEAH!!
MINORI, LOOK!!
I TOTALLY KILLED IT!
WE'VE GOT BIGGER CON-CERNS THAN THAT.
WHAT?! SERI-OUSLY?!
WE'RE ALMOST OUT OF KETCHUP...
ACK!
YOU'RE RIGHT! SCREW MY HIGH SCORE, WE NEED KET-CHUP!
OR THE OMURICE IS DOOMED!

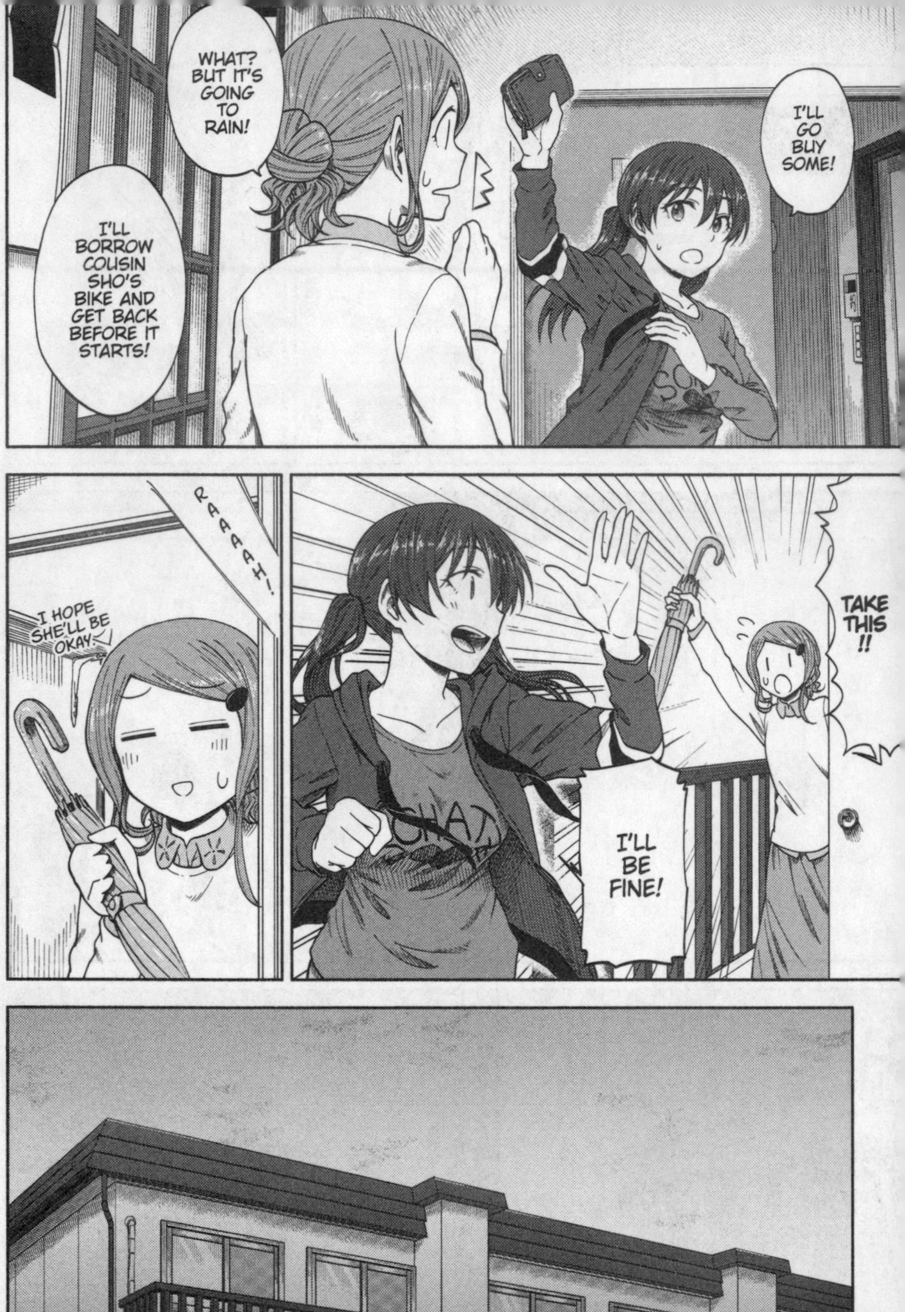
I'LL GO BUY SOME!
WHAT? BUT IT'S GOING TO RAIN!
I'LL BORROW COUSIN SHO'S BIKE AND GET BACK BEFORE IT STARTS!
TAKE THIS!!
I'LL BE FINE!
RAAAAAH!
I HOPE SHE'LL BE OKAY.

THE LAUNDRY!

HERE IT COMES!

OH NO!

PLIP
PLIP
PLIP

CHOP
CHOP

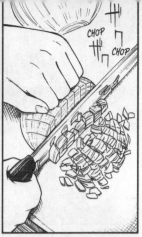

NANA-CHAN'S TIMING COULDN'T HAVE BEEN WORSE...

ゴォォォ ァ ァ ァ ァ ァ ァ

SHAAAAAA

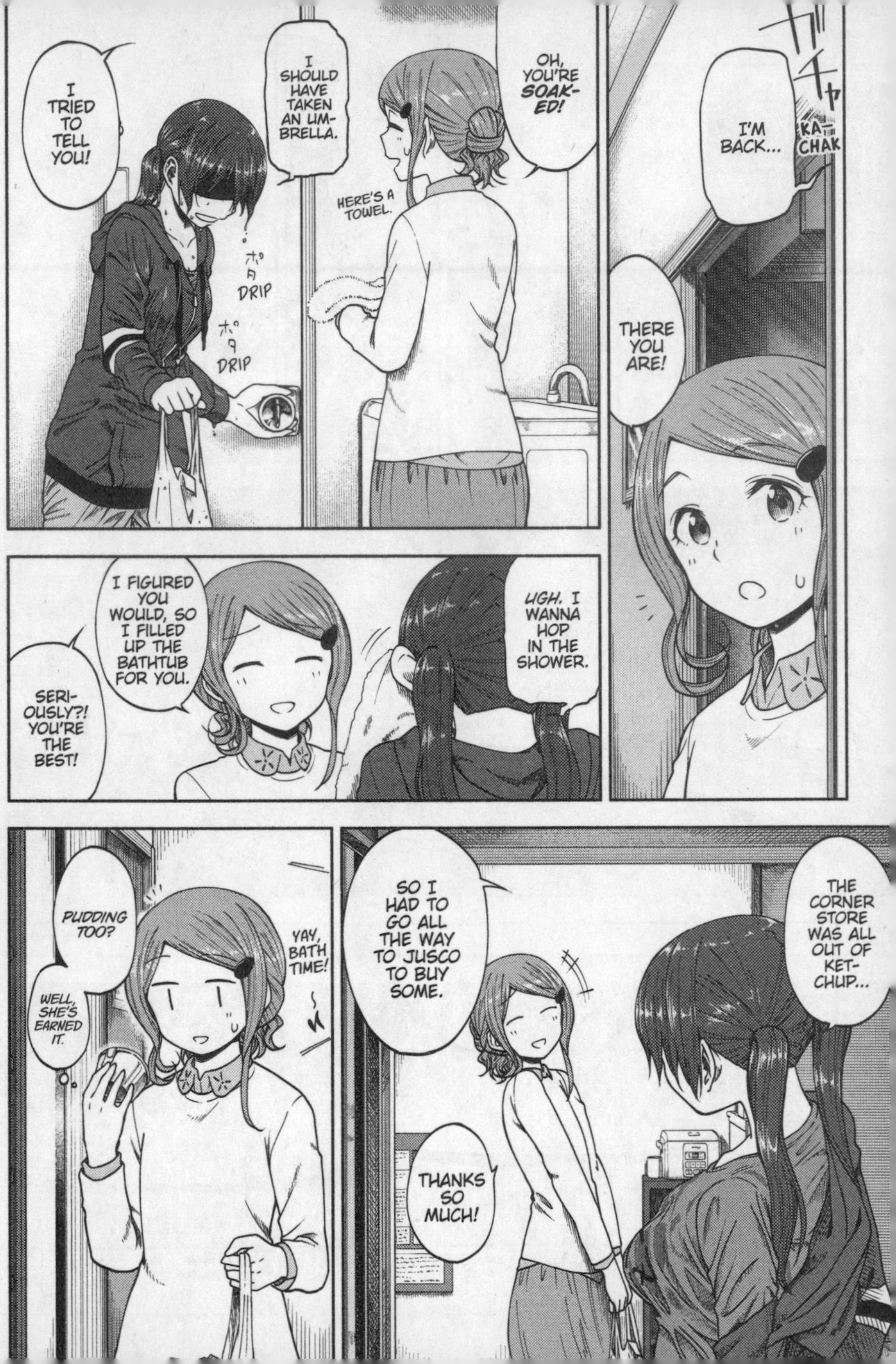
KA-CHAK
I'M BACK...
THERE YOU ARE!
OH, YOU'RE SOAK-ED!
I SHOULD HAVE TAKEN AN UM-BRELLA.
I TRIED TO TELL YOU!
HERE'S A TOWEL.
DRIP
DRIP
UGH. I WANNA HOP IN THE SHOWER.
I FIGURED YOU WOULD, SO I FILLED UP THE BATHTUB FOR YOU.
SERI-OUSLY?! YOU'RE THE BEST!
THE CORNER STORE WAS ALL OUT OF KET-CHUP...
SO I HAD TO GO ALL THE WAY TO JUSCO TO BUY SOME.
THANKS SO MUCH!
YAY, BATH TIME!
PUDDING TOO?
WELL, SHE'S EARNED IT.

HAAH...

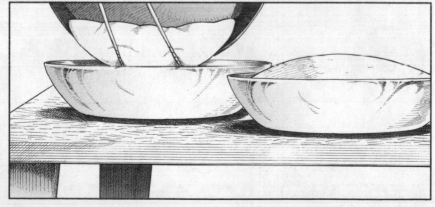

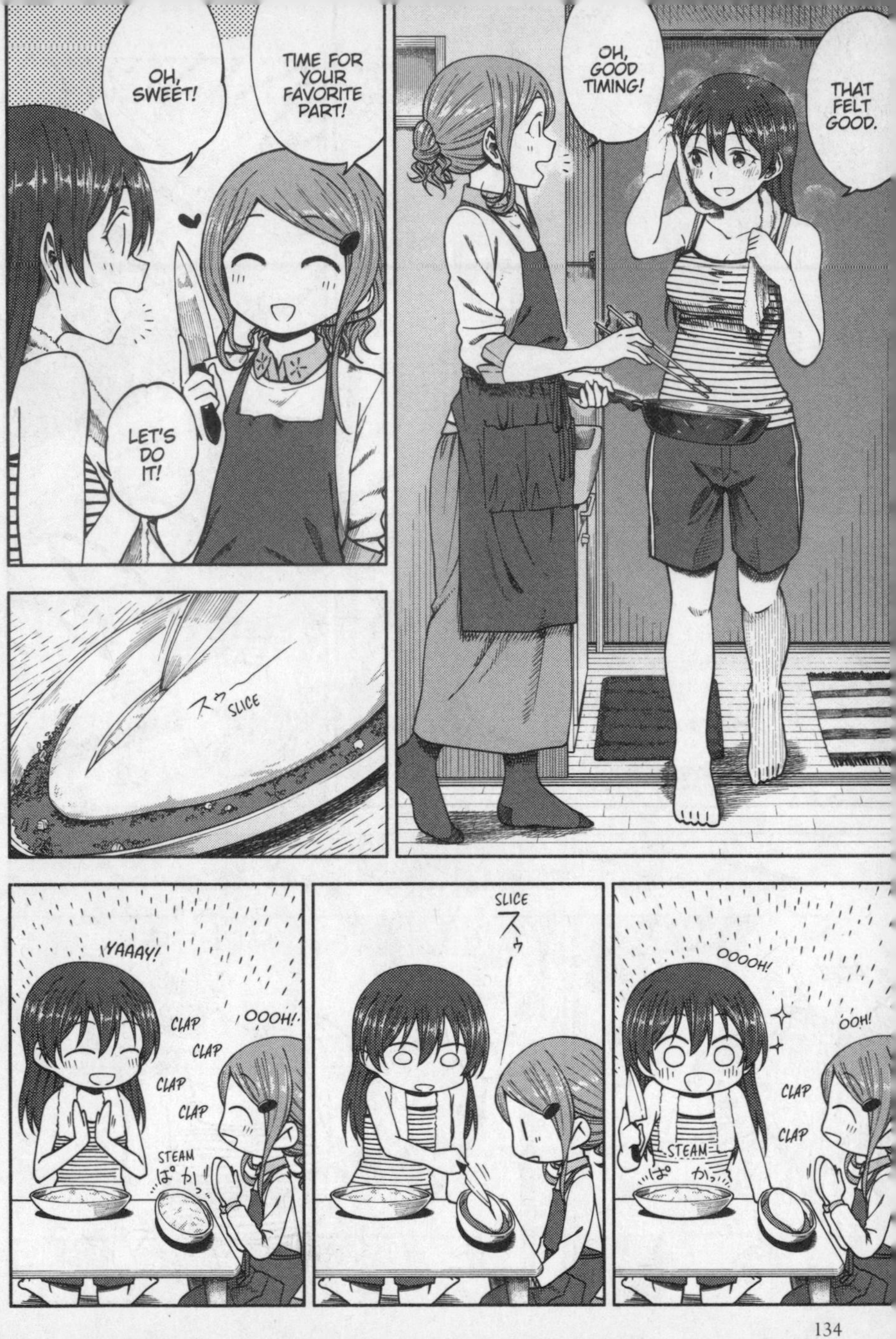
THAT FELT GOOD.
OH, GOOD TIMING!
TIME FOR YOUR FAVORITE PART!
OH, SWEET!
LET'S DO IT!
スゥー SLICE
OOOOH!
OOH!
CLAP
CLAP
STEAM
ぱかっ
SLICE
スゥー
YAAAY!
OOOH!
CLAP
CLAP
CLAP
CLAP
STEAM
ぱかっ

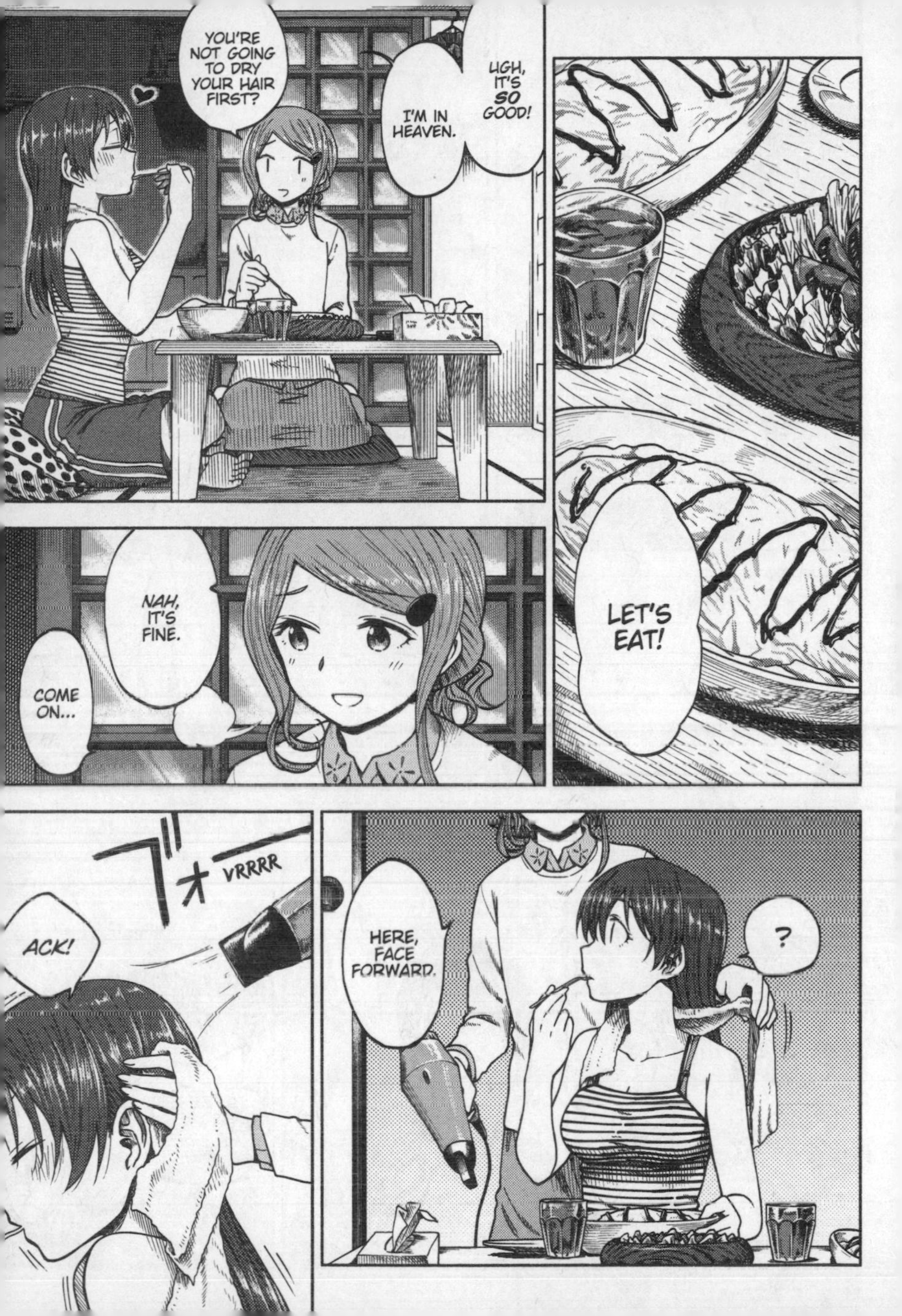
LET'S EAT!
UGH, IT'S SO GOOD!
I'M IN HEAVEN.
YOU'RE NOT GOING TO DRY YOUR HAIR FIRST?
NAH, IT'S FINE.
COME ON...
?
HERE, FACE FORWARD.
VRRRR
ACK!

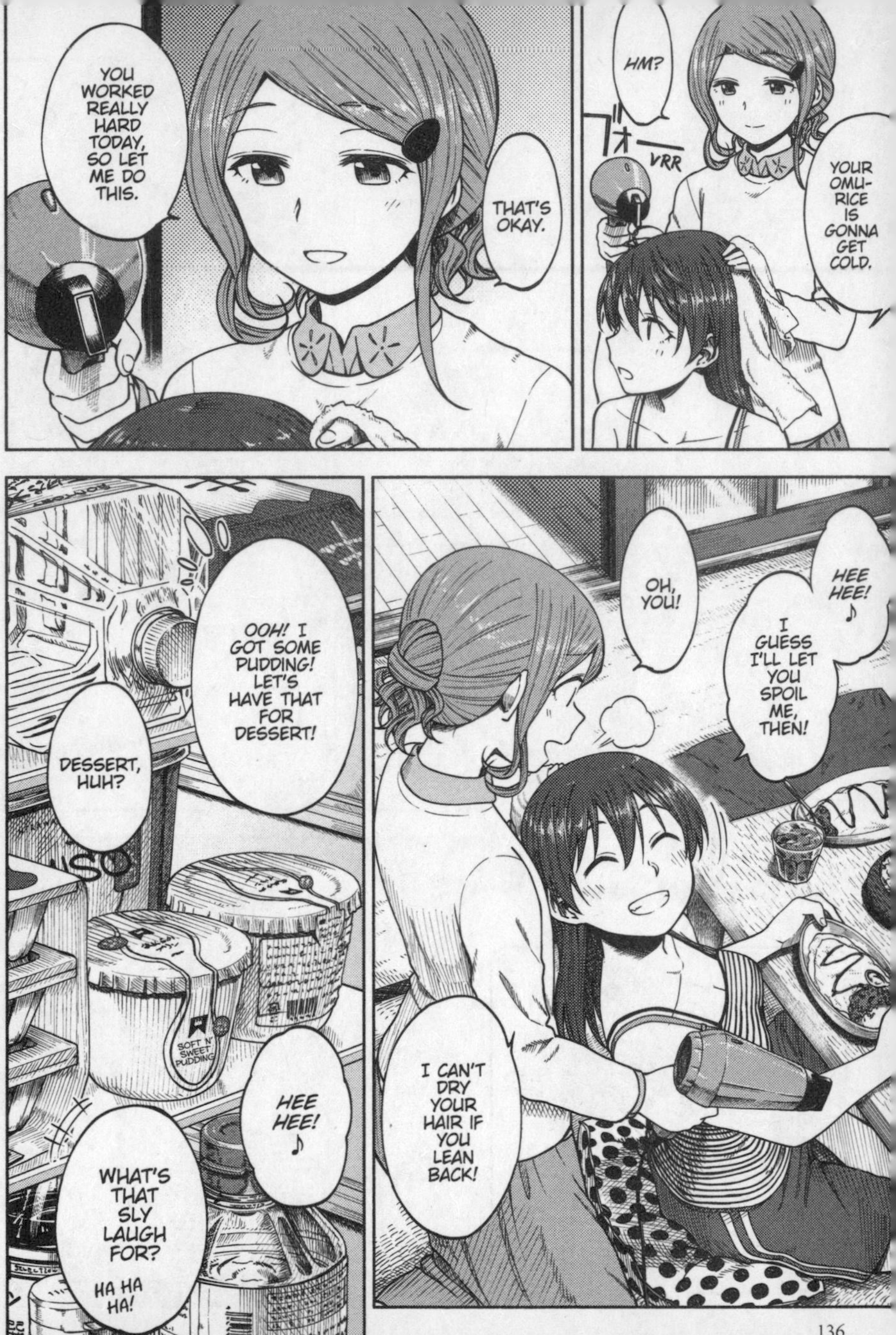
HM?
VRR
YOUR OMU-RICE IS GONNA GET COLD.
THAT'S OKAY.
YOU WORKED REALLY HARD TODAY, SO LET ME DO THIS.
HEE HEE! ♪
I GUESS I'LL LET YOU SPOIL ME, THEN!
OH, YOU!
I CAN'T DRY YOUR HAIR IF YOU LEAN BACK!
OOH! I GOT SOME PUDDING! LET'S HAVE THAT FOR DESSERT!
DESSERT, HUH?
SOFT N' SWEET PUDDING
HEE HEE! ♪
WHAT'S THAT SLY LAUGH FOR?
HA HA HA!

Our Wonderful Days

story & art by Kei Hamuro

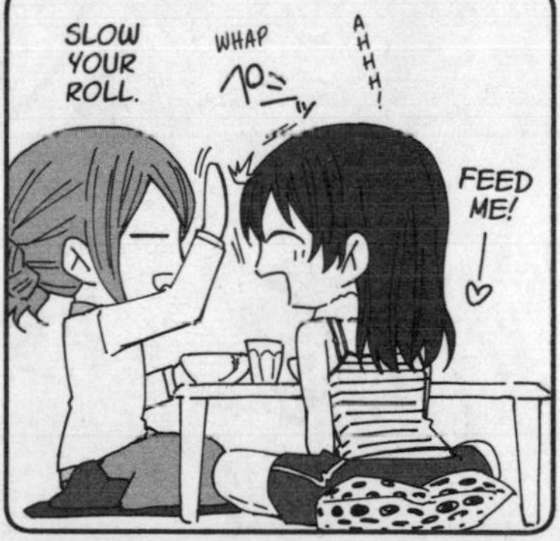
SLOW YOUR ROLL.
WHAP
AHHH!
FEED ME!

Our
Wonderful
Days * Tsurezure
       Biyori

Chapter 6
A Bit of Rain

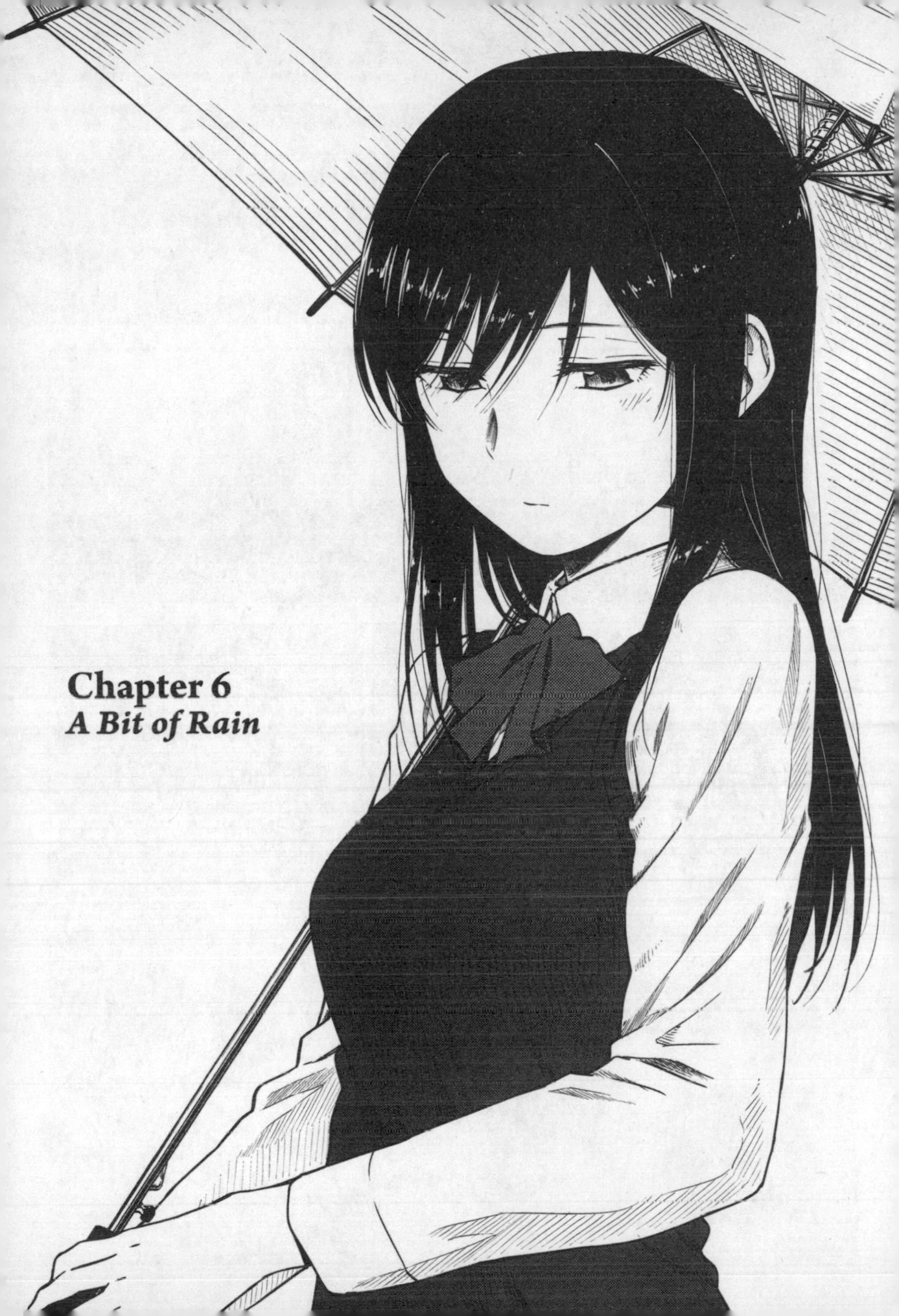

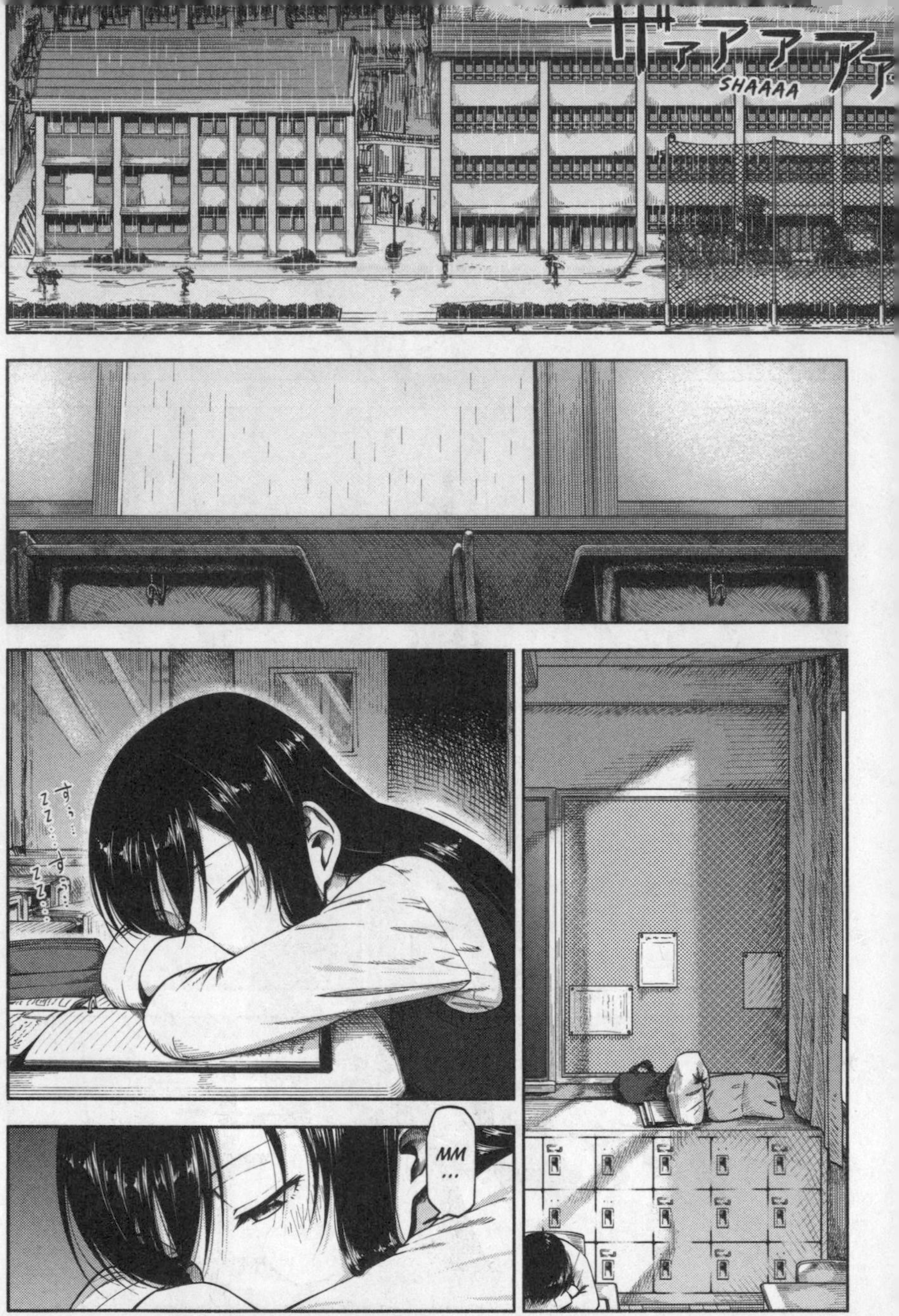
ザァアアア
SHAAAA
すぅ…
ZZ…
すぅ…
ZZ…
MM …

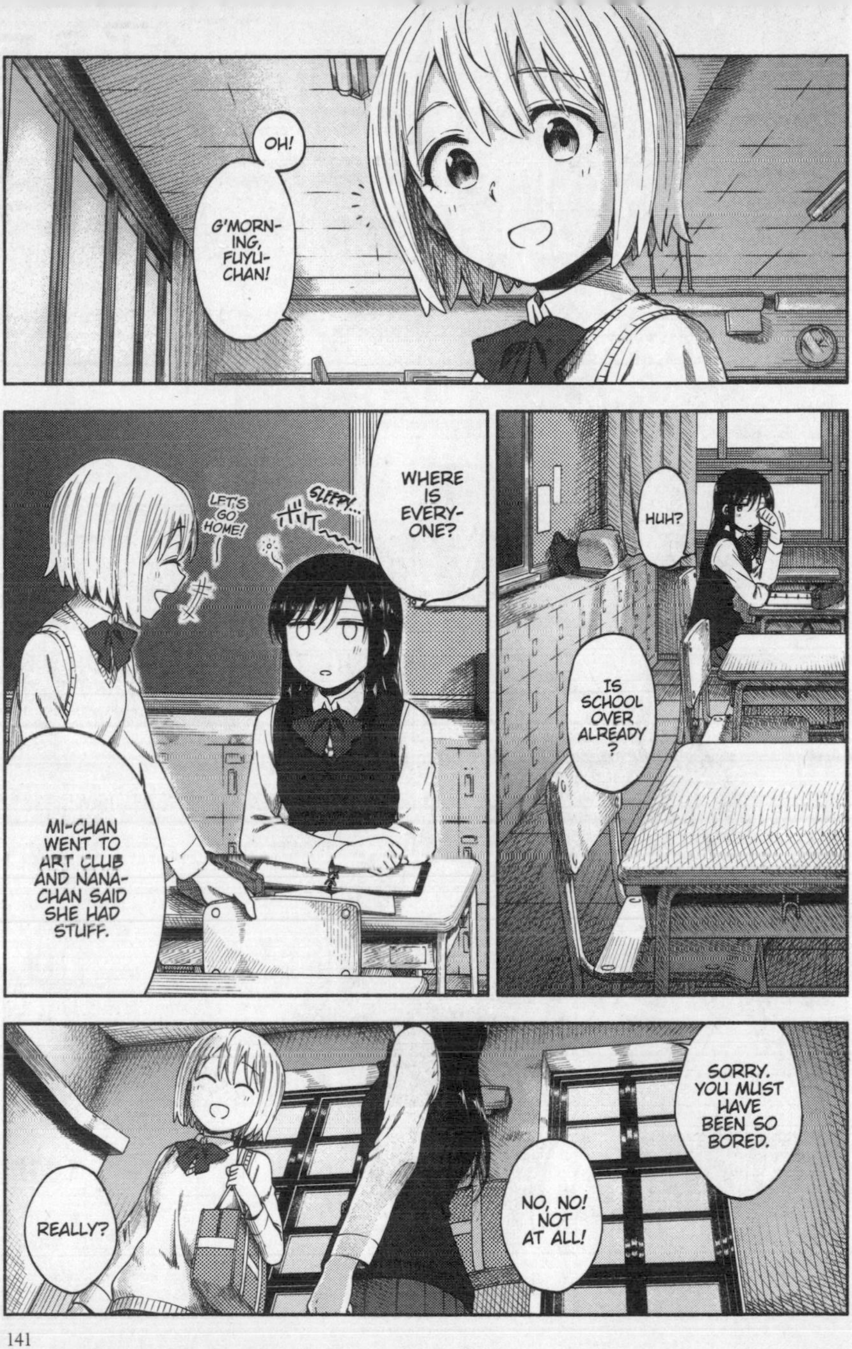
OH!
G'MORNING, FUYU-CHAN!
HUH?
IS SCHOOL OVER ALREADY?
WHERE IS EVERYONE?
SLEEPY...
LET'S GO HOME!
MI-CHAN WENT TO ART CLUB AND NANA-CHAN SAID SHE HAD STUFF.
SORRY. YOU MUST HAVE BEEN SO BORED.
NO, NO! NOT AT ALL!
REALLY?

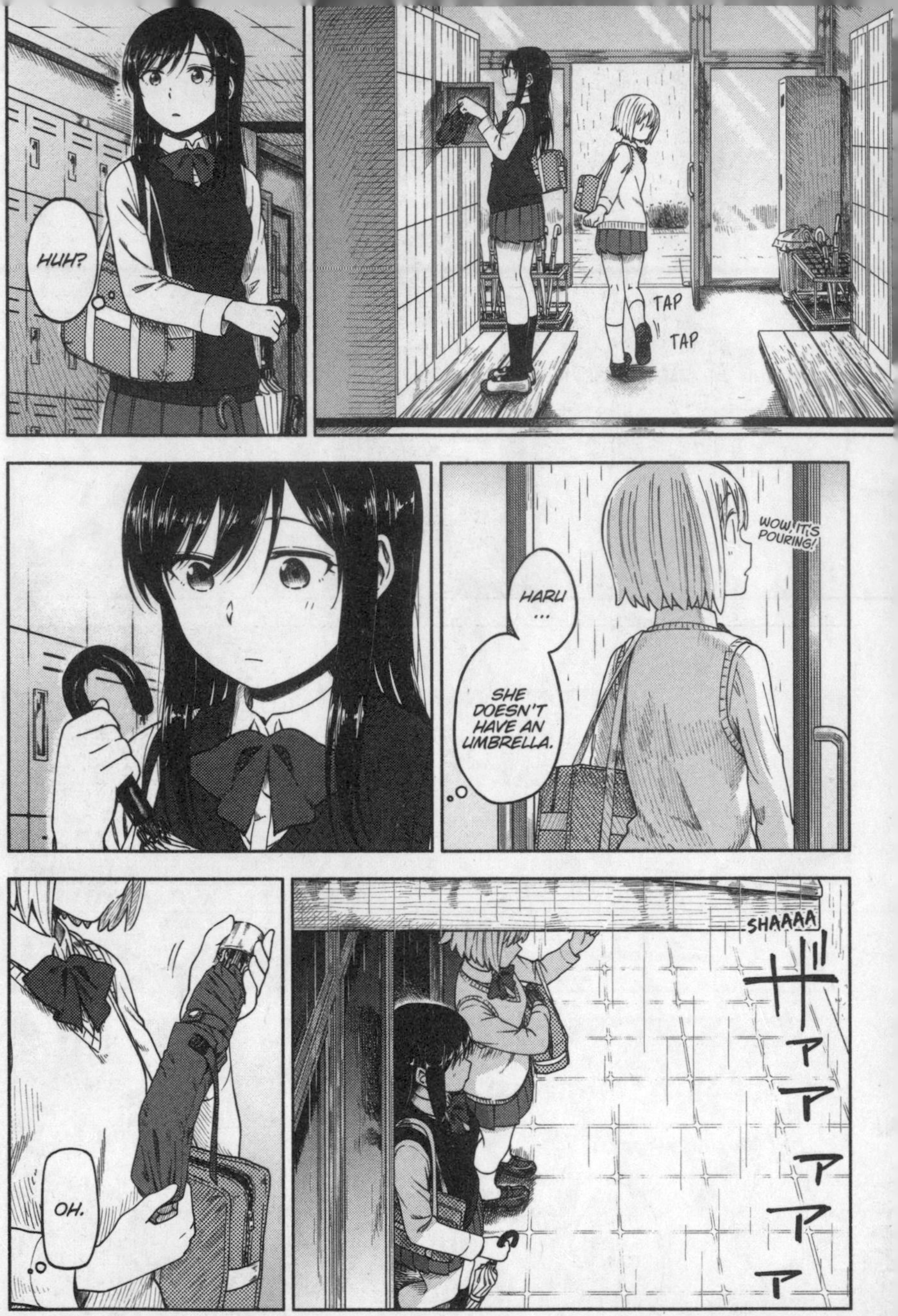
TAP
TAP
HUH?
WOW, IT'S POURING!
HARU ...
SHE DOESN'T HAVE AN UMBRELLA.
SHAAAA
ザァァァァァ
OH.

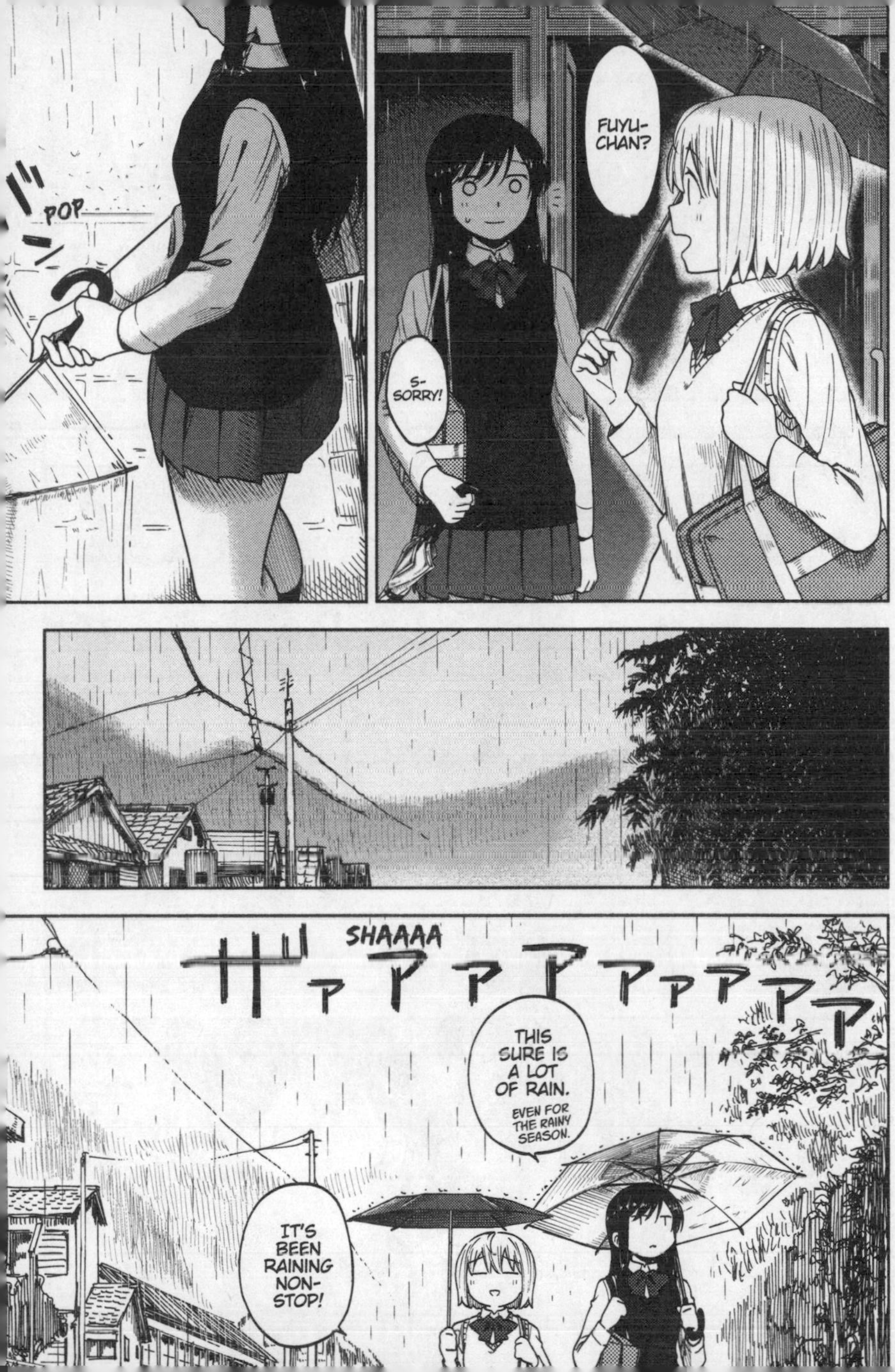
FUYU-CHAN?
S-SORRY!
POP
SHAAAA
THIS SURE IS A LOT OF RAIN.
EVEN FOR THE RAINY SEASON.
IT'S BEEN RAINING NON-STOP!

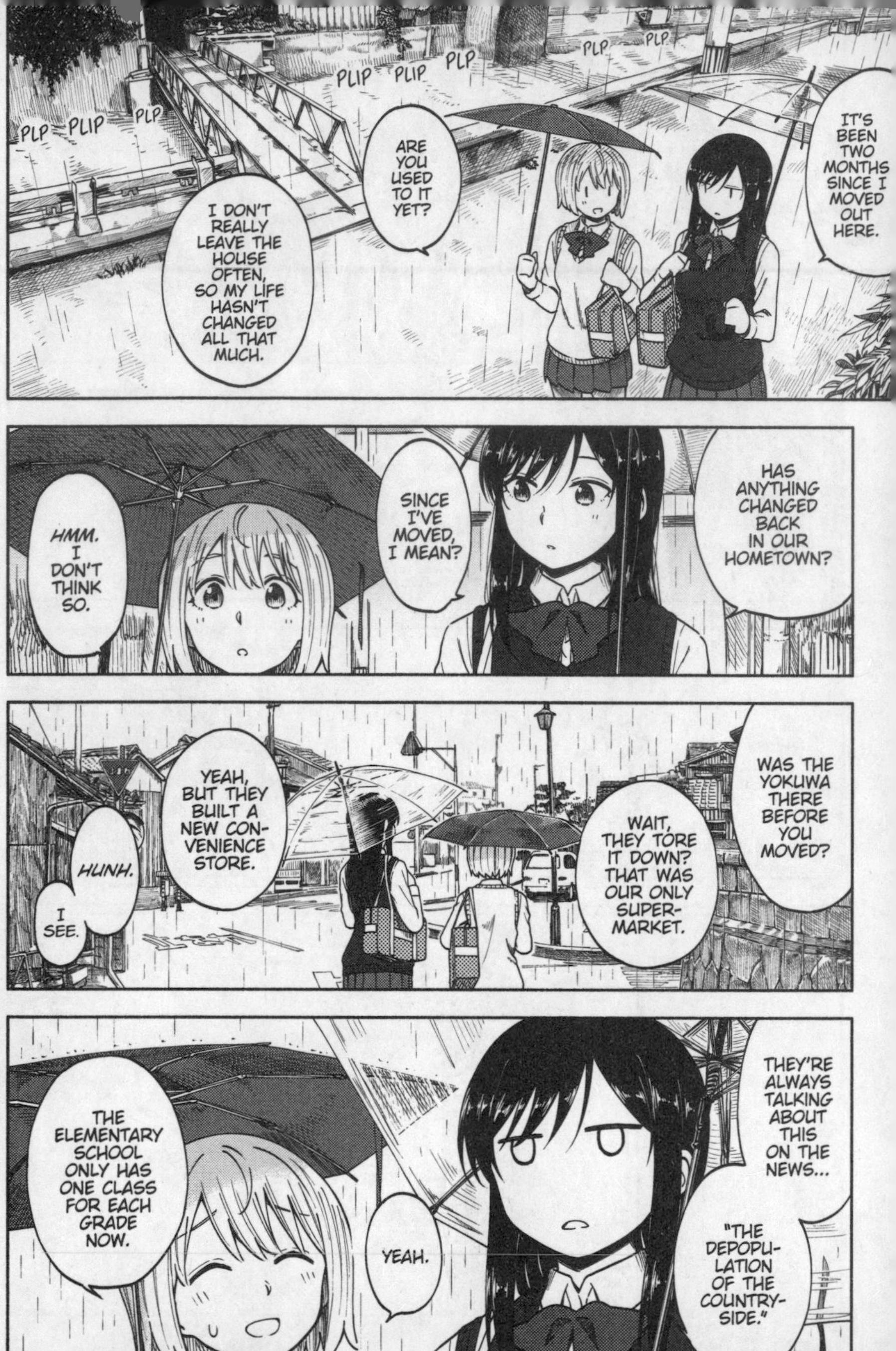
PLP PLP
PLP PLIP PLIP
PLP PLIP PLP
IT'S BEEN TWO MONTHS SINCE I MOVED OUT HERE.
ARE YOU USED TO IT YET?
I DON'T REALLY LEAVE THE HOUSE OFTEN, SO MY LIFE HASN'T CHANGED ALL THAT MUCH.
HAS ANYTHING CHANGED BACK IN OUR HOMETOWN?
SINCE I'VE MOVED, I MEAN?
HMM. I DON'T THINK SO.
WAS THE YOKUWA THERE BEFORE YOU MOVED?
WAIT, THEY TORE IT DOWN? THAT WAS OUR ONLY SUPER-MARKET.
YEAH, BUT THEY BUILT A NEW CON-VENIENCE STORE.
HUNH.
I SEE.
THEY'RE ALWAYS TALKING ABOUT THIS ON THE NEWS...
"THE DEPOPU-LATION OF THE COUNTRY-SIDE."
YEAH.
THE ELEMENTARY SCHOOL ONLY HAS ONE CLASS FOR EACH GRADE NOW.

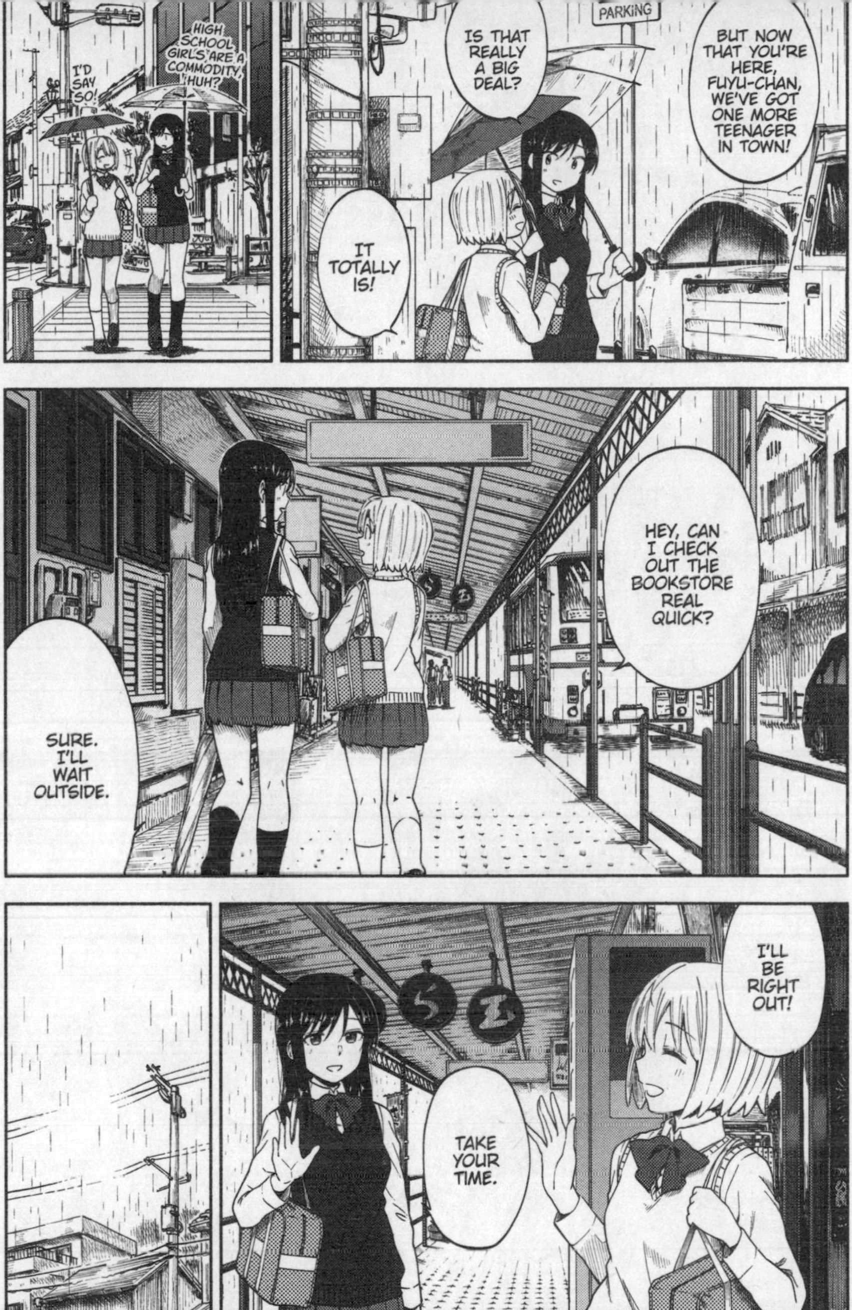
PARKING
BUT NOW THAT YOU'RE HERE, FUYU-CHAN, WE'VE GOT ONE MORE TEENAGER IN TOWN!
IS THAT REALLY A BIG DEAL?
IT TOTALLY IS!
HIGH SCHOOL GIRLS ARE A COMMODITY, HUH?
I'D SAY SO!
HEY, CAN I CHECK OUT THE BOOKSTORE REAL QUICK?
SURE. I'LL WAIT OUTSIDE.
I'LL BE RIGHT OUT!
TAKE YOUR TIME.

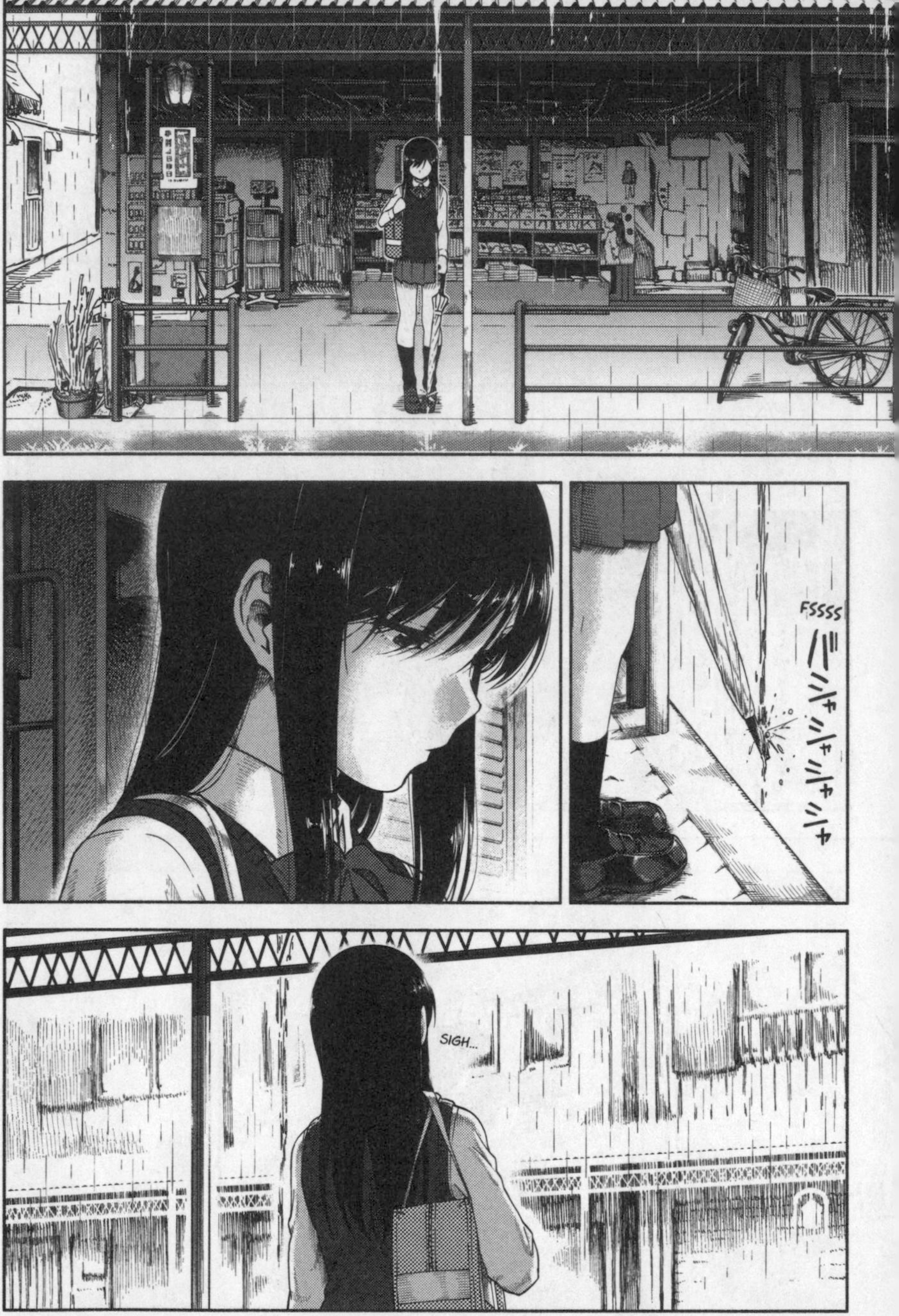
FSSSS
バシャシャシャシャ
SIGH...

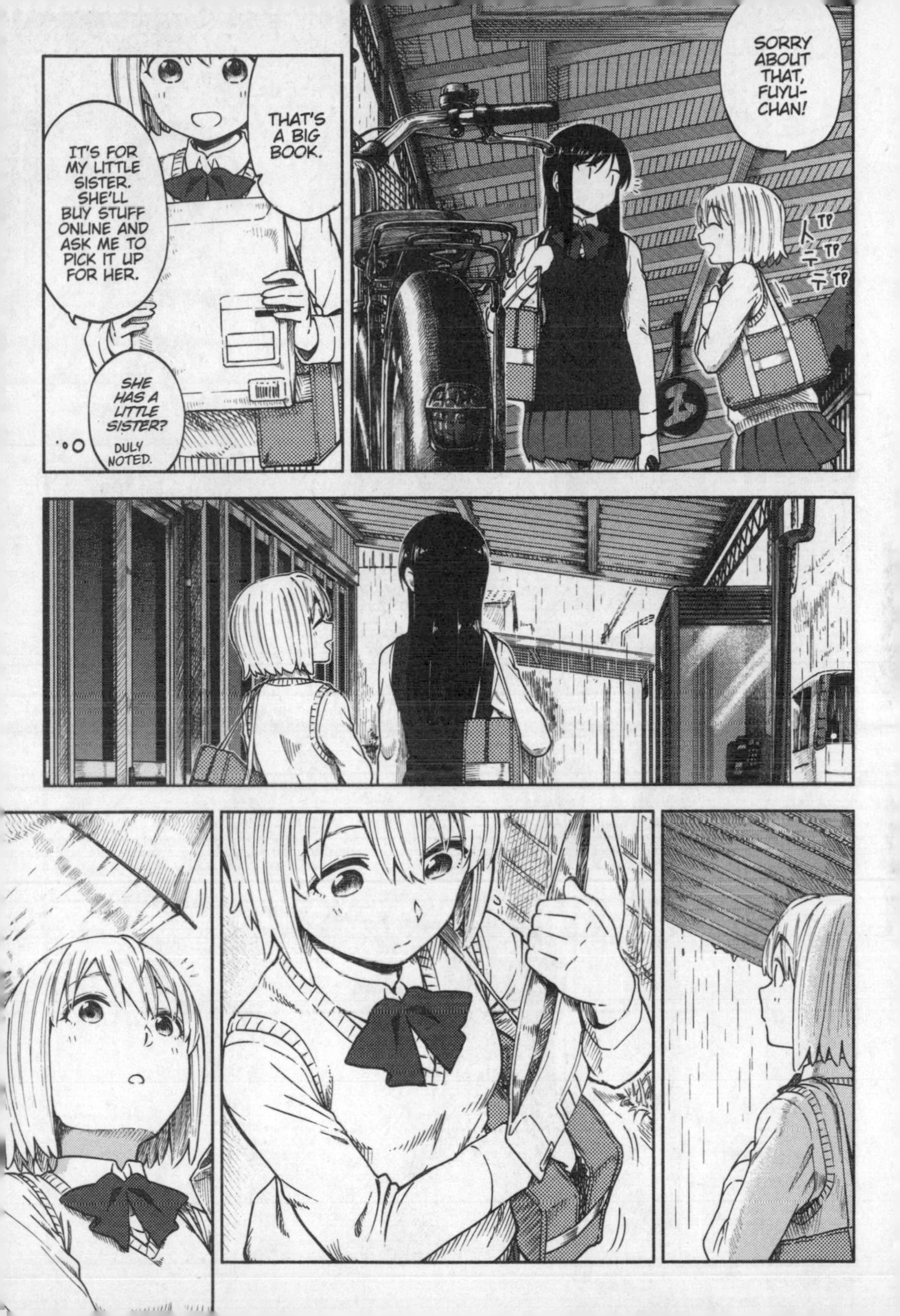
SORRY ABOUT THAT, FUYU-CHAN!
TP TP TP
THAT'S A BIG BOOK.
IT'S FOR MY LITTLE SISTER. SHE'LL BUY STUFF ONLINE AND ASK ME TO PICK IT UP FOR HER.
SHE HAS A LITTLE SISTER?
DULY NOTED.

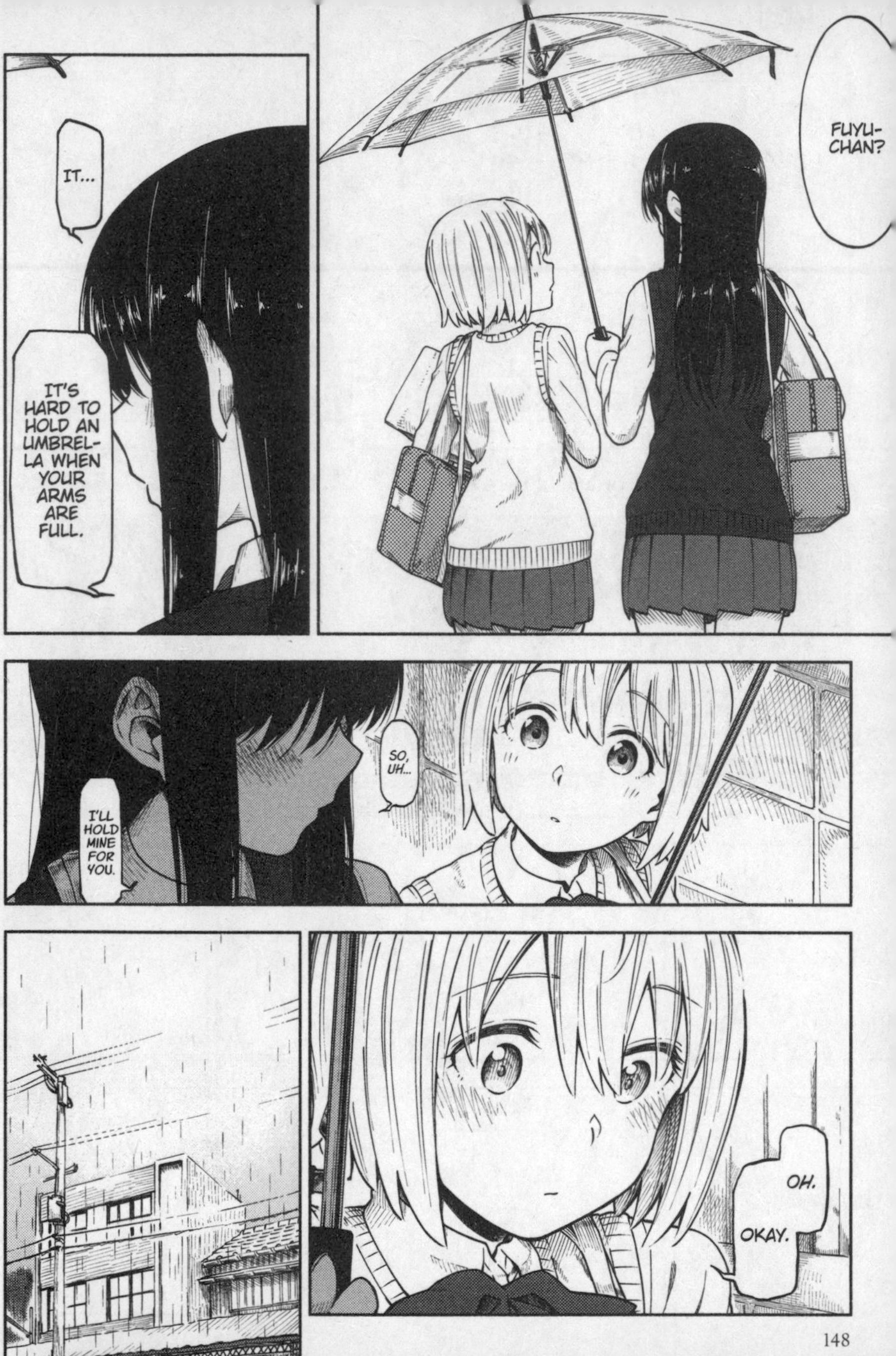
FUYU-CHAN?
IT...
IT'S HARD TO HOLD AN UMBREL-LA WHEN YOUR ARMS ARE FULL.
SO, UH...
I'LL HOLD MINE FOR YOU.
OH.
OKAY.

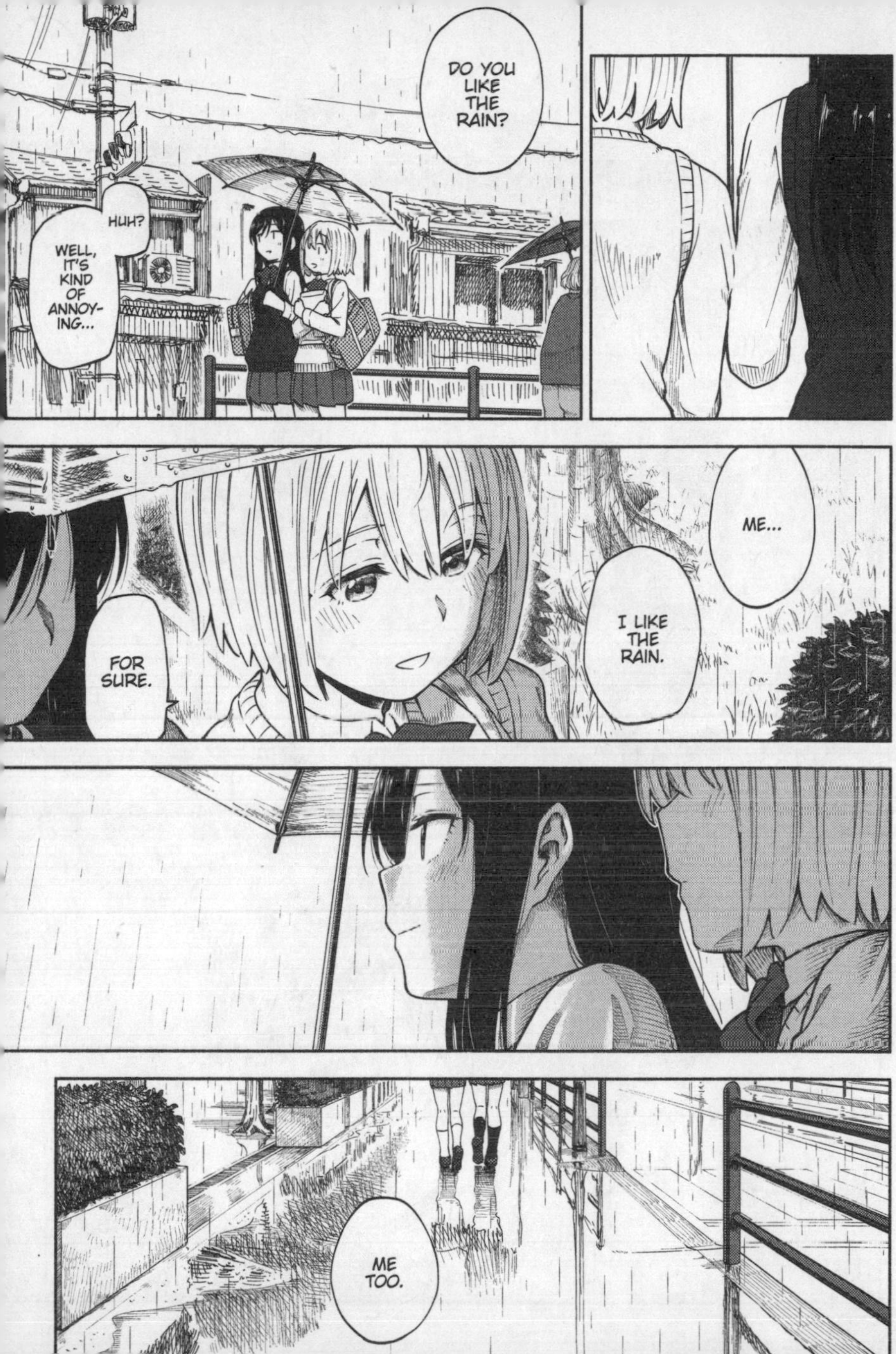
DO YOU LIKE THE RAIN?
HUH?
WELL, IT'S KIND OF ANNOY- ING...
ME...
I LIKE THE RAIN.
FOR SURE.
ME TOO.

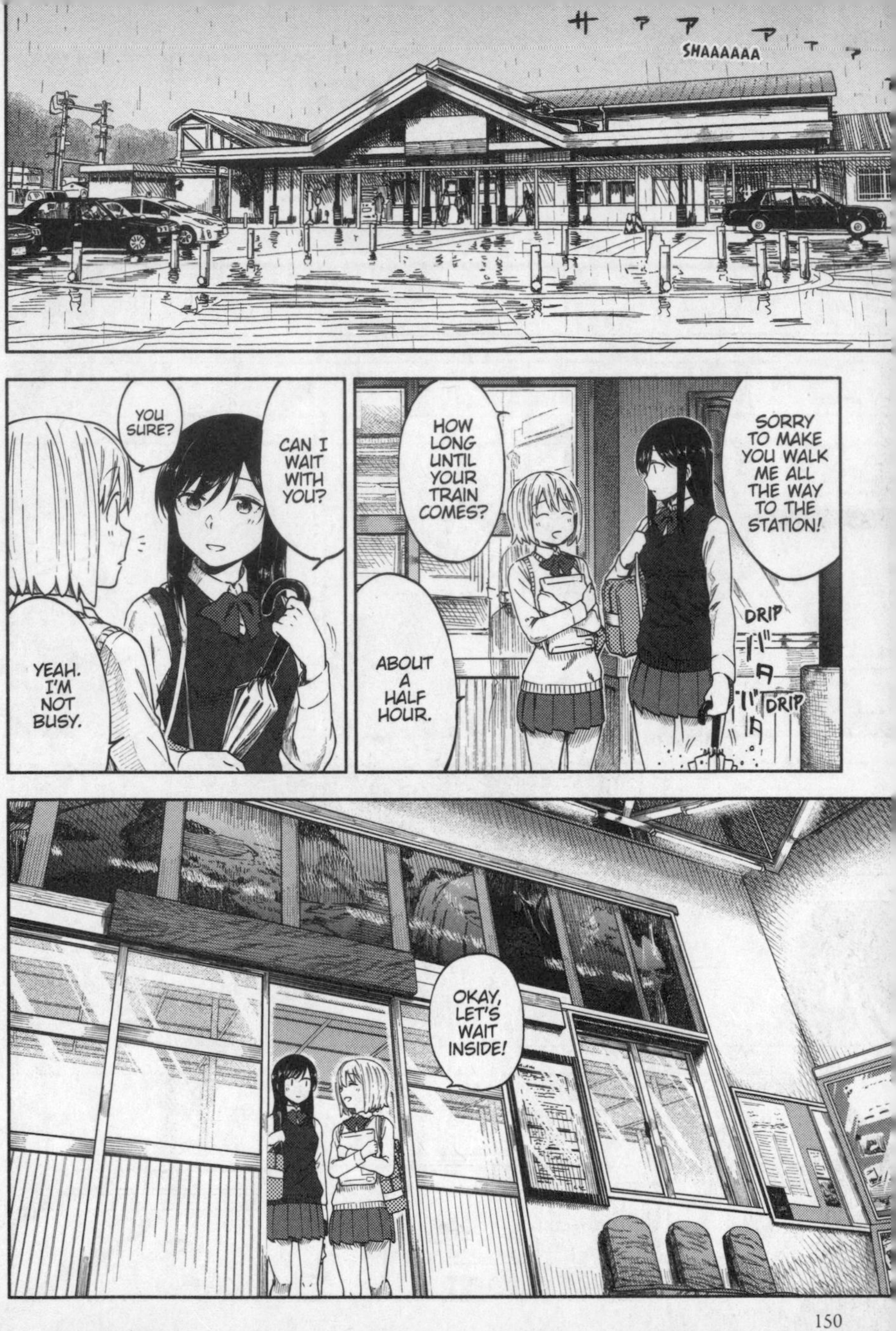
SHAAAAAA
SORRY TO MAKE YOU WALK ME ALL THE WAY TO THE STATION!
HOW LONG UNTIL YOUR TRAIN COMES?
ABOUT A HALF HOUR.
DRIP
DRIP
CAN I WAIT WITH YOU?
YOU SURE?
YEAH. I'M NOT BUSY.
OKAY, LET'S WAIT INSIDE!

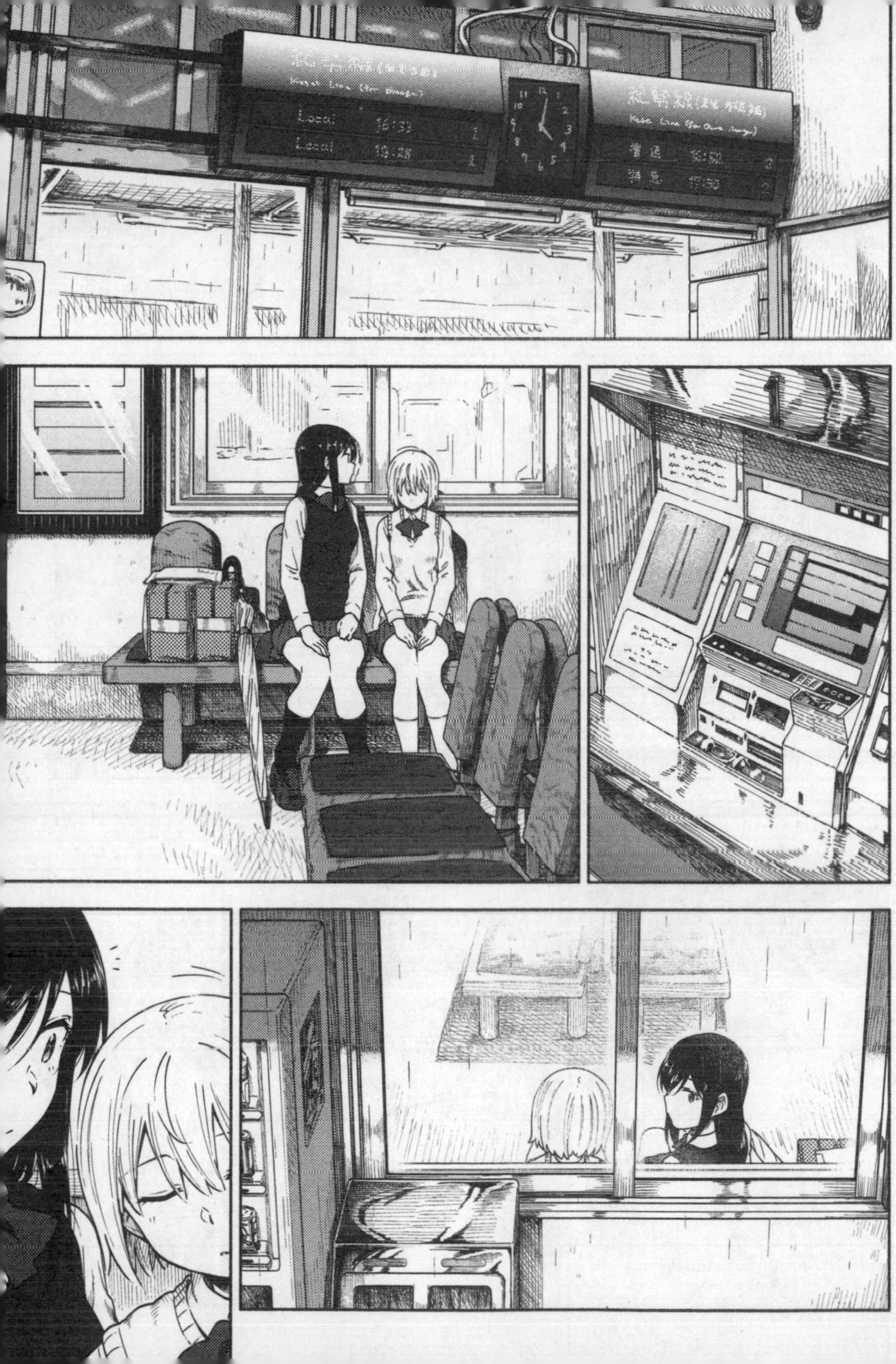
Local
Local
1

HARU
?

ZZZ
ZZZ

· · · · ·

AND
WARM.

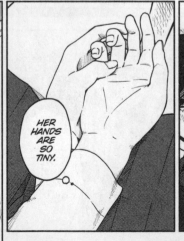

HER
HANDS
ARE
SO
TINY.

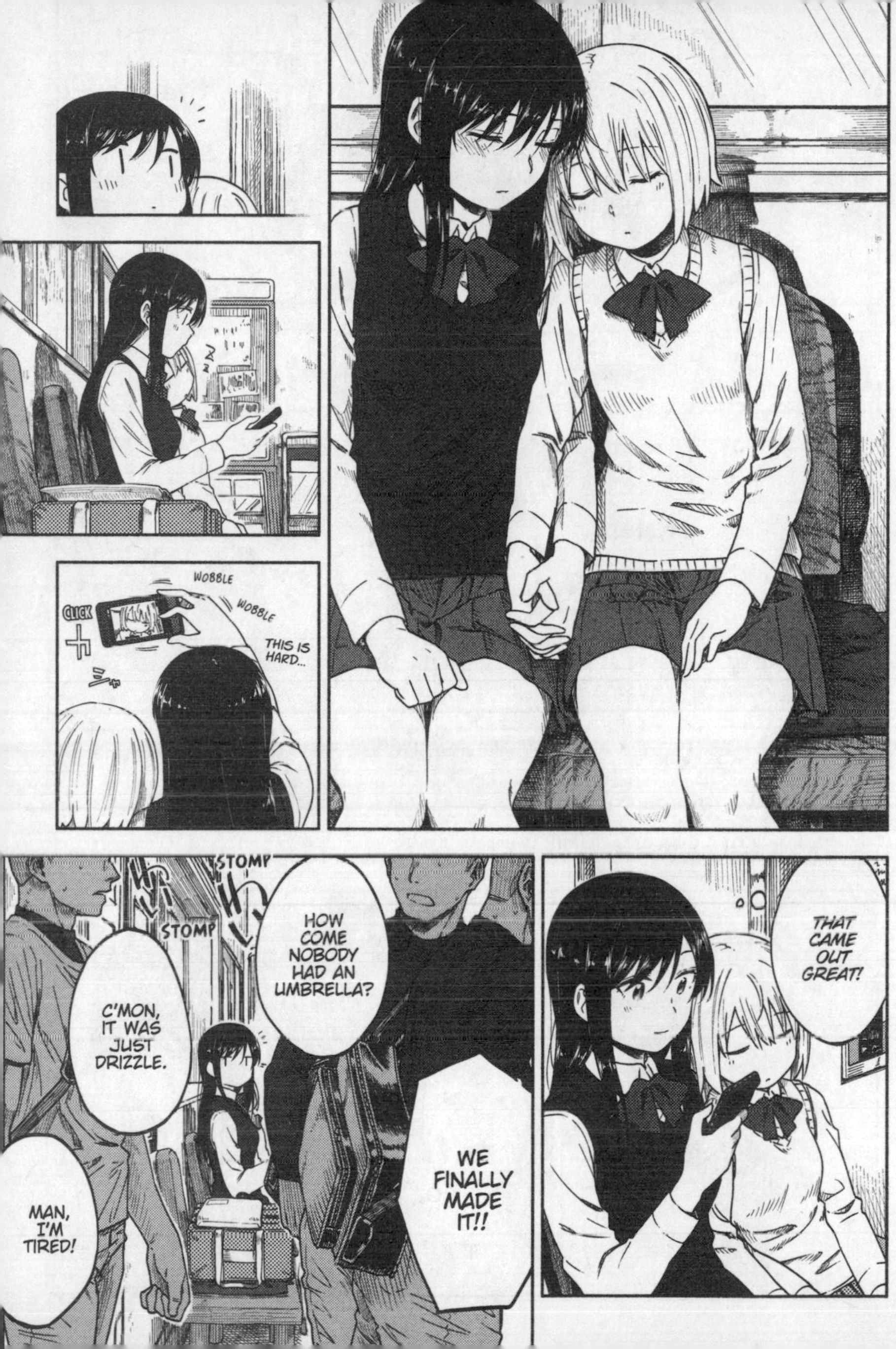
WOBBLE
WOBBLE
CLICK
THIS IS HARD...
THAT CAME OUT GREAT!
STOMP
HOW COME NOBODY HAD AN UMBRELLA?
STOMP
C'MON, IT WAS JUST DRIZZLE.
WE FINALLY MADE IT!!
MAN, I'M TIRED!

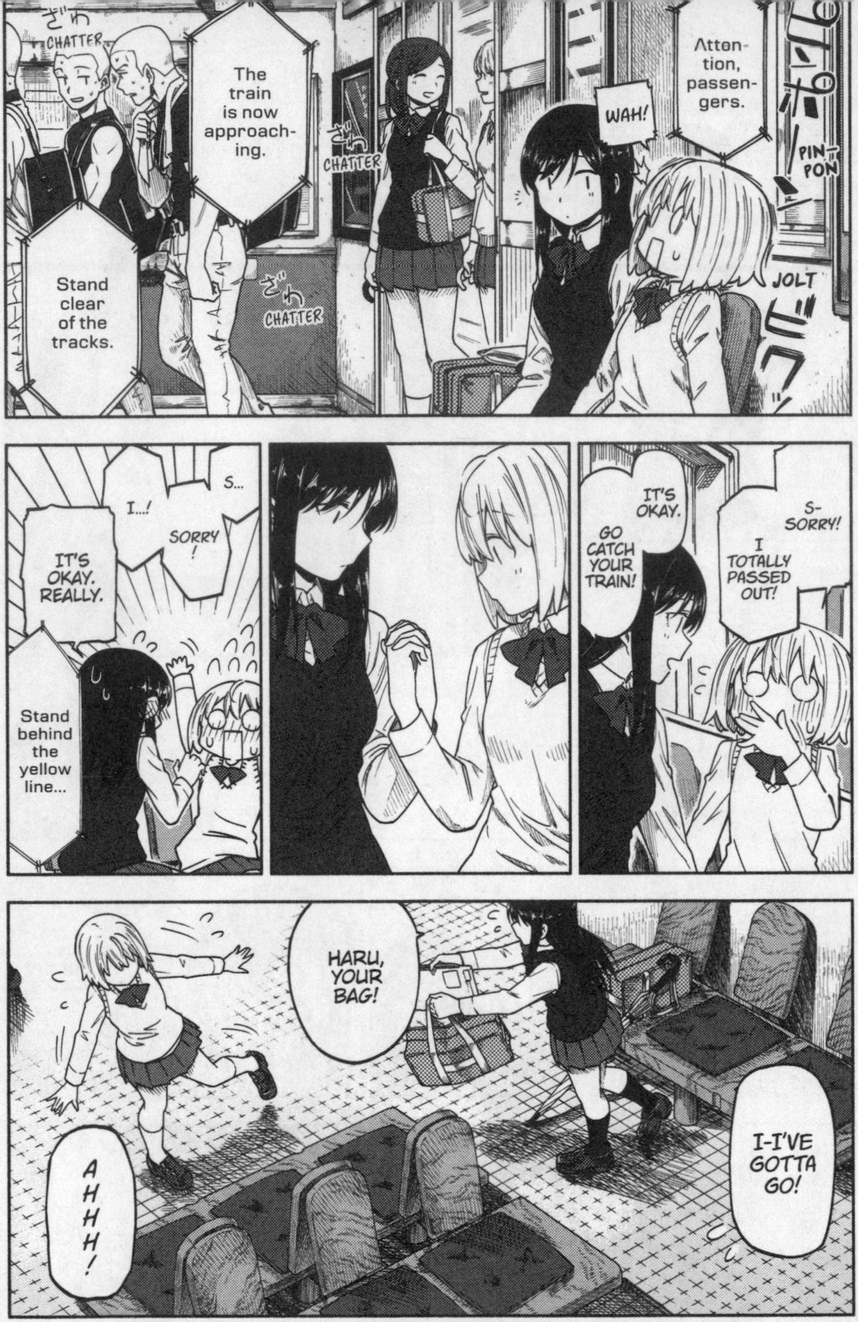
Attention, passengers.
PIN-PON
WAH!
JOLT
The train is now approaching.
CHATTER
CHATTER
CHATTER
Stand clear of the tracks.
S-SORRY! I TOTALLY PASSED OUT!
IT'S OKAY. GO CATCH YOUR TRAIN!
S...
I...!
SORRY!
IT'S OKAY. REALLY.
Stand behind the yellow line...
HARU, YOUR BAG!
I-I'VE GOTTA GO!
AHHH!

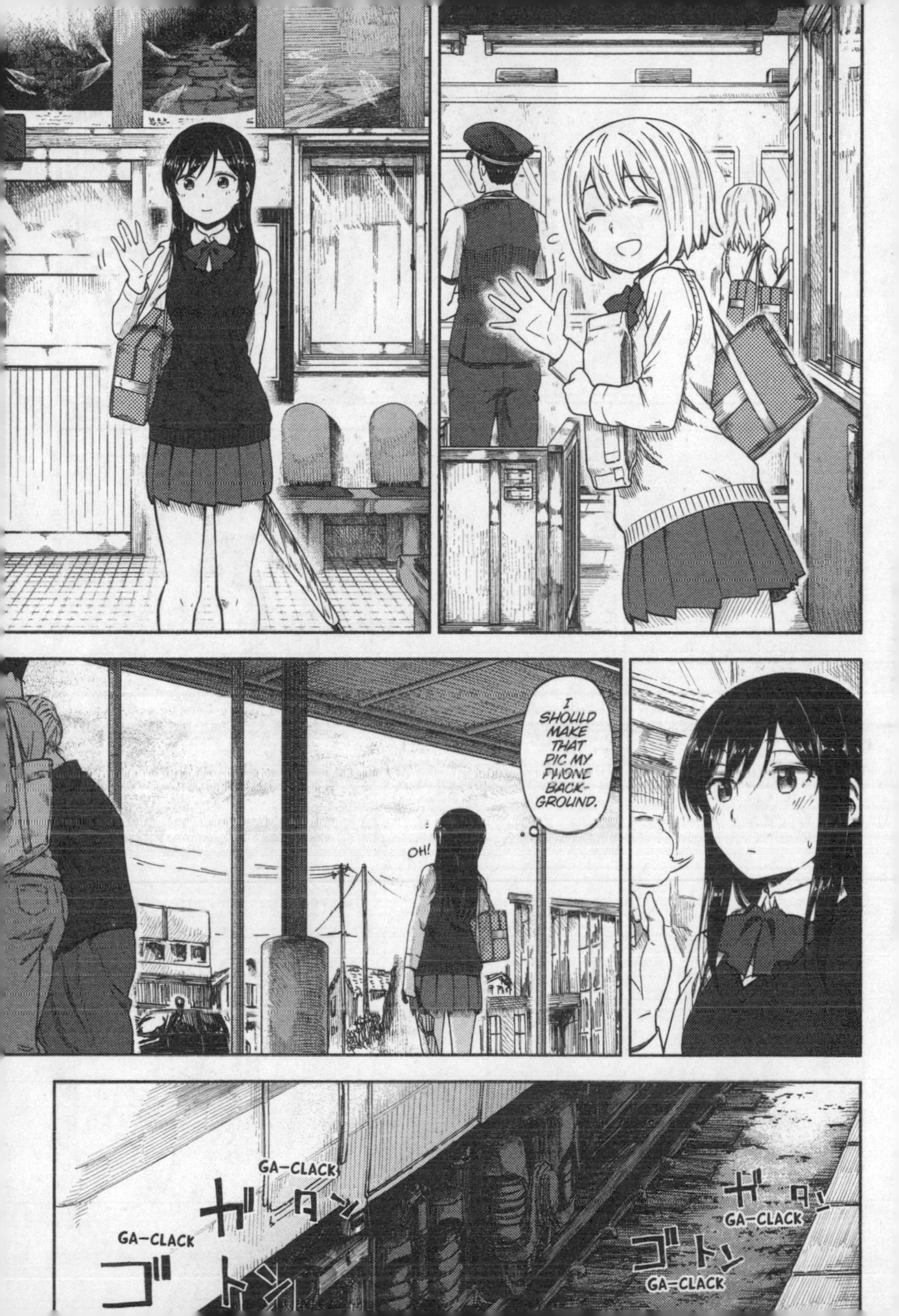
I SHOULD MAKE THAT PIC MY PHONE BACK-GROUND.
OH!
ガタン
GA-CLACK
ゴトン
GA-CLACK
GA-CLACK
ガタン
GA-CLACK
ゴトン

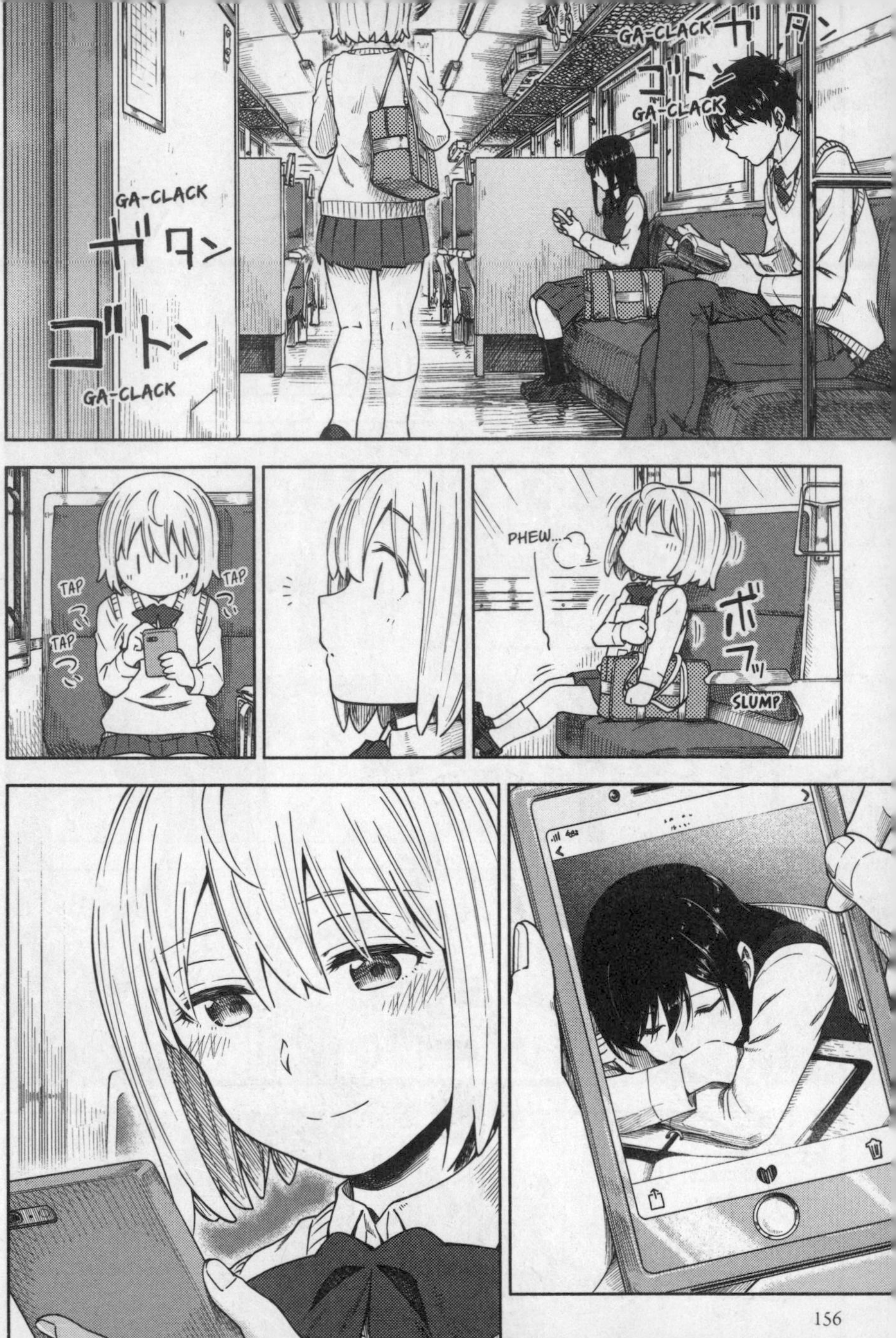

GA-CLACK ガタン
ゴトン
GA-CLACK
GA-CLACK
ガタン
ゴトン
GA-CLACK
PHEW...
ボフッ
SLUMP
TAP
TAP
TAP

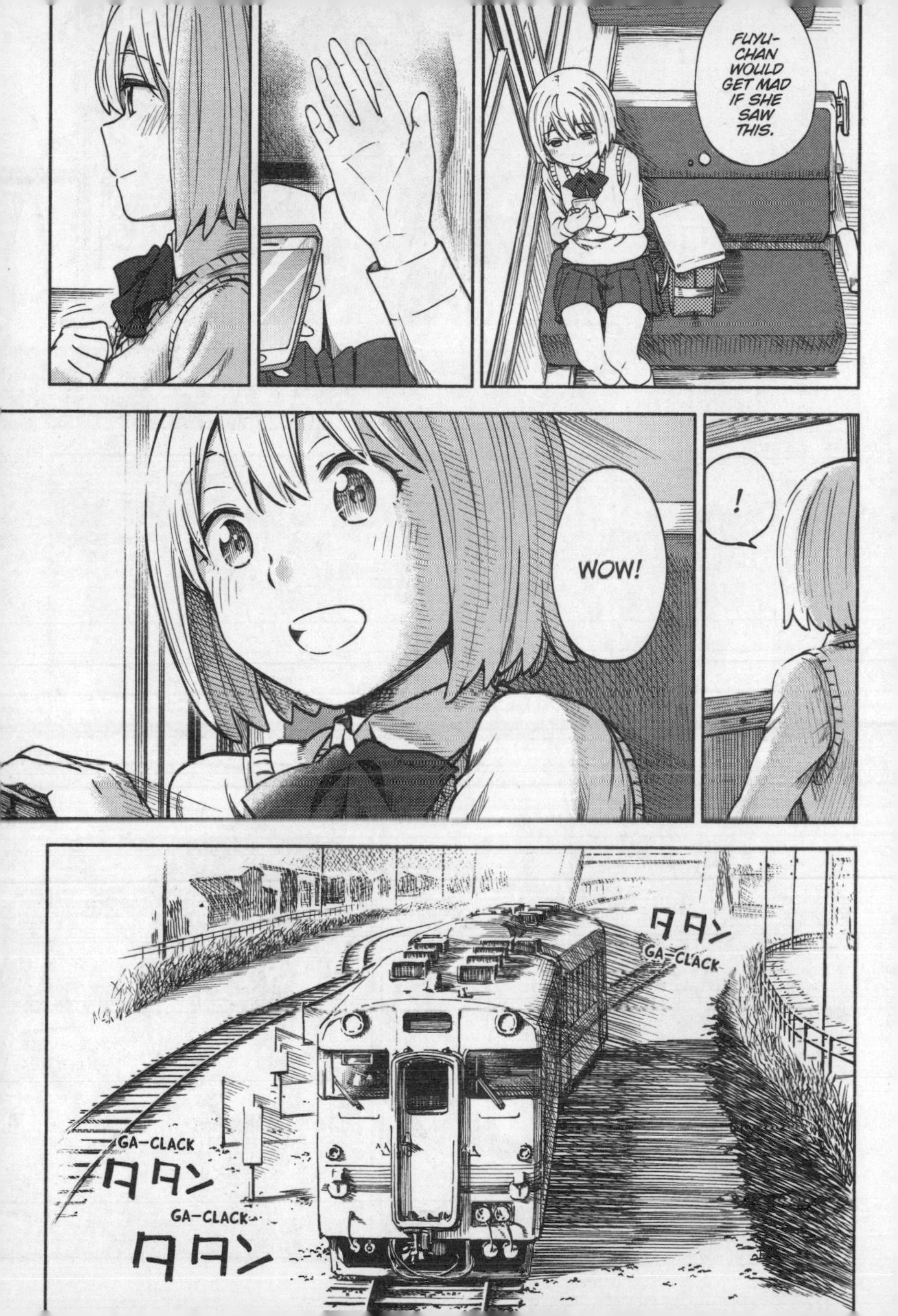
FUYU-CHAN WOULD GET MAD IF SHE SAW THIS.
!
WOW!
タタン
GA-CLACK
GA-CLACK
タタン
GA-CLACK
タタン

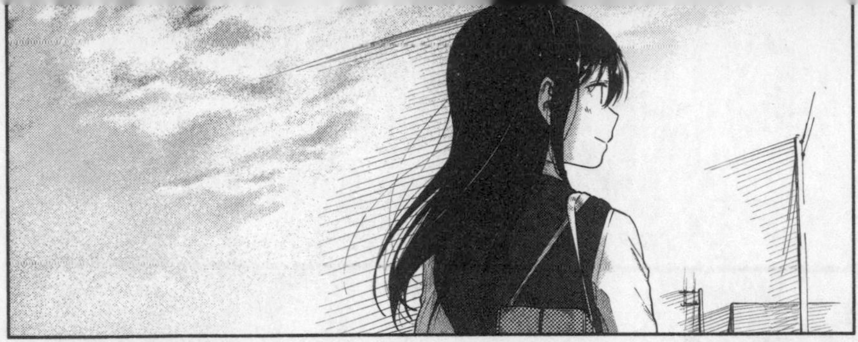

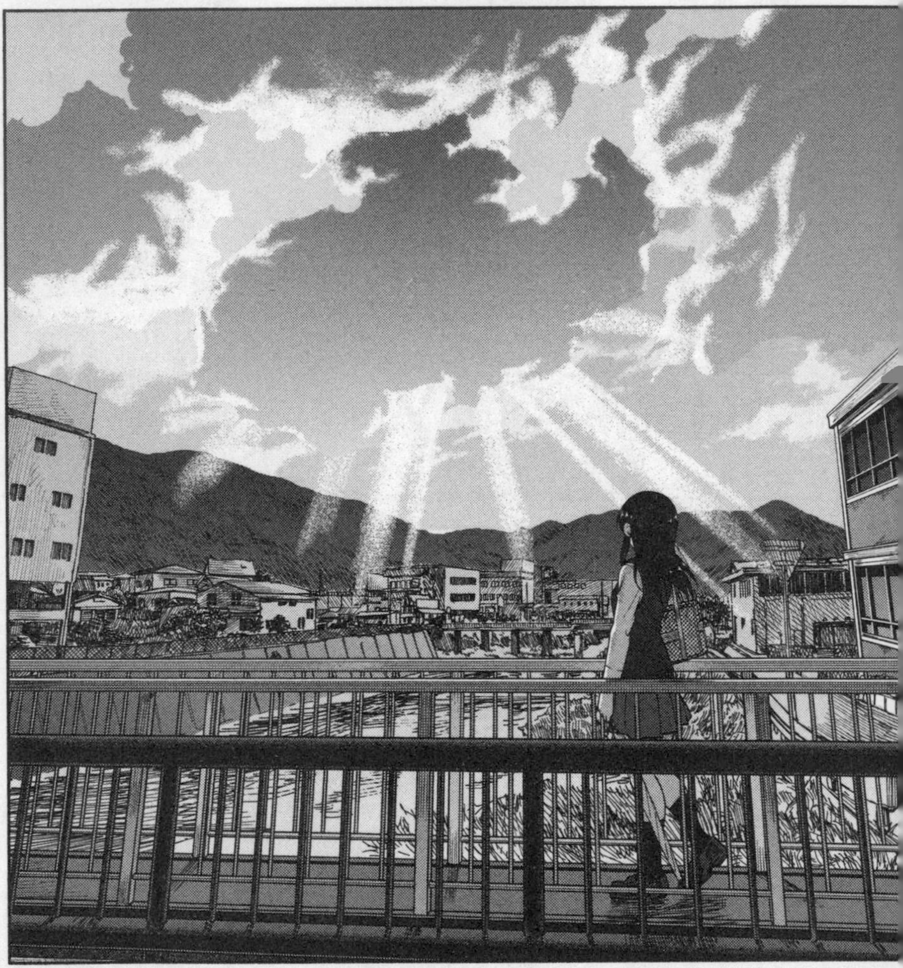

To be continued...

Our Wonderful Days

story & art by Kei Hamuro

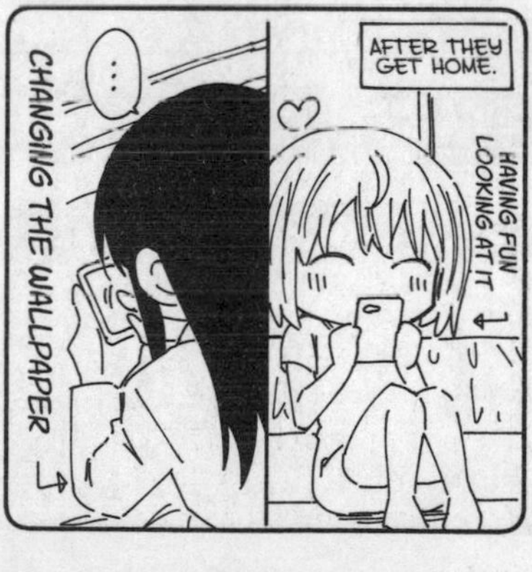
AFTER THEY GET HOME.
HAVING FUN LOOKING AT IT
…
CHANGING THE WALLPAPER

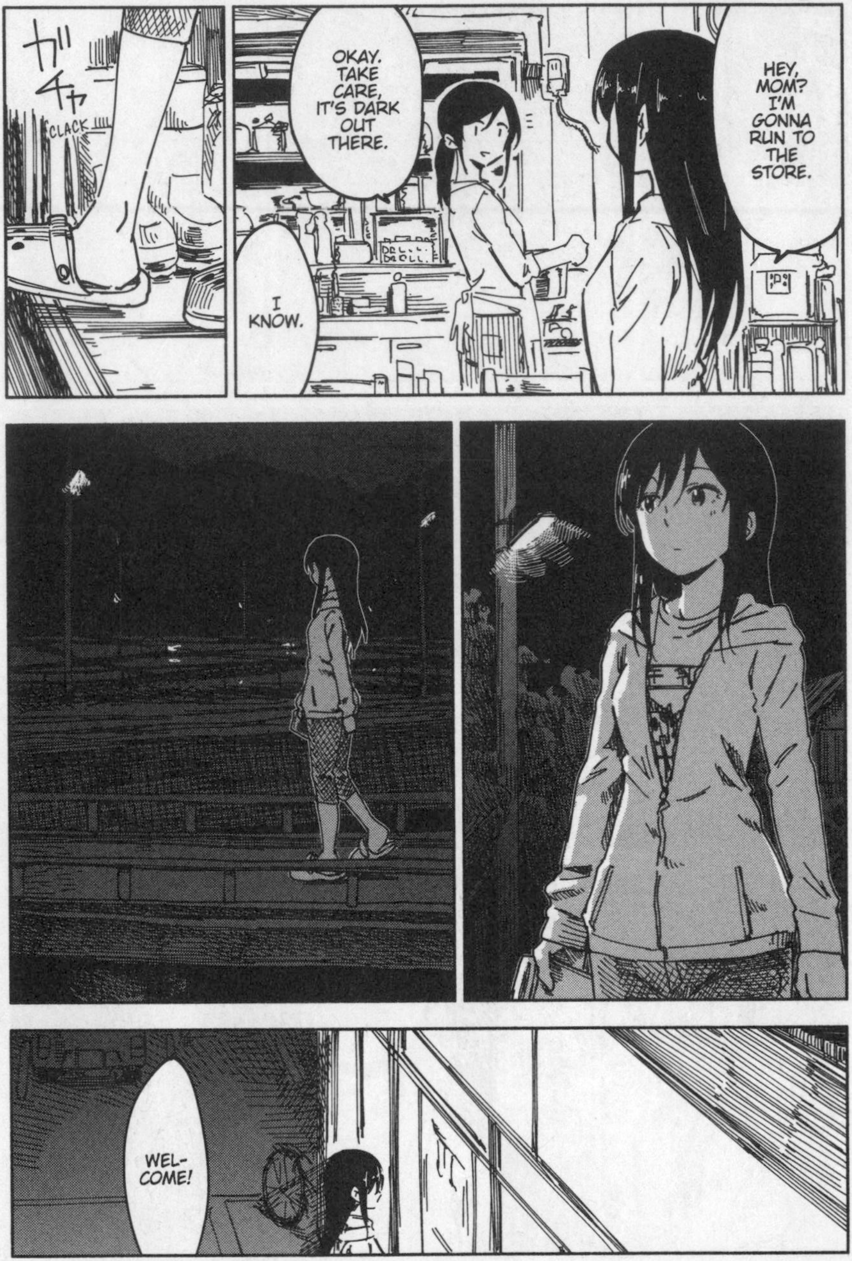
HEY, MOM? I'M GONNA RUN TO THE STORE.
OKAY. TAKE CARE, IT'S DARK OUT THERE.
I KNOW.
ガチャ
CLACK
WEL-COME!

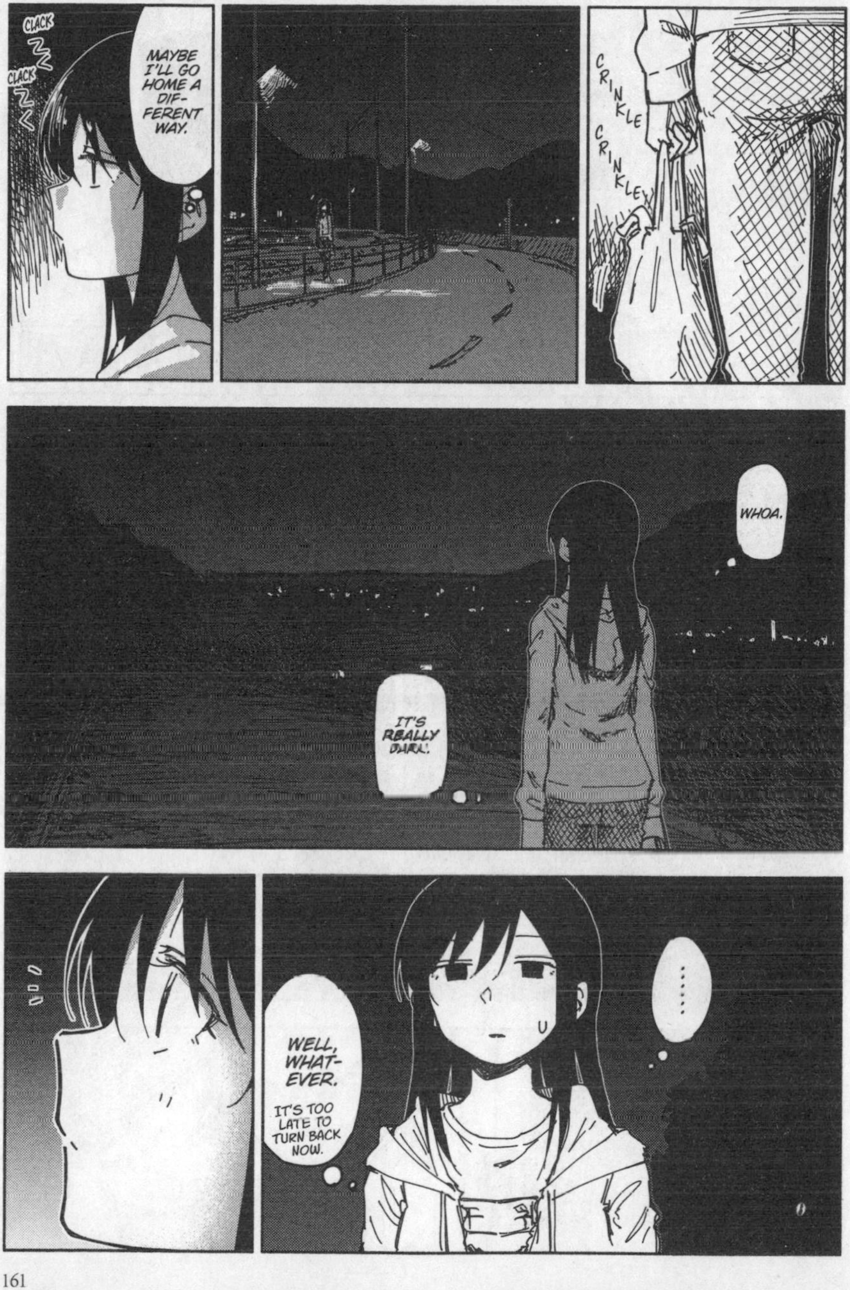
CRINKLE
CRINKLE
CLACK
CLACK
MAYBE I'LL GO HOME A DIF-FERENT WAY.
WHOA.
IT'S REALLY DARK.
......
WELL, WHATEVER.
IT'S TOO LATE TO TURN BACK NOW.

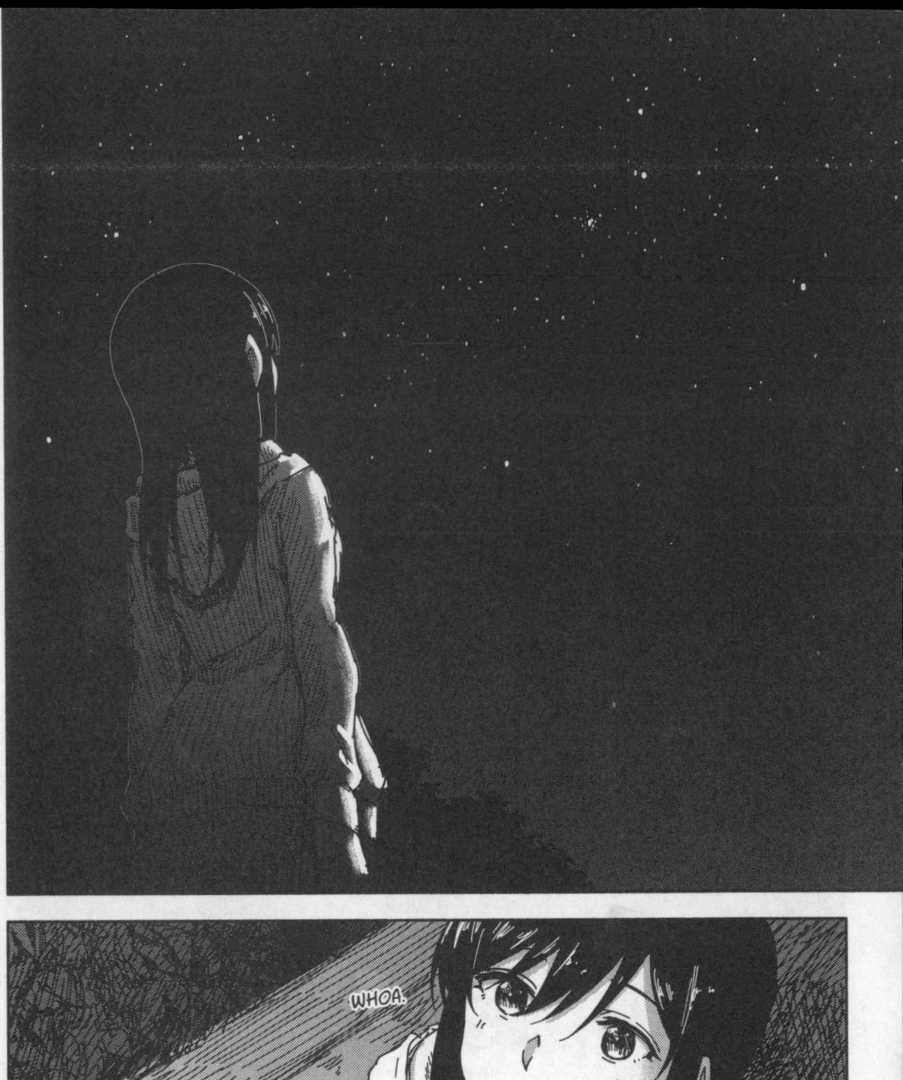

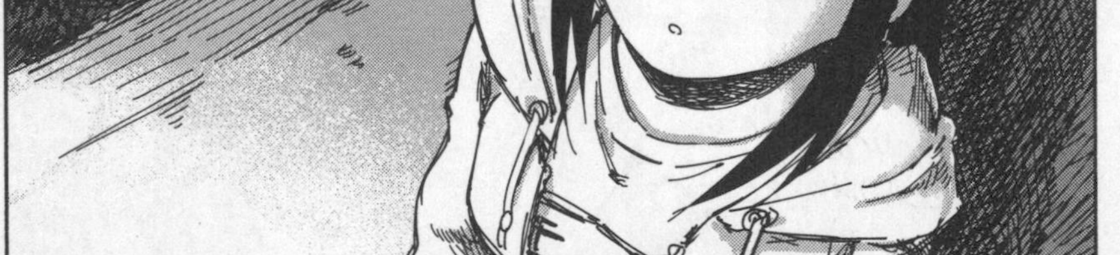
WHOA.

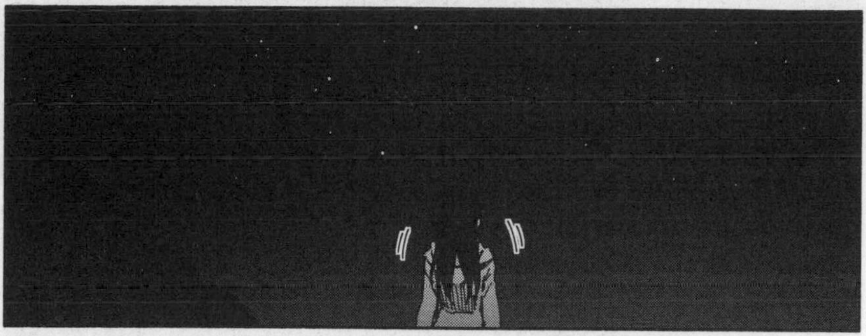

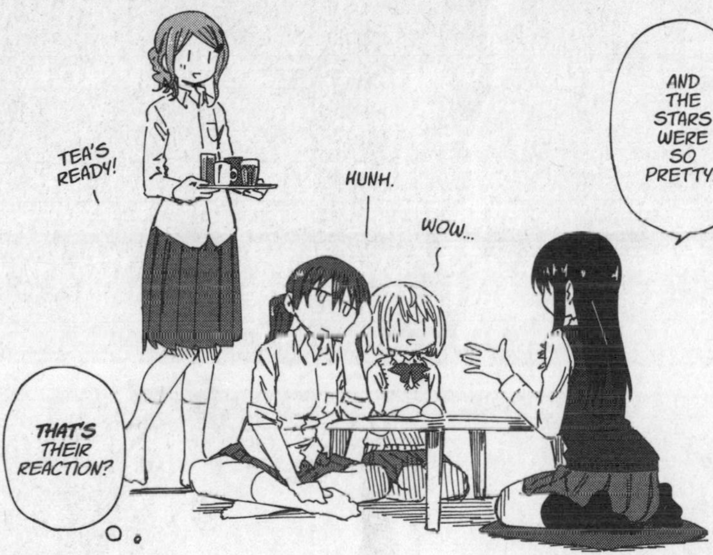
AND THE STARS WERE SO PRETTY!
WOW...
HUNH.
TEA'S READY!
THAT'S THEIR REACTION?

THANK YOU
FOR READING!

Kei Hamuro

Our Wonderful Days
Tsurezure Biyori

OUR WONDERFUL DAYS: A DIFFERENT LOOK! TURN OF THE CENTURY!

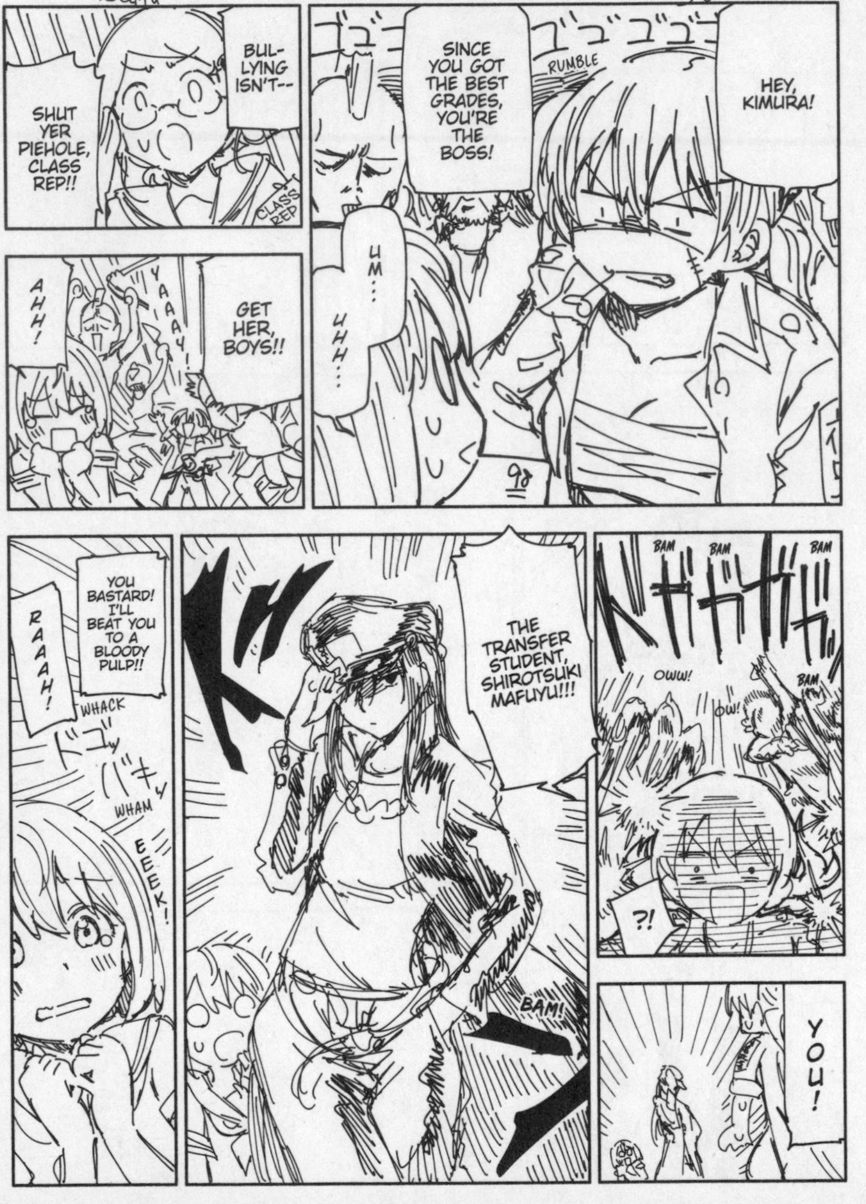
HEY, KIMURA!
RUMBLE
SINCE YOU GOT THE BEST GRADES, YOU'RE THE BOSS!
UM... UHH...
BUL-LYING ISN'T--
SHUT YER PIEHOLE, CLASS REP!!
CLASS REP
GET HER, BOYS!!
YAAAAY!
AHH!
BAM
BAM
BAM
OWW!
BAM
OW!
?!
YOU!
THE TRANSFER STUDENT, SHIROTSUKI MAFUYU!!!
BAM!
YOU BASTARD! I'LL BEAT YOU TO A BLOODY PULP!!
RAAAAH!
WHACK
WHAM
EEEK!

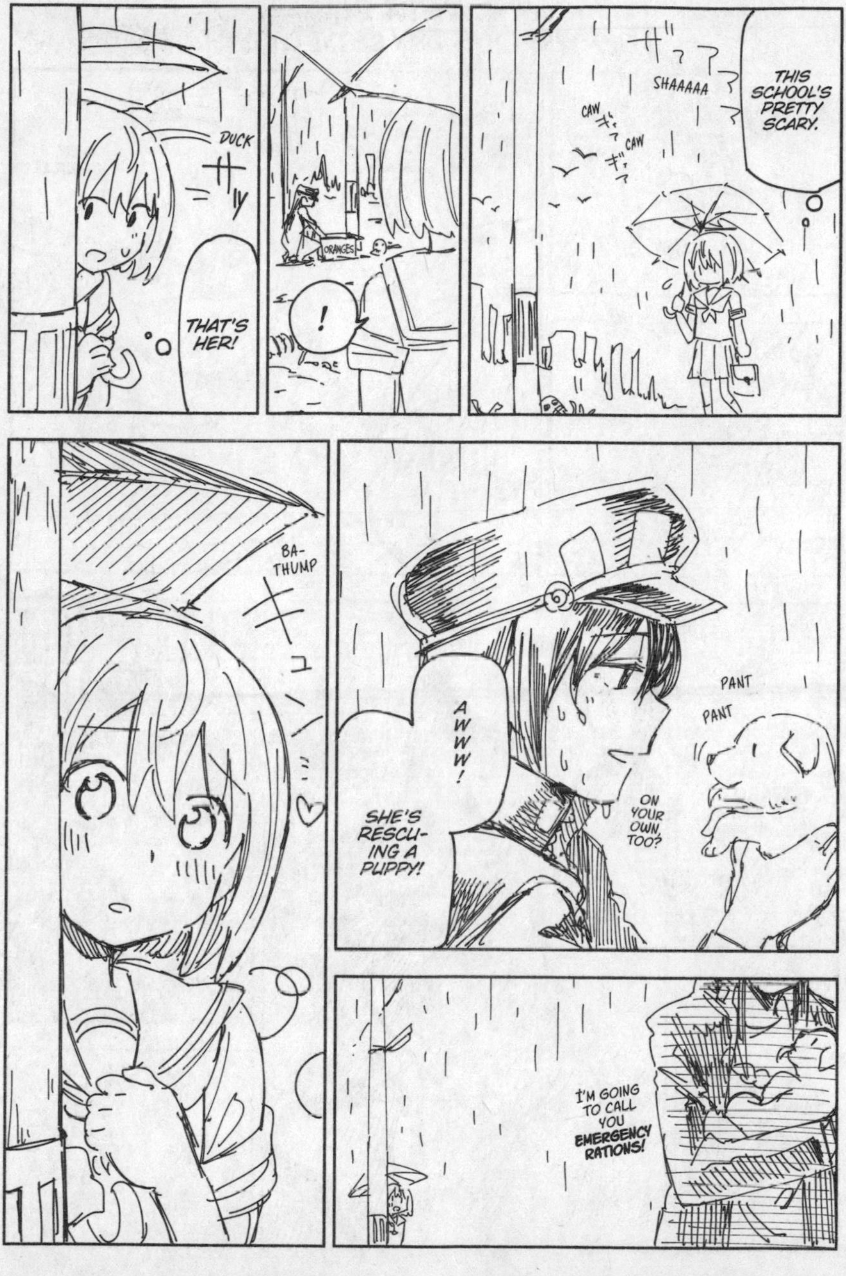
SHAAAAA
CAW
CAW
THIS SCHOOL'S PRETTY SCARY.
ORANGES
!
DUCK
THAT'S HER!
PANT
PANT
ON YOUR OWN TOO?
AWWW!
SHE'S RESCU-ING A PUPPY!
I'M GOING TO CALL YOU EMERGENCY RATIONS!
BA-THUMP

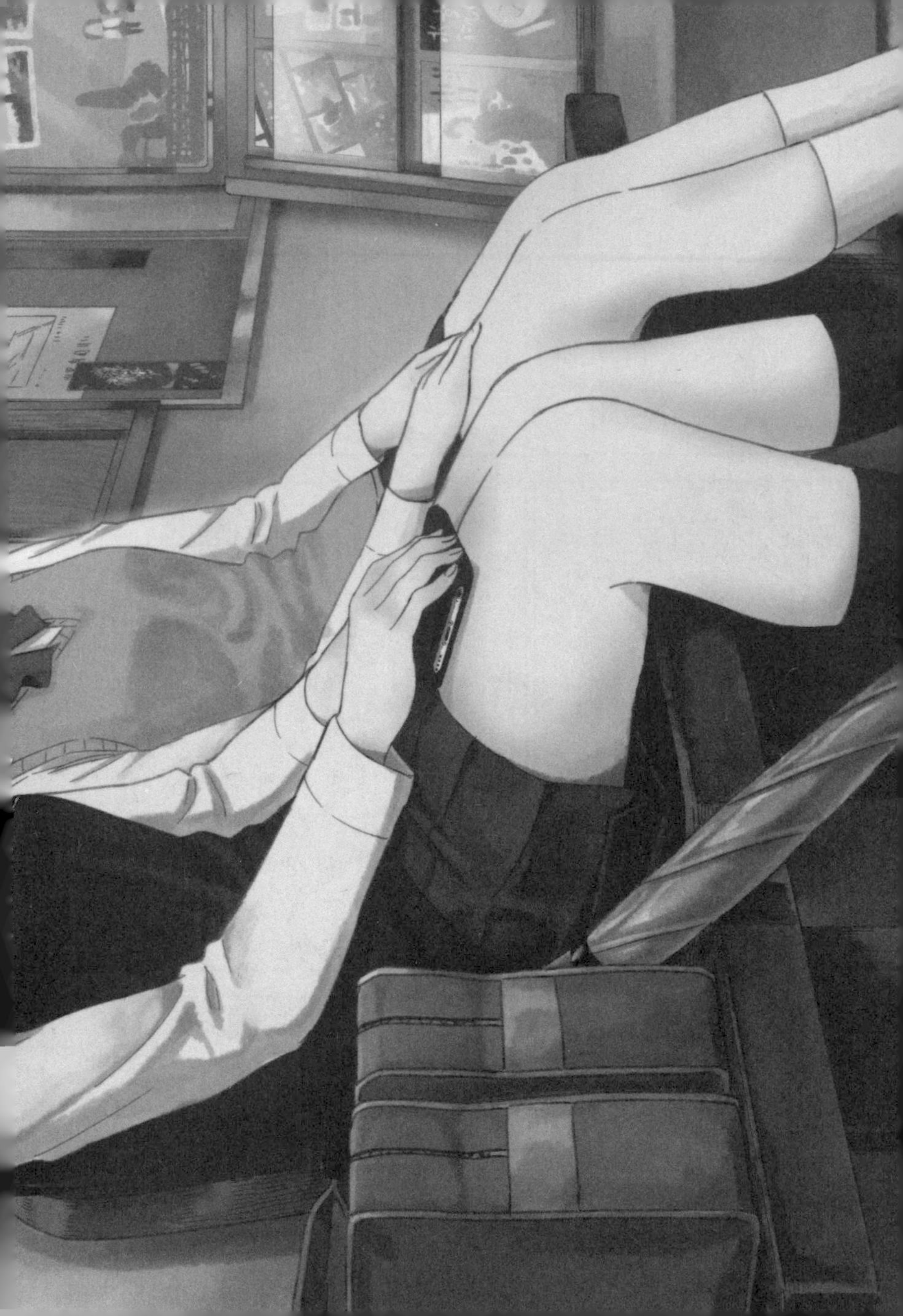

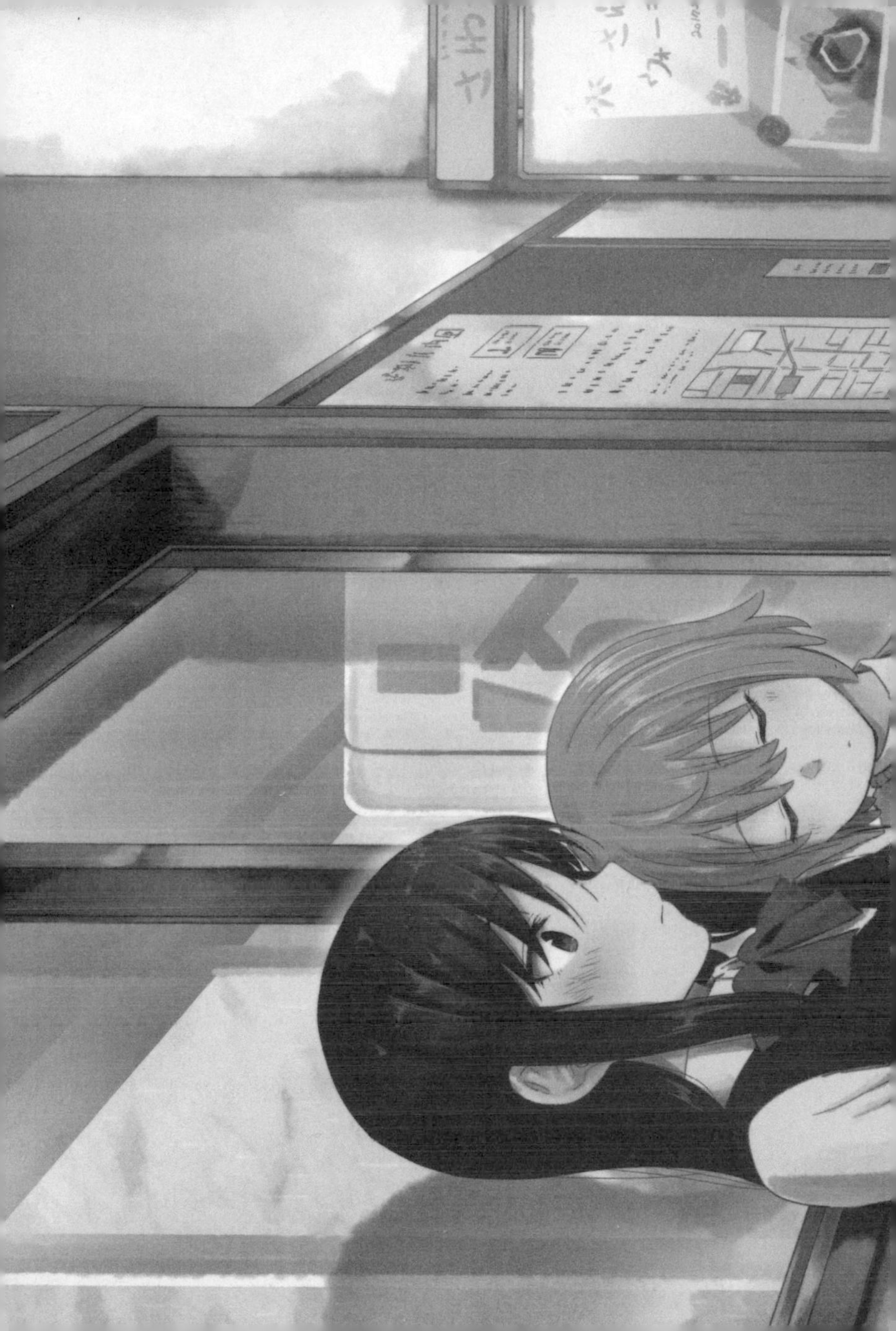

Our Wonderful Days
Tsurezure Biyori

SEVEN SEAS ENTERTAINMENT PRESENTS

Our Wonderful Days

Tsurezure Biyori

story and art by KEI HAMURO

VOLUME 1

TRANSLATION
Katrina Leonoudakis

ADAPTATION
Asha Bardon

LETTERING AND RETOUCH
Erika Terriquez

COVER DESIGN
KC Fabellon

PROOFREADER
Stephanie Cohen
Cae Hawksmoor

EDITOR
Shannon Fay

PRODUCTION MANAGER
Lissa Pattillo

MANAGING EDITOR
Julie Davis

EDITOR-IN-CHIEF
Adam Arnold

PUBLISHER
Jason DeAngelis

OUR WONDERFUL DAYS: TSUREZURE BIYORI VOL. 1

First published in Japan in 2018 by ICHIJINSHA Inc., Tokyo.
English translation rights arranged with KODANSHA.

Seven Seas press and purchase enquiries can be sent to Marketing Manager Lianne Sentar at press@gomanga.com. Information regarding the distribution and purchase of digital editions is available from Digital Manager CK Russell at digital@gomanga.com.

ISBN: 978-1-64275-338-7

Printed in Canada

First Printing: November 2019

10 9 8 7 6 5 4 3 2 1

FOLLOW US ONLINE: www.sevenseasentertainment.com

READING DIRECTIONS

This book reads from ***right to left***, Japanese style. If this is your first time reading manga, you start reading from the top right panel on each page and take it from there. If you get lost, just follow the numbered diagram here. It may seem backwards at first, but you'll get the hang of it! Have fun!!

1
2
3
4
5
6
7
8
9

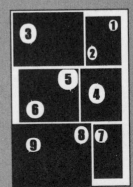